THE BUSINESS GUIDE TO THE UNIX SYSTEM

D1401634

THE BUSINESS GUIDE TO THE UNIX SYSTEM

Jean L. Yates
Sandra L. Emerson

Addison-Wesley Publishing Company
Reading, Massachusetts • Menlo Park, California
London • Amsterdam • Don Mills, Ontario • Sydney

Marshall Henrichs, Cover Design

Disclaimer of Warranties and Limitation of Liabilities

The authors have taken due care in preparing this book and the programs in it, including research, development, and testing to ascertain their effectiveness. The authors and the publishers make no expressed or implied warranty of any kind with regard to these programs nor the supplementary documentation in this book. In no event shall the authors or the publishers be liable for incidental or consequential damages in connection with or arising out of the furnishing, performance, or use of any of these programs.

UNIX™ is a trademark of Bell Laboratories. *The Business Guide to the UNIX System* is not sponsored or approved or connected with Bell Laboratories. All references to UNIX in the text of this book are to the trademark of Bell Laboratories.

Library of Congress Cataloging in Publication Data
Main entry under title:

The Business guide to the UNIX system.

    1. UNIX (Computer operating system) 2. Business—
Data processing. I. Yates, Jean.
HF5548.4.U53B87   1984   650'.028'5425   83-11802
ISBN 0-201-08848-7 (pbk.)

ISBN 0-201-08848-7
ABCDEFGHIJ-HA-8987654

Dedicated to Dean MacMurray Kaiper
and Julia Kaiper Yates

PREFACE

The UNIX* operating system is an increasingly popular business tool on mini and microcomputers. To learn to use UNIX software you no longer have to plow through a fourteen-inch pile of technical manuals. This book will provide you, the business computer user, with beginner training on the UNIX system.

By using clear tutorial examples, this book allows you to learn the UNIX system without continual access to a staff person who already knows the system.

Chapter 1 introduces you to the UNIX system. History and application of UNIX software to business are described.

Chapter 2 starts the tutorials, explains concepts, and teaches basic skills. Notations used throughout the rest of the book are described in this chapter.

Chapter 3 teaches you UNIX text editing, a skill basic to using all other UNIX software. The **vi** editor is covered.

Chapter 4 explains one of the most popular parts of UNIX software for business people, the file and directory system. You learn to build your own "electronic file cabinet" using UNIX commands.

Chapter 5 expands on the UNIX file and directory system discussion in Chapter 4. Advanced techniques for manipulating, sorting, and classifying files are given.

Chapter 6 covers the UNIX shell. The shell program can be programmed by business people to automatically perform tasks that take a long time at the keyboard. You can customize your UNIX system in this chapter. You can search through

* UNIX™ is a trademark of Bell Laboratories.

files for words and manipulate files and directories with shell procedures.

Chapter 7 teaches you to use electronic mail, the calendar and "tickler" file, and how to use UNIX software with a modem to remote locations. On-line documentation and tutorials are also described here.

Chapters 8 and 9 show the powers of the **nroff** text formatting program. Chapter 8 gives you the basic skills, and Chapter 9 shows you how to use macro packages for advanced formatting.

Chapter 10 teaches the new UNIX computer owner how to manage and maintain a system. Oriented to micro users without an on-staff system manager, the chapter covers system backup, assignment of usernames and passwords, routine duties and problems.

Four appendices give you additional information. Appendix A covers basic computer terms not described in the text. Appendix B is a glossary of UNIX terms. Appendix C is a useful bibliography on UNIX documents. Appendix D is a resources section on UNIX hardware, software, and services.

ACKNOWLEDGMENTS

This book is the result of a team effort by the staff and associates of Yates Ventures, a Los Altos-based firm specializing in research on standard software. All members of the firm contributed to the project.

Special acknowledgment is due to the following individuals for their outstanding effort. Joanne Clapp managed word processing and document production. Melinda Rowe managed the completion of the overall project and worked extensively with the publishers. Caren Weisglas and Caryn Dombroski performed technical edits on the manuscript. Leon Starr performed the final style edit. Eileen Skrabutenas prepared the Resources section. Sylvia Washington performed the exercises in the book.

Thanks to the University of California at Berkeley for access to their UNIX system and to Intel for their loan of a 330X microcomputer. Appreciation is extended to Microsoft Corporation, specifically Mark Ursino, John Ulet, and Gordon Letwin for their valuable suggestions and overall support of Yates Ventures' efforts.

And finally, we acknowledge the Yates Ventures mascots, still shredding paper and marking pages with pawprint comments from the feline viewpoint.

Los Altos, California
December 1983

J.L.Y.
Yates Ventures

CONTENTS

3   CREATING AND EDITING DOCUMENTS   49

4 THE UNIX FILE AND DIRECTORY SYSTEM   135

5 THE UNIX FILE AND DIRECTORY SYSTEM, PART 2   181

6 # MAKING THE SHELL WORK FOR YOU   231

7 COMMUNICATING WITH YOURSELF AND OTHER USERS   283

8 FORMATTING TEXT FILES AND DOCUMENTS 323

9 ADVANCED TEXT FORMATTING WITH nroff 361

1

THE UNIX* SYSTEM FOR BUSINESS USERS

The UNIX operating system, developed by Bell Laboratories, is now widely distributed with small business computer systems. The UNIX system has a library of over 200 document preparation, business computing, and programming tools. After reading this chapter, you can decide if UNIX software fits your business computer needs.

The UNIX Operating System

Bell Laboratories and the UNIX System History
   The C Language

The UNIX System and the Small Business Computer
   Text Entry and Editing Programs
   Spelling Check Program
   Filing Documents
   Formatting Documents
   Information Retrieval and Automation of Tasks
   Electronic Mail and Networking

Is the UNIX System for You?
   The User Interface

Getting Started

* UNIX™ is a trademark of Bell Laboratories.

THE UNIX OPERATING SYSTEM

Operating system software controls and directs a computer's actions. Like an electronic traffic light, operating systems observe the flow of electronic data through the "streets" of the computer. They make sure that data gets to the right place, and they stop electronic "traffic jams" from forming. Imagine a tiny electronic traffic cop, standing on the intersection of the gold lines on the green boards inside your computer, and the data as even smaller cars speeding along the gold "freeways." UNIX, CP/M, and MS-DOS operating software are typical of computer "traffic cops" used in microcomputers to keep everything running smoothly.

The UNIX operating system is a popular *multiuser* operating system for powerful 16-bit business microcomputers. 16-bit micros use microprocessors, single-piece electronic devices, as their computer brain, or *CPU*. In contrast to 8-bit microprocessors like the Apple II's 6502 or Tandy Model 1's Z80, 16-bit micros include the IBM PC's 8088 and Tandy System 16's 68000. A multiuser operating system lets more than one person, at different terminals, interact with the computer at the same time.

Occasionally, UNIX systems have been adapted as single-user systems. Single-user systems allow only one person at a time to interact with the computer. Most single-user micros run either CP/M from Digital Research, Inc., or MS-DOS from Microsoft Corporation.

The UNIX operating system is a chameleon; its many forms and flavors are adaptations of minicomputer research and development-oriented software to commercial needs. Originally developed by Bell Telephone Laboratories, the UNIX system is now distributed by over 100 computer and software vendors. Some versions of the UNIX system are unique to microcomputers; some have been specifically reworked for engineers, typesetters, the government, and other special kinds of computer users. This book describes the most popular features of the system and avoids discussion of versions specific to one computer or type of user. There may be some differences between your computer's UNIX system and what is described here, but they will be small. The most universal parts of the UNIX system in their most common forms are covered in this book.

The principal organizations promoting the movement of the UNIX system to microcomputers are Microsoft Corporation of Bellevue, Washington, whose XENIX product is available on 8086, Z8000, and 68000-based microcomputers; UniSoft Systems of Berkeley, California, whose product is available on 68000-based microcomputers; and individual computer vendors who move the UNIX system to such computer systems as Onyx and Plexus.

The UNIX operating system, originally developed for minicomputers, is now available on microcomputers and mainframes as well. However, as you see in Fig. 1.1, most UNIX system

Fig. 1.1 Projected Installations of the UNIX System, by Size of Computer (Based on Cumulative UNIX Licenses through December 1986)

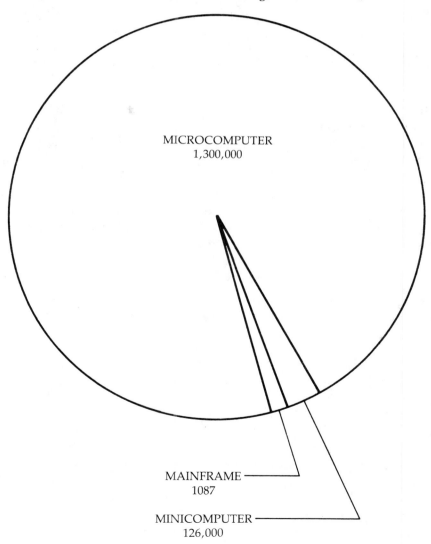

MICROCOMPUTER
1,300,000

MAINFRAME
1087

MINICOMPUTER
126,000

users will be microcomputer owners, and this book primarily addresses that audience. The microcomputer owner using the UNIX system has a unique set of needs, different from those of the traditional user. Many UNIX microcomputer owners are confronting a multiuser operating system for the first time and are unfamiliar with the special conditions required to maintain such a software system. The UNIX operating system was not developed for beginning users; consequently, the uninstructed user loses much of the system's power.

This book offers step-by-step explanations of useful office tasks performed with the UNIX system. Before starting to use the system in Chapter 2, investigate the history of the system in this chapter and read some important information on deciding to purchase a UNIX-based microcomputer.

BELL LABORATORIES AND THE UNIX SYSTEM HISTORY

The Bell System is one of the world's largest computer users, and Bell Laboratories, one company in the Bell family, develops much of its software. Bell Labs has generated thousands of software programs for Bell System use in the last ten years. The UNIX operating system is one of the most popular.

The UNIX system evolved over ten years, from origins as a software program for text editing and formatting. First developed around 1970, today it is a massive set of programming tools for software development, text preparation, and communications, in addition to its operating system functions.

The developers of the UNIX system pioneered the concept of "portability." Portable software can be moved from one type of computer to another. If Bell decides to use a new computer, they want to move existing software to it, not rewrite the programming. You probably feel the same way. So many computer users like portability that it is today a major selling point of UNIX software.

The C Language

The C language, also developed at Bell Labs, makes UNIX software portable. UNIX is written in C, a language designed for big software programs that can be independent of any particular kind of computer. They can be moved easily to many types of computer systems. Many microcomputer software companies develop application software in C, often working in conjunction with the UNIX tools, programs specifically designed for efficient C programming.

Bell Labs continues to enhance UNIX software and to release periodic updates. System V was released in 1983, and with it Bell announced support for microcomputer versions as well as the previously available minicomputer-oriented product. In the future, Bell may introduce more micro and business software. Until then, over two hundred independent software companies offer application software packages, such as spreadsheet/"calc," accounting and inventory control programs.

THE UNIX SYSTEM AND THE SMALL BUSINESS COMPUTER

What can you, a business professional, do with the UNIX operating system? The answer is, a great deal. The UNIX system is an operating system *plus*. It includes many programs that usually must be purchased separately.

Some of the useful functions accomplished with UNIX software in a business environment include electronic mail and communications, electronic file cabinet development, data and file manipulation and control, and text processing and *text formatting*. You can even perform your own typesetting, if you have a typesetting machine. UNIX file manipulation and man-

Fig. 1.2   Bell Labs

The new Altos 586 microcomputer offers affordable, fast 16-bit processing to accommodate five users, expandable to eight. Integral networking capability permits expansion to serve hundreds of users. Versions include both dual floppy and Winchester hard disk.

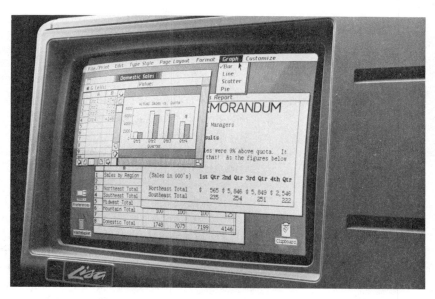

Lisa's™ high resolution screen can display up to four integrated software applications simultaneously. Shown here are (clockwise, left to right) LisaGraph™, LisaWrite™, and LisaCalc™. Across the top of the screen is the menu bar that lists the options available to start a specific task. After a selection is made, the menu bar's pull down feature displays additional options for completing the task.

The Radio Shack System 16 runs the MicroSoft XENIX version of UNIX.

agement tools will sort and select within files as well as sort and select among files themselves. An on-line dictionary to check spelling and word usage in any document is part of the UNIX system.

Text Entry and Editing Programs

The UNIX system provides two types of *text editing* programs: *line-oriented* and *screen-oriented*. The UNIX editing programs are the primary means of creating text and program files, whether documents are edited line-by-line or a screenful at a time on the terminal's video display. The editing programs allow text to be entered and modified without constant retyping, so that final drafts are letter-perfect before they are printed.

You can tell the UNIX system to perform several tasks at once. For example, you can send a document to the printer while you continue to use an editing program. Several different documents may be combined. Sections of text can be moved, copied, or deleted. These "cut-and-paste" features and the ability to run several tasks at one time make the UNIX system text editing software efficient and powerful.

Spelling Check Program

Once a document has been entered and modified with an editing program, it may be checked for typographical errors and spelling mistakes using the UNIX on-line dictionary. You can even build custom dictionaries of terms for your special needs.

Filing Documents

UNIX provides a built-in filing system. Within certain restrictions, the naming of files and the specific organization and categorization of them is done by you, not the system. The UNIX system is like a filing system of manila folders in a filing cabinet, except the indexing, copying, sorting, and rearranging of documents is under computer control.

Formatting Documents

The UNIX system provides a document formatting program to generate printed and typeset documents. The document formatting program *right-justifies* text, creates uniformly indented paragraphs, and gives you a great deal of control over page design. When used with a set of formatting commands known as a macro package, UNIX formatting programs make it easy to produce polished documents for publication. Creation of charts, tables, and mathematical expressions are handled by two special UNIX programs.

Self-service typesetting is a powerful and unique capability of the UNIX formatting program. The number and quality of UNIX-compatible typesetting machines is increasing, and the ability to prepare text for computer typesetting can save money and time in the production phase of printed documents. Brochures, pamphlets, and articles can be typeset using the same commands you learn for regular document formatting. If you own a small UNIX micro, you probably can't justify purchasing a typesetter. You can send your disks to some companies with typesetters, and the charges are much lower than if you sent them printout.

Information Retrieval and Automation of Tasks

UNIX file management programs can recognize patterns of letters in text. You can organize groups of documents by key words or other patterns and then file, index, modify, copy, or remove them by group. Files may also be grouped by name, date, or other criteria.

UNIX information retrieval and indexing features speed routine filing tasks. You can automate your most commonly performed computer tasks by storing sets of commands in a file to be executed at your convenience. First you determine the sequence of procedures you perform most frequently. For example, you may do the same things every morning when you arrive at work. You might routinely change the UNIX electronic "date stamp," check for electronic mail to you on the system, send an electronic message to a colleague that you have arrived at work, and turn on the editing program for the day's text processing. Using a UNIX technique called a "shell script," you can store and automatically rerun the many keystrokes you take to perform this typical morning's tasks. You prepare a special electronic file containing the keystrokes and call it a one-word name. Then just type in the name in the morning and the computer goes to work for you!

Electronic Mail and Networking

You can reduce paperwork and traffic between offices by sending memos, documents, and financial data electronically with the UNIX system. Copies of messages are automatically indexed, filed, dated, and addressed. The electronic mail program sends or forwards messages to lists of users. You can set a calendar management and reminder program to greet you every morning with a list of appointments for the day.

Electronic mail may be sent within one office or over a network, enabling rapid communication with UNIX systems in branch offices, or with other companies, libraries, and universities. Other programs allow work to be performed on a remote UNIX machine.

IS THE UNIX SYSTEM FOR YOU?

What factors should you consider when deciding if the UNIX system is for you? First and foremost, consider the increased complexity of the software. Power and increased capabilities come with a price, and that price is a longer learning curve for UNIX operations than for the very simple single-user operating systems micro owners have used in the past. You may find the UNIX system to be well worth the extra learning time, once you read this book and the instruction manuals included with your system.

Consider the availability of UNIX *application packages*. Until recently, it was much easier to find good packaged software for CP/M or MS-DOS than for UNIX. As a business person, you want a solution to your business needs, not a computer course. You are looking for the best available packaged applications, and if those are under XYZ operating system, that's what you will buy. You can now find many good UNIX application packages, but they may not meet your needs, particularly if you want something with limited appeal.

Using the UNIX system, you will soon have access to hundreds of formerly minicomputer application programs moved down to UNIX micros. These programs are more powerful and sophisticated than many microcomputer equivalents. For example, many minicomputer general ledger/accounting systems allow you to create unlimited numbers of subledgers, and run very large account receivables and payables. Packages moved to UNIX micros include such hard-to-find microcomputer software as cost accounting, manufacture resources planning, and inventory/cash flow control and analysis. These kinds of sophisticated and useful packages were previously unavailable on microcomputers because the operating system and hardware power were not sufficient to run them. The new UNIX-based microcomputers that are now available provide this capability. Your access to sophisticated programs is expanded when you choose the UNIX system for your company's computer.

The User Interface

If you are learning to use computers with a micro, you are probably accustomed to seeing cryptic commands and information on the screen, and then translating the information for yourself. The UNIX system is not just cryptic; it is a bigger, more sophisticated, and flexible system. Because of its complexity, the UNIX system requires some degree of simplification to allow you to interact with it—a relationship commonly referred to as the user interface. XENIX, UniPlus + ® from UniSoft, and other implementations of the UNIX system all now incorporate some user interface features that make the system easier to use. In some cases, you interact with the UNIX system through very easy-to-understand "menu" systems, as seen in Fig. 1.3.

With other implementations of the UNIX system, you may still deal with the traditional cryptic "%" or "$" prompt indicating the command line, but you have better on-line or instructional "help" information, or have manuals to assist you in learning the system.

Fig. 1.3   A Menu-Driven Fortune Systems Screen

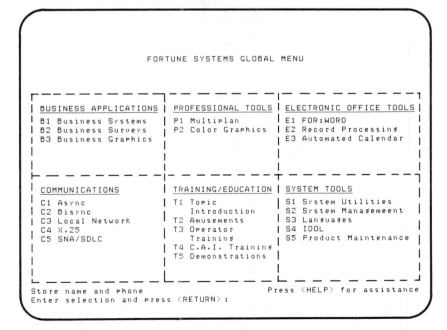

The global menu lists all available software.

In the future, the UNIX operating system, in its various forms and flavors, will become a keyword for access to large numbers of business application software packages. As with CP/M, UNIX will be a keyword. Because the UNIX system software and application packages that run on it will be solutions to many business computer users' needs, the way you interact with it will become more and more simple. Eventually, a number of UNIX-based programs will hide the UNIX system from you entirely, and you will only have to interact with it if you want the additional powers and capabilities that the "raw" operating system offers.

GETTING STARTED   In this book, we assume that you want to learn more about the UNIX system than the application programs that run on it. We give you information that allows you greater flexibility in handling and manipulating your data files, sending and receiving mail and communications among users of the system, and using UNIX tools and functions that make it a uniquely powerful operating system *plus*. You don't have to use all of these tools to use the application programs that are available on the UNIX system. But if you want some of the additional power and capabilities that we have described in this chapter, this book's easy-to-understand tutorials and practical examples will get you started performing tasks that have stymied you in the past and prompted the comments "Now, why can't I just do that? It seems like it should be so easy."

As an operating system that evolved in response to many end-users' interactions and comments—especially the Bell System, one of the largest end-users of computers in the world—the UNIX system contains many features that end-users have demanded. Implemented inside the UNIX system, these features relate directly to features that you, the small business system user, also demand. This book covers the easier, most popular of the hundreds of UNIX programs that can be used in offices.

The rest of this book contains information and interactive tutorials on using the UNIX system in a business environment. We assume that you have basic knowledge of such computer terms as "disk drive" and "CPU." If you don't, we have presented some basic information in Appendix A, or you may refer to any good textbook on microcomputer systems. We don't assume that you know any UNIX system lingo, and we explain the special terms "pipes," "filters," and "hierarchical file structure," plus others that you may have heard talked about without much explanation. There is a glossary at the end of the book, and glossary items in the text are all italicized.

This book is just as applicable to minicomputer and mainframe business systems as to microcomputers. If you are using a business-oriented minicomputer or mainframe, you have some advantages that the micro owner doesn't. You will be able to talk to the data processing managers, system administrators, or other professional data processing personnel who maintain the system in your company. Since this book is directed to people who may not have such resources, we discuss software and interaction with the computer in greater detail than might be needed by those mini users who can seek help from the staff who maintain their system.

2 GETTING STARTED IN THE UNIX* SYSTEM

This chapter introduces the basic commands you will use every time you run your UNIX system. The opening and closing rituals and the process of creating document files will soom become second nature to you.

Lessons Fit into Your Work Day

Avoiding Problems

Notation Conventions Used in the Text
    Italics
    Implementation Dependence—The [@. . .@] Symbol
    Command Notation
    Command Names
    Blanks and Spaces in UNIX Notation
    The Cursor—▯

Understanding Example Screens—What You Type, What You See in Response

Notation Conventions for Special Keys
    The ESCape key—ESC
    The RETURN key—⟨CR⟩
    The CONTROL Key—On Some Keyboards, CTRL
    The "INTERRUPT" key—RUB, DEL, ERASE, or BREAK
    The LINEFEED key—LF
    Non-Printing Characters—⟨CR⟩, %, ESC, Password

* UNIX™ is a trademark of Bell Laboratories.

Getting started with the UNIX system is no different than getting started in any other field of study. You begin slowly, learn the fundamentals, and gradually increase your knowledge and skills. This chapter covers the UNIX basics: entering and leaving the system, correcting typing errors, and what to do if the computer seems "stuck." Before beginning lessons, you learn basic UNIX terminology. One section of this chapter, Notation Conventions, has been marked to stand out for easy access. "Notation Conventions" describes the special UNIX symbols and words used in this book. It will be referred to frequently as you learn the UNIX "language."

LESSONS FIT INTO YOUR WORK DAY

This chapter is divided into lessons. Each lesson will usually take 15 to 60 minutes of work. A brief description of the subject, a summary of the new information you will learn, and the approximate time you will spend at the terminal is stated at the beginning of each lesson. You are probably fitting your UNIX education into your work day. The "standalone" and relatively short lessons do not require long uninterrupted periods at the terminal. Lessons longer than a half hour tend to be fatiguing. After you have completed one lesson at the terminal, it is advisable to take a short break.

Each lesson will provide you with new information and will show how it relates to your job. You will learn the essentials of the UNIX system first, and immediately begin useful work. The knowledge acquired applies directly to business computer users.

Before starting this and the following chapters, read the outline on the title page. It overviews the material in each lesson and gives you an idea of the chapter content. Please read over the material in each lesson before starting to work at the terminal.

It is important that you are seated at the terminal to do the work in the lesson. Just as the only way to learn math is through the point of a pencil, the only way to learn to use a computer operating system is by pounding the keys.

AVOIDING PROBLEMS

Beginning computer users are often afraid that they will "break" the computer by something that they type at the keyboard. You cannot break the computer hardware, but you can hurt the software and the information that has been entered if you indiscriminately use information in the advanced sections of this book. Files of letters, data, and information can be erased by doing the wrong thing at the terminal when you are using the system as a *superuser*. **NEVER** play around with the UNIX system while logged in as superuser. If there is a *system manager* who takes care of the computer at your office, ask him or her for information. If not, look in the manuals for your computer and make sure you are not a superuser.

You learn from your mistakes; and with computers, typing in mistaken information may make the system come to a stop. Causing a "hang up" is a common experience for the beginning user, and is to be expected. Beginning and experienced users make mistakes, and the last lesson in this chapter shows you what to do when a "hang up" occurs.

Notation Conventions Used in the Text

Before starting the lessons, become familiar with the notations, conventions, and basic UNIX terms in this section. Study this information to understand the symbols and terms used in the rest of the book. You may want to put a clip on the beginning of this section, as you will refer to it frequently.

Italics

Words or phrases shown in *italics* can be found in the glossary at the end of the book. Terms in the glossary are generally marked only at their first occurrence. Terms that appear only occasionally may be marked more than once.

Implementation Dependence—The [@. . .@] Convention

Whenever the symbols [@. . .@] enclose text in this book, the UNIX feature described is *implementation dependent*. Computer manufacturers have not all implemented UNIX software the same way. Your particular computer may or may not offer these features.

Command Notation

An outline style is used to describe commands and the actions you perform to initiate them. You can read the command lines as complete, terse sentences. For example, the following command,

```
ls -lr Directory1 Directory2<CR>
```

is read, "enter (type) ls -r Directory1 Directory2 and press the carriage return." Because commands in this book are shown in **boldface**, you can quickly scan the page for command instructions. The details of the command sentence are described in a later section of this chapter.

Command Names

Although we encourage you to think of command lines as sentences, many UNIX commands bear little resemblance to the English words they represent. To help you remember the functions of these commands, the full command name is placed in parentheses after the command's *mnemonic*. The important letters in the command name are highlighted in boldface type, as shown in the following examples:

```
cd (change directory)
chmod (change mode)
cat (catenate)
mkdir (make directory)
```

When a command appears many times in a chapter, its full name following the mnemonic may be shown only once or twice. If a command has not been mentioned for several pages, we will refresh your memory by restating its full name. Some command names, **date**, **echo**, **file**, **find**, **kill**, **mail**, **passwd**, **sort**, **spell**, etc., have clear meanings after you have studied the lessons.

Blanks and Spaces in UNIX Notation

Blanks and *spaces*, although not represented by printed characters on the screen, are real characters in the UNIX system. If you are having difficulty getting the UNIX system to understand your commands, there is a good chance that you are either putting blanks where they do not belong, or have not put them where they are expected to be. For example, the UNIX system will not accept the command.

```
ls-r l Directory1 Directory2<CR>
```

because a blank is required between the command (**ls**) and its options (**r** and **l**). However, simply adding the space after **ls**,

```
ls -r l Directory1 Directory2<CR>
```

will not work either. Just as the UNIX system requires a space after the command, it cannot accept one between its options without a separate hyphen for each option. If you remove the blank, the command will be correct:

```
ls -rl Directory1 Directory2<CR>
```

You must always put one blank where expected, but if you accidentally type two or more, the system will ignore the extras. Important: In some cases we have used the symbol ⱡ to indicate a space or blank where it might not otherwise be obvious.

The Cursor—⬚

Video display terminals customarily indicate the point on the screen where the next typed character will appear by illuminating the spot or area. This illuminated spot is called the *cursor*. The exact appearance of the cursor varies from machine to machine, and some application programs have their own cursor size and shape. The most common cursor is a solid rectangle or an underline. Some cursors blink; on some terminals the user is allowed to select the cursor character, whether it should blink and, if it blinks, what its blink rate should be. Our symbol for the on-screen cursor is ⬚.

Understanding Example Screens—What You Type, What You See in Response

When using a book to interact with a computer, it can be exasperating to relate the contents of your screen to the text. Descriptions of what *should* happen are often confusing. Because pictures are worth more than a hundreds of words, each lesson in this book contains screen illustrations that reflect exactly what you should be typing and seeing in response. As much as possible, what you see is what you get.

Characters that you are to type are shown in **boldface**. *The system's response to your typed input is shown in normal (not bold) type.*

Sometimes large blocks of text (letters, mail lists) are used to demonstrate commands. Part of the text not relating to the actions being learned may be omitted. Three dots aligned vertically on the left side of the screen indicate that part of the screen display is missing.

```
$ cat jobreply
Letter to Andrea Applicant
from General Manufacturing Co.
   .
   .
   .
Sincerely yours,
Mary Jones,
Manager, General Manufacturing Co.
$ ▯
```

The **$** is a shell prompt. The shell prompt notifies you that the system is ready to receive your next command. The shell is explained in the section on "Concept—The UNIX Shell."

Notation Conventions for Special Keys

The ESCape Key—ESC

The symbol **ESC** (usually the way the key is named on the keyboard) means that you should press this key. Escape has several functions, all relating to exiting one program or command for another.

The RETURN Key—⟨CR⟩

The return key tells the computer that you want it to take the information just typed and perform the appropriate action on it. It is like a green light to the computer to go ahead and start working. When a carriage return is required, it is noted by ⟨**CR**⟩. You never have to guess. If no carriage return symbol is shown, none is required.

The CONTROL Key—on Some Keyboards, CTRL

The control key is just a shorthand method of telling the computer what to do. By pressing the control key and another key (usually a letter) simultaneously, you quickly tell the system to perform an action. In contrast, typing out the commands represented by the *control character* might take one or more lines of typing words and numbers. The control key is indicated by a "caret" (^) symbol, and the combination of control and another key, the control character, looks like "^G or ^S." Every combination of the control key plus another key (^A, ^B. . .^Z) represents a different action. You can see that the control keys are very powerful, and offer you many different "shorthand" options. Control keys are used extensively in UNIX, and although learning them will take a little initial effort, they will soon become second nature to you.

The "INTERRUPT" Key—RUB, DEL, ERASE, or BREAK

Sometimes it is necessary to *interrupt* a command in progress. An interruption makes the system stop whatever it is doing at the moment and return to the shell prompt. (Remember the shell prompt from the last section.) The interrupt key on your keyboard may be called RUBOUT (RUB), DELETE (DEL), ERASE, or occasionally, BREAK. We refer to this "key" as the interrupt. On-screen interrupts are called **INTR**. Your system may respond with the printed message "interrupt" when the key is pressed.

The LINEFEED Key—LF

LINEFEED is a key seldom used on modern video terminals, but it is occasionally used by the UNIX system. UNIX software was developed on terminals that printed on paper, not on a video display. When using a paper printout, linefeed tells the paper to advance. Since video terminals just erase and reprint over and over on the same "TV" surface, linefeed is not needed. However, the UNIX system is so big, and UNIX "gurus" like every single feature so much that linefeed remains in the system.

     The last lesson in this chapter uses linefeed. The linefeed character does not print on the screen; it will be shown as **LF** in any discussion.

Non-Printing Characters—⟨CR⟩, ^, ESC, Password

Carriage return, line feed, control characters, your password, and *escape* are characters which do not print on the screen and are highlighted within a gray frame. The first instance of this in the tutorials is noted and explained again.

BASIC TERMS IN THE UNIX SYSTEM

Among UNIX afficionados and beginners alike, the language of the system is considered terse. However, experienced UNIX users often express their pleasure in, and even semifanatical devotion to, the language. Beginners' responses are sometimes quite different, ranging from confused to frustrated.

Yes, the *UNIX command language* is a new vocabulary; like any new learning experience, gaining fluency in "UNIXese" will take some practice. The only way you will learn the UNIX command language is to use it. The lessons in this book are designed to put the commands to work, so that you will perform useful tasks while learning. Before beginning the lessons, however, the overall plan and principles of the UNIX system must be touched on. Although you will not understand everything the first time through, studying and returning to this section will put the commands that you learn in perspective. With experience you will feel less like you're driving a car in the fog with no lights and more like you're looking out the window, holding a roadmap, seeing the lay of the land.

Concept—The UNIX Shell

The usefulness of the UNIX *shell* to your business data processing is so great that a full chapter has been devoted to it. At this point it is important to master its essential features. (You will fill in the details in Chapters 6.)

The concept of the shell is different than most computer features you have learned in the past. It is easiest to understand by using an analogy.

The shell can be compared to the membrane surrounding a living cell. If you remember your high school biology, the cell membrane is a rather smart entity, controlling the flow of food materials and information (remember DNA?) in and out of the cell. It protects the cell from damage by monitoring and stopping destructive material, and is in itself a complete system. Inside the cell are the nucleus, which controls the whole cell, and various assisting entities that perform specific tasks related to normal life and growth.

In UNIX, the shell is like a cell membrane, containing and protecting the programs and *kernel* software. The kernel (the UNIX nucleus) contains the programs that activate the hardware system. The shell takes information and data that is presented to it, and decides if it should be allowed to enter the system, where it should go, and what to do with the resulting response it gets from the kernel and related software.

"Shorthand" commands that you give the system (including control characters and command lines) are expanded by this smart shell program to many lines of information, often sent to several different areas of the UNIX system. The shell also keeps track of where *you* are, and returns the response to *your* terminal, even if there are many inputs from different users at the same time.

The shell is sometimes called a command interpreter; it takes your typed request (command) and figures out what you want (interprets).

Fig. 2.1 Shell-Kernel Symbolic Structure

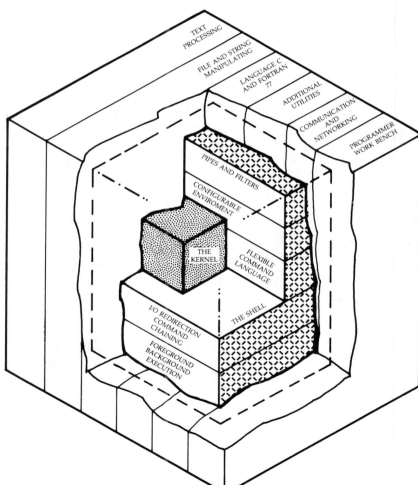

The Shell Does More Than One Thing at a Time

The shell can handle more than one simple command at a time. You don't have to type just one input and wait for a response. You can give it a whole sequence of information in one line, and it is smart enough to read the line and see what you want. It directs the system's programs and kernel to perform the whole sequence without requiring more inputs from you until it is complete. For example, you could tell it to format a document, print it, and turn off all in one *command line*.

The Shell Prompt ($)

Whenever the UNIX system is ready to accept a command, it displays the shell prompt ($).

The shell prompt is a visible indicator that the shell program is active and ready to accept your commands. In this book we indicate the shell prompt by the dollar sign symbol ($) since this symbol is most common to UNIX systems. However, the symbol is not universally used. Some systems use the percent symbol (%) for the shell prompt. You can make the substitution in your book. Some microcomputer manufacturers use yet other symbols for the shell prompt. You will determine yours by using your system.

The Command

Commands instruct the computer to perform some clearly defined task or operation. The command sequence has two steps. First, the command name and any desired options or *arguments* are typed on the command line. Second, pressing the return key (⟨**CR**⟩) executes the command. This command sequence may be compared to the grammatical structure of a sentence. The parts of the command sentence are given in a very precise vocabulary and arranged in a specific order.

The *Command Line*

The command line comprises all the characters, including blank spaces, that you use to build your command. The command line is typed after the shell prompt, on the same line.

The *Command Syntax*

The order and format in which most commands are typed on the command line is referred to as the command syntax.

The Command Sentence

Commands may be thought of as simple sentences used to address the computer. Once you have mastered the concept of the command sentence, your sessions with the UNIX system will quickly become conversations. Let's examine the following English sentence: UNIX, list Directory1 and Directory2. This command is telling the UNIX system to list two directories, in this case, files of telephone numbers. This sentence may be analyzed as follows:

SUBJECT	ACTION (Verb)	OBJECTS
UNIX	list	Directory1 Directory2

The format of this sentence: subject, verb, object is like the English language, and is the basic format for all UNIX commands. Since the UNIX system is the subject of all commands, it is never stated. However, it is implied in UNIX command language; you can read the shell prompt as shorthand for "UNIX."

The verb of the sentence has the same function in UNIX command language as a verb does in English. Commands (verbs) are usually abbreviated. Here, the verb "list" is abbreviated as **ls**. The shorter commands are, the less work it is to type them. There is also less chance of making a typographical error.

Arguments

We have now examined the subject (UNIX) and verb (command) in the command sentence. The next object or *argument* is what the command verb acts on. There may be more than one argument in the UNIX command sentence. Most of the time, the argument is just a file of information. You are telling UNIX to do something to a file of data or text. Now make the sentence

UNIX, list Directory1 and Directory2

into a command sentence. First, since we said the subject, UNIX, is always understood, we can drop it; second, list is shortened to **ls**, a UNIX program. The "official" UNIX sentence becomes:

```
ls Directory1 Directory2
```

We have just told the system to list the contents of the two phone lists.

Options

The ability to modify the meaning of the command verb adds power to the UNIX system. In English, such modifiers are called adverbs. In UNIX command language, they are called *options*. Options add refinements to the actions of the command verb. In the example above, we could have said,

```
UNIX, list "long" Directory1 and Directory2
```

The word long is an option (adverb). In the UNIX command vocabulary, "long" means to list not just summary information about the directories but all the information pertaining to them. Again, the word "long" is abbreviated to l, so that the "list long" command becomes

```
ls -l Directory1 Directory2
```

Hyphens in the Command Line

Note the hyphen before l. Most options in UNIX command language must be separated from the command verb by a blank space, and they are usually preceded by a hyphen (-).

Just as there can be any number of adverbs in an English sentence, so a UNIX command sentence can have many options. For example, if we wish to reverse the order in which the information is listed, we can add the letter "r" (for reverse) to the options. The command then appears as

```
ls -lr Directory1 Directory2
```

Some commands have many arguments, and some have none. A few commands perform one function with arguments and quite another function without. The UNIX system is very large, and there are hundreds of commands and options. Their exact usage varies, but the concepts that you have learned here give you a framework for understanding the variations covered later in this book.

To review, the usual syntax of a UNIX command sentence is

```
prompt command [(options). . .] arguments. . .
```

STARTING THE LESSONS

The rest of this chapter contains interactive lessons. You can learn the UNIX system only by experience. You *must* type in the lessons on your computer and experience the responses to become proficient. When the lessons require you to enter characters or words, enter them exactly as shown and observe the results. Do not omit any steps.

Each lesson follows a step-by-step format. The usual order of these steps is:

Step 1   The procedure for executing the command is stated: type **date**.

Step 2   The screen display is shown as it appears before the command is typed.

Step 3   The command is shown exactly as you should type it.

Step 4   The screen display is given as it appears after the command is executed and the results have appeared on the screen. A typical example of this procedure is given below:

Type the command **date**.   (STEP 1)

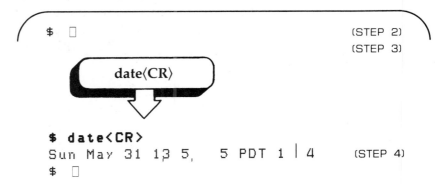

$ **date<CR>**
Sun May 31 13 5,   5 PDT 1 | 4   (STEP 4)
$ ☐

It is usually clear in the examples where a given procedure begins and ends; in some cases, a double rule makes the end of the sequence obvious. In later chapters, the size of some displays requires representing them differently, and these representations are explained as they occur.

Making Notes on Questions and Problems

Write in this book! (unless it belongs to someone else). When questions or problems arise (and they undoubtedly will), note them. Make sure to note your questions and the steps that led to them. Write down any messages that the computer gives you, and note any hardware changes like lights or buzzers.

If you have problems, you can talk to your system manager, computer technician, or, for many micros, call the manufacturer's 800-hotline. They will want you to recreate exactly the displays and circumstances that prompted the problem. Take down specific information they give you so you know what to do the next time the problem happens. They'll get justifiably angry if you call them again because you don't remember what they told you!

Setting Up to Get Started

Before beginning your first session at the terminal, make certain of several things specific to your brand of computer. See that your system is in the *multiuser mode*, not the *single-user mode*. If you are working on a large system or accessing the UNIX system via a *modem*, it is unlikely that you will be in single-user mode. If you are working on a microcomputer, look in the manuals and follow instructions to get into the multiuser mode when you are *not* a superuser. DO NOT use this book to learn the UNIX system while you are superuser or you may destroy files!

LESSON 2.1:	How to Get Into and Out of Your UNIX System
NEW KNOWLEDGE:	Use of login (user name, password), and logout commands; the **date** command
APPROXIMATE TIME:	20–25 minutes

We cannot cover turning on all of the 100+ computers using UNIX software; you must carry out the preliminary operations of powering up and gaining access to your UNIX system by using the computer manuals. It is assumed that you are now sitting in front of a terminal display similar to the following. (The company name or other legends that appear are called the system "banner.")

```
GENERAL MANUFACTURING COMPANY UNIX SYSTEM
login:  ☐
```

The login Command— password and username

Initial contact with the UNIX system is always made through the login command. In the display shown above, you are being asked to "introduce yourself" by typing in your *username*. Every user of the UNIX system must be assigned a username, sometimes called a *login name* or *account name*. You will usually be assigned your own name or some variant or abbreviated spelling of it as your username. You will also be assigned a *password* to accompany your username if your company requires passwords.

The UNIX system maintains an internal list of every authorized user. Your first contact with the UNIX system will be the process of verifying your username and password. If you are using a big UNIX system and have not yet been assigned a username or a password, contact the person in your organization who is responsible for system management. If you are using a micro, consult your system documentation for instructions on establishing usernames and passwords. You are probably free to use any words you choose. If you have a username, you are ready to begin.

```
login: chris<CR>
```

You should now see the following display on the monitor:

```
login chris
password:
```

The appearance of the word "password" in the display tells you that the UNIX system requires a password. The system wants to be certain that the person at the terminal is an authorized user. The password is your secret ID, known only to you and the computer. In a big system, you are assigned an initial password when you receive your username. In some cases, the system manager will not assign you a password, assuming that you want to create one of your own. No one knows your password. If you forget it, you will need a new one.

When carrying out Step 2, your password will not be printed on the screen as you type it. Bystanders cannot learn it by looking over your shoulder. We use "accountdiv" as our password.

Entering the password

```
login: chris<CR>
password: accountdiv<CR>
```

If you make an incorrect entry during login, the UNIX system will not inform you that the procedure was incorrect until both the username and password have been entered, nor will it tell you which of the two was incorrect. If you make an error in entering username or password, simply enter a double carriage return ⟨**CR**⟩⟨**CR**⟩ and try again.

After you log in successfully, some large systems will respond with messages from the system manager, such as scheduled maintenance, changes to system files, or a "logo" (identifying graphical pattern). The system manager handles the display seen at login. The diagram below shows a typical result of a successful login.

```
login: chris<CR>
Password: accountdiv<CR>

(1) We are getting short of disk storage
space.
Please remove all old files as soon as
possible.

(2) The system wil be shut down from 12
midnight Saturday to 8 am Sunday for
scheduled maintenance.
$  □
```

The presence of the system messages together with the shell prompt, **$**, indicates that you have correctly logged on the UNIX system. The cursor is now positioned next to the **$** to indicate where your typed commands will appear. Suppose, however, you receive the following display:

```
login: Chris<CR>
Password: accountdiv<CR>
Login incorrect
login:
```

Capital Letters

What's wrong? Notice that your accurate username "chris" is composed of all lowercase letters, but the login name used in the example begins with a capital C. The UNIX system will not recognize either your login name or your password unless they are both exactly identical to the ones assigned. Capital letters count here!

The date Command—
Error Messages

If you have logged in successfully, you are now ready to have the UNIX system go to work for you. Let's try a simple command. The date command tells the system to display the current time and date. Type **date⟨CR⟩**.

```
$ date<CR>
Sun Aug 8 22:04:09 PDT 1984
$ □
```

What happens if you enter a command incorrectly? You receive an *error message*. Make a deliberate mistake to see an error message. Type *dote* instead of *date*. You should see the following display:

```
$ dote<CR>
dote: Command not found.
$ □
```

When you entered the word "dote," you used a word not in UNIX's command vocabulary. The system searched all of its internal lists for a command "dote," and, failing to find it, informed you that the command was not found.

Not all errors are simple typographical mistakes. If you enter the command correctly, but enter an incorrect option, you will see an error message. The UNIX system will usually inform you of your error as shown in the display below:

```
$ date -t<CR>
date: bad conversion
$ □
```

The system interpreted this command as an attempt to set the date rather than as a simple request to display it. The syntax shown is not the correct one for setting the date. The system issued an error message and returned to the shell prompt.

You will discover that error messages in the UNIX system are terse, leaving it up to you to find out the exact nature of the error. Lengthier and more specific error messages might be considered desirable, but more detail requires the retention of more information in the computer and slows it down. A great deal of work is being done with the UNIX system to make its error messages more informative, particularly on micros.

The logout Command

We will conclude this first lesson with the *logout* procedure. Just as you inform the UNIX system that you wish to use it by logging in, you must formally leave the system by "logging out." If you fail to log out, anyone who works at your terminal will have access to your files, and if you are paying for computer time, your account may be billed for the time between your login and logout. On microcomputers, not logging out before turning off the power can result in problems with your files. Combine our discussion of logout with the instructions in your manual for logging off and shutting down your system.

Many beginning computer users mistakenly assume that if they turn off the machine, they have somehow automatically logged out; this is no more the case than turning the computer on automatically logs you in. The only possible exception to this rule is if you are accessing the UNIX system through a telephone and modem. The system will probably log you out automatically when you hang up the telephone. Consult your system manager to verify this.

Logout by typing control-d: ^d. Remember that control characters do not appear on your screen.

```
$  ^d
login:
```

You know that you have logged out correctly when UNIX prompts you to log in again.

Other Ways to logout

Not all systems use control-d to log out. On UNIX systems using the UC Berkeley UNIX adaptation, you may be instructed to use the explicit command **logout**. The logout command eliminates confusion and prevents you from accidentally logging yourself out. The system message appears:

```
% ^d
use "logout" to logout.
% logout<CR>
login: ▯
```

Before going on to Lesson 2.2, practice logging in and out, even trying some incorrect entries to see what happens.

LESSON 2.2:
NEW KNOWLEDGE:
APPROXIMATE
TIME:

Correcting Typing Errors on the Command Line
Use of the @ and # characters

10–12 minutes

This is a short lesson that provides two helpful tools. The @ and # symbols let you correct typing errors while entering a command.

Erasing a Line

Typing @ (the at symbol) cancels the entire command line. This single character is called *line kill* or simply "kill." When it is typed, the cursor will jump to the next line, but the incorrect line is still seen on the screen. Alternatively, some computers backspace over the entire line and wait on the same line for the correct input. In either case, you retype the entire command correctly. The kill command is especially useful when you have already typed a number of characters but realize that the entire command is not the one wanted, or that there is an error in the first few characters of the line. Using the @ command, you can just cancel the entire line and start over.

Erasing a Character

If you have only typed one or two incorrect characters, you can cancel individual characters by typing the pound symbol, #, *erase*. Erase negates the character immediately preceding it on the line.

It is also possible to "cancel" the command line by pressing the carriage return. The system attempts to execute what you have entered, and is not able to do so. It sends you an error message and a prompt symbol for starting over.

The following exercises demonstrate the use of these two characters. Step 1 shows the word "testwords." The word has no significance, and you may use any letters or words you wish.

NOTE: *As in all of the exercises in this book, we assume that you have your system up and running, that you have successfully logged into the UNIX system, and that the shell prompt is on the screen.*

The line kill Command, @

Type in your example letters or words and then the @ symbol. When the cursor reaches the point at which the @ character was entered, observe that the display changes to one of the two below.

```
$ testwords@
$  □
```

or

```
$  □
```

NOTE: *The @ character may not work on your system. If this is the case, you will have to consult your system manager to find out which character is used instead. The control-X key is often used as a kill character.*

The erase Character, #

Assume that you intended to execute the date command but have actually typed "datt." To correct the error, type "#" (which negates the second "t"), then type the correct letter, "e." You should see the display below.

```
$ datt#e<CR>
Mon May 3 08:04:15 PDT 1984
$  □
```

The system's response is the date and time, which confirms that your corrected command was interpreted as **date⟨CR⟩**.

Each time the # symbol is typed, it negates the directly previous character. For example, if you had typed the final "e" of the date command, you would have to cancel both it and the extra "t." Your display would then appear as:

```
$ datte##e<CR>
$ Mon May 3 08:06:15 PDT 1984
$  
```

Incidentally, the @ and # characters may be used during login; you may find them difficult to use when entering your password since it is not displayed on the screen.

LESSON 2.3:   Changing Your Password
NEW KNOWLEDGE: Use of the **passwd** command
APPROXIMATE
TIME: 10 minutes

If you suspect that someone has learned your password, you will want to change it. Most users like to change passwords periodically just to be safe. When you change passwords, use an everyday word that relates to your work and that you are not likely to forget. Some users have set up a password based on code or arcane symbols only to later forget it. They then need to go through the unnecessary experience of asking the system manager to log in as *superuser* and delete their password.

A password can be as short as four characters if it contains a mixture of uppercase and lowercase characters, or six characters if it is all one case. A password of six to ten characters is ideal. Any more than ten characters increases the probability of a typing error.

You change your password with the **passwd** command. This command can also be used to install a password for the first time on some systems.

Changing Your Password   Type **passwd⟨CR⟩**.

```
$ passwd<CR>
Changing password for chris
Old password: accountdiv<CR>
New password: financial<CR>
Retype new password: financial<CR>
$ ▯
```

The next time you log in, the UNIX system will recognize your new password, "financial." Since you are unable to see your new password as you type it, the computer prompts you twice, compares the two entries, and gives you an error message if the two entries don't match exactly.

The following display shows the response to this.

```
$ passwd<CR>
Changing password for chris
Old password: acountdiv<CR>
Sorry
$ passwd<CR>
Changing password for chris
Old password: accountdiv<CR>
New password: financial <CR>
Retype new password: finacial<CR>
mismatch--password unchanged
$ 
```

LESSON 2.4:	Reviving a Stalled Terminal
NEW KNOWLEDGE:	Procedures to follow when the system stops
APPROXIMATE	
TIME:	30 minutes

A stalled terminal will soon become as simple for you to handle as changing a typewriter ribbon is today. No computer system is perfect: from time to time they fail. When they do, you are the first to know. You are not expected to "fix" the machine, but often the only thing wrong is that the system is "hungup," that is, in a condition that suspends the execution of instructions. This condition can usually be handled right at the terminal. Unless you have dealt with computer systems before, some of the instructions described here may be new to you. Just read them through carefully, and consult manuals, more experienced users, or system managers if needed.

Reviving a Dead Terminal

Most frequently, the terminal appears dead—make sure it is turned on! If on, it may prevent you from logging in. Sometimes, the terminal will freeze up in the middle of a session. It may print nonsense, or it may not print anything, completely ignoring your commands.

Control-q—^q

Try entering control-q (^q). Your problem might be a suspended display caused by entering a control-s (^s). Wait for at least a minute to get a response after ^q. If lots of people are using the system, it will respond slowly.

The Interrupt Key—The Forced Quit Signal, ^\

If you are sure that the response you are awaiting will never occur, or if you do not want to wait any longer, you can interrupt the command in progress by pressing the interrupt key. This signal is usually generated by a key labeled RUB, RUBOUT, DEL, DELETE, or ERASE. (*Do not* use the BREAK key; it may log you out!) Although rarely the case, the "forced quit" signal (^\) may terminate the program that is causing the terminal to "hang."

Escape—ESC

If you have been using an edit program (next chapter), you may be stuck in text entry mode. Press **ESC** twice. If the terminal's beeper (bell) sounds, you are probably in the "open" or "visual" mode of the editor. Typing a single capital "Q" should bring you back to command mode and allow you to recover. If the beeper does not sound, type in one or more lines consisting of a period by itself: .⟨**CR**⟩. This step takes you out of text entry mode and returns you to the editing command level, where you should be able to interact with the system.

Cables and Connectors

When the terminal does not print anything you type and does not sound the bell, there may be a problem in the mechanical connectors in your equipment. Check that all cabling and plugs are firmly in place. If you are using the UNIX system via a modem, make sure that the carrier light on the modem is still on; if it is not, the system has logged you out. You will have to redial and log back in.

Control-d—ˆd

If you are willing to run the risk of logging out, enter ˆ**d**. Several programs instantly terminate upon receiving a control-d.

Log In Again

As a final resort, try to log out and log back in. If you are using a desktop system, you may have to turn off the computer. Pull all floppy disks out of the drives before turning off the power or you may not have data on the floppy any more.

Ask for Help

If all of the foregoing measures fail, go to the system manager and ask for help or call the 800 number of the computer manufacturer.

CUSTOMIZING YOUR TERMINAL WITH stty

When you log in, the UNIX system makes certain assumptions about the kind of terminal you are using. Specific functions are arbitrarily assigned to certain keys. (Actually, the keys themselves are not assigned, but rather the system's interpretation of the internal codes generated by the keys.) What do you do if you don't like the key assignment or if your keyboard is missing one of the keys the UNIX system is expecting? The system is very flexible: it allows keys (codes) to be reassigned to your liking. This may be necessary if you're accessing the system via telephone, since the UNIX system can't possibly know in advance what kind of terminal is calling in.

Because video terminals generate a backspace cursor motion with 'control-h', which erases the previous character, many UNIX users want to trade the **#** erase character for control-h. Control-h is visually desirable as an erase character because it causes the video terminal to move the cursor backwards over the unwanted characters as it cancels (usually erases) them, allowing you to retype over them. Unlike **#**, control-h or backspace does not leave a trail of extra characters on your screen.

The command **stty** (**s**et **t**ele**ty**pe), reassigns keys, changes tabs, and governs a host of other terminal characteristics.

First we will show how to use **stty** to ascertain the current assignment of keys, then how to use it to customize the erase character, the line kill character, and other functions. You may assign almost any key to a function, but assigning functions to control characters assures continued availability of the full upper- and lowercase character set in your work.

The behavior of **stty** is extremely dependent on your system. Since the terminals of desktop UNIX systems may be custom designed for the particular system, such systems may not offer you a full list of terminal features that can be changed.

stty, when stated in simple command form *without arguments*, will display a list of important terminal options together with the current value of these options. The command can also be used to **set** these options. This dual role of **stty** will become clearer in the examples below. For now, type **stty⟨CR⟩** to see a list of your terminal's characteristics. Here's what you might see on a typical multiuser system.

```
$ stty<CR>
speed 9600 baud
erase = '#'; kill = '@'
even odd -nl echo -tabs
$ 
```

This display shows how some of the important features
on the terminal are currently set. Those of interest to use now
all appear on the line below 'speed 9600 baud.' This line shows
the UNIX system's *default values* for erase (**#**) and line kill (**@**).

**Resetting Erase, Kill,
and Interrupt Characters**

Reassign the erase key first:

```
$ stty erase ^h<CR>
$ 
```

The '^h' will not appear on your screen as you type it.
(As you may remember from our discussion of control characters,
a control command is issued by holding down the control key
and simultaneously pressing the desired letter, in this case
'**h**'.) If you choose, you may type the two printing characters
'^' (caret) followed by 'h', by surrounding them with double
or single quotation marks. Although you are usually permitted
to enter either upper- or lowercase characters, **stty** may display
them only in uppercase. Verify the change with **stty** ⟨**CR**⟩:

```
$ stty<CR>
speed 9600 baud
erase = '^H'; kill = '@'
even odd -nl echo -tabs
$ 
```

Practice using **^h** as an erase character. Try typing a *definitely*
incorrect command, such as **datsnafu**. Before ⟨**CR**⟩, backspace

the cursor to the '**t**' and then type **e** ⟨**CR**⟩. You'll get the familiar
date response.

```
         5 backspaces          "e"          <R>
datsnafu[ ] =========>  $ dat[ ] ====> $date<CR>
$ datsnafu^h^h^h^h^he<CR>
Mon May 3 09:45:12 PDT 1983
$ ▯
```

If your terminal contains a **BACKSPACE** key, it is exactly
equivalent to a ^h. If characters are not visually erased as you
back up over them, remember that they actually are canceled
as far as the computer is concerned. If you would like them
visually erased also, you must set some other **stty** option.
Consult your system manual for more information.

Next, let's change the 'line kill' function from @ to control-
x (^**x**). You could choose a different control character if you
wish; however, ^**x** is a common choice for the line kill character.
It is changed with exactly the same command sequence as the
erase character, but this time the individual characters are
entered, surrounded by quotation marks. Again, verify that
the change has been installed:

```
$ stty kill '^x'<CR>
$ stty<CR>
speed 9600 baud
erase = 'H'; kill ='^U'
even odd -raw -nl echo -tabs
$ ▯
```

Now, when you have made an error that cannot easily
be corrected by backspacing, simply type ^**x** to tell UNIX to
ignore everything you've typed since the last ⟨**CR**⟩. The cursor
will usually drop to the line below the flawed line, but a new
shell prompt will **not** appear.

Finally, users of systems using UC Berkeley UNIX® may find the default value for the interrupt character, the **delete** key, to be awkward because its use requires the hand to leave the home area on the keyboard. A common substitute for the interrupt character is control-c. If you so choose, reassign your interrupt character as well to your liking and verify as before.

The changes you have just made in the system's view of your terminal are, of course, not a permanent part of the UNIX system. When you next log in you'll find all the keys reassigned back to their default values.

Now you are ready to go further into the UNIX system. The material covered in the next chapter provides you the basic tools to create text files and documents. Approximately 75 percent of your use of the UNIX system will be spent with procedures and commands covered in Chapter 3.

3 CREATING AND EDITING DOCUMENTS

You use the editing programs to create all text and program files on the UNIX* system. Familiarity with an editing program is essential to using the UNIX system's powers.

Steps in Text Editing

Overview of Text Editors and Word Processors

Text Formatting Versus Word Processing

Text Editing and Files

The UNIX System of Editors: ed, ex, and vi
    The Edit Buffer
    Lesson 3.1: Command Mode and Text Entry Mode.
                 Entering and Exiting **vi**. Inserting text
                 The **vi** (filename), **i**, **w**, and **wq** commands
    Lesson 3.2: Cursor Motion, Part 1
                 Use of the **h**, **j**, **k**, **l**, **G**, **(** and **)** cursor
                 motion commands; deleting and replacing
                 with the **x**, **dw**, **dd**, and **r** commands
    Lesson 3.3: Cursor Motion, Part 2
                 Use of the **w/W**, **b/B**, and **e** commands
    Lesson 3.4: Advanced Cursor Motion, Part 1
                 Use of the ^ (caret), **0** (zero), **$**, **M**, and **( )**
                 (parentheses) commands; an additional use
                 of the **G** command

* UNIX™ is a trademark of Bell Laboratories.

Editing Options
The Window Option in **vi**
Line Numbering (**nu**) in **vi**
Ignorecase (**ic**) Option in **vi**
The Wrapmargin (**wm**) in **vi**

The UNIX system provides all the tools you need to develop a powerful automated office. Facilities for electronic file cabinet creation, electronic mail, calendar and rolodex functions, text editing and formatting, mail list management, accounting data storage, and other features exist in UNIX software. Common to all is the basic skill of creating and editing files, usually documents, but sometimes data-like mail lists and accounting information.

Before you can use the file handling facilities of UNIX software, you must be able to proficiently edit the information within those files. This chapter gives you the basic skills needed to move on to learning UNIX programs for the office functions listed above.

STEPS IN TEXT EDITING

The procedures of computerized editing are no different than those of "manual" editing. Steps in computer-text creation include:

- writing a rough draft
- making changes and corrections to the text
- adding new text to the original draft
- moving paragraphs to make the text flow more smoothly
- printing the finished copy after all the changes have been made
- filing a copy of the finished document so that it can be recalled and edited.

Text editors, including those discussed in this chapter, automate these procedures, speeding up and expanding your text processing powers. With a text editor, much of the redundant work is done by the computer. You are free to utilize more advanced features to improve your productivity.

OVERVIEW OF TEXT EDITORS AND WORD PROCESSORS

Before starting to use the editor, let's take a few minutes to examine exactly what a computerized text editor is and why it is superior to the conventional methods of producing and editing text. A special type of text editor called a *word processor* is compared with the editors of the UNIX system in this section.

An editor is a program that lets you enter text, make changes to it, and store it for future use. Text editors take much less time to use than a conventional typewriter. Nowhere in industry is the equation *time = money* more dramatically demonstrated than in the time saved by electronic editing.

Text editors offer many automatic features. They can check and correct spelling errors, find and replace misspelled words or phrases you want to change, and perform many related tasks.

When making changes to a document using a typewriter, the entire document must often be retyped. When the text is only a single page long, such retyping is a minor irritation. When the document is several pages or more, retyping can be a time-consuming and exhausting experience. In contrast, with a text editor you never need to retype text that is already correct. You make only corrections, changes, or additions. The text editor lets you rearrange text any way you wish with a few keystrokes.

TEXT FORMATTING VERSUS WORD PROCESSING

Text editors require an additional program to create finished, printed documents. Formatting text, including justification of margins, change of line spacing, and manipulations of a document's appearance is handled by a text formatting program. In the UNIX system, formatting is provided by a program called **nroff**. The details of this program are covered in Chapter 8, Formatting Text Files.

The UNIX text editor, **vi**, and the UNIX text formatter, **nroff**, are two separate programs. In other text processing programs, editors and text formatters are combined into one program, commonly called a word processing program.

Some word processing packages are very easy to use. Word processors on the market differ, each emphasizing features for a specific kind of use. The principal tradeoffs between editor/formatters and word processors are summarized here.

Word processors provide an edge in speed: formatted text is produced as you type, and many text revision operations are either automatic or very simple. In contrast, the UNIX system offers a greater number of operations related to data editing, two of which are particularly valuable: first, you can move within a really large file more quickly than in all but the most expensive word processors; second, many different blocks of text can be saved or set aside for inclusion at some later point without leaving a file. There are few word processors that offer these features, part of the file and data manipulation aspects of the UNIX system. An economic factor: editors come with most UNIX systems at no additional cost, which cannot be said for most word processors.

TEXT EDITING AND FILES

The file is the basic storage unit used by the UNIX system to contain information. Every document or collection of data that you type into your computer is considered a file. Think of files in much the same way you think of the common office file folder, as a manila folder of information about clients or accounting.

A document file created with a text editor has associated with it a name to identify it for future reference, just as you would label the tab on a manila folder file before putting it into the file cabinet. The name you give a document in editing is called a *filename*. We will refer to document and file interchangeably in this chapter.

THE UNIX SYSTEM OF EDITORS: ed, ex, AND vi

There are two general types of editors: line editors and screen editors. Although they both create or edit text, each does it in a different way. A line editor operates on a single line of text at a time. Specific commands are issued to recall the line to make changes to it. Still other commands must be issued to write the corrected line back into the file. This procedure has to be carried out for each line of text.

With a screen editor (or "full-screen editor") several lines of text are displayed at one time. Screen editors usually offer more automatic features to speed text production.

UNIX systems generally have three editors:

- **ed** (pronounced "e-dee") is a basic line editor. It lacks prompts and error messages, and is considered to be difficult to learn by many users. It is intended for use by programmers who reference text by line numbers.

- **ex** (pronounced "e-ex") is a line editor developed by the University of California at Berkeley. **ex** has all the functions of **ed**, plus additional commands. **ex** has informative prompts and useful options like automatic line numbering and automatic indentation. It is still a programmer's editor, and is not often used for text creation.

- **vi** (pronounced "ve-eye" and short for "**vi**sual") is a screen editing version of **ex**. Since **vi** is a descendant of **ex**, most **ex** commands are in **vi**.

The **vi** editor is faster and easier to use than the line editors **ed** and **ex**. Under some rare circumstances, the use of **vi** is not practical. If your access to the UNIX system is via a modem at 300 baud, you may find **vi**'s responses unacceptably slow. Then you must consider the use of **ed** or **ex**. However, **vi** is now almost universally available for UNIX systems, and is the most popular text editor for businesses with UNIX systems. Text editing instruction in this book is for **vi** only.

The Edit Buffer

The concept of the *edit buffer* is not the simplest introduced here, but is important so you understand why the system reacts as it will when you start editing. Fig. 3.1 shows the relationship of the edit buffer to the text production sequence.

1. A file is requested from disk.
2. Disk file is copied in the buffer.
3. Editing changes are made to file copy in the buffer.
4. When editing is complete, a request is made to write the new version onto disk.
5. Buffer file is written over old disk file. Disk now has new version in permanent storage.

The text typed with a UNIX text editing program is not automatically saved as you type it. It sits in an area of the computer's short-term memory. *All the work that you do with the text editor takes place in the edit buffer, and is temporary.* Text is not saved permanently until you execute a "write" command, which places the contents of the buffer in permanent storage.

Think of the edit buffer as a working storage area. Think of the contents of the buffer as your working copy. Once a file has been stored, you can recall a copy of it and make changes. Yet the disk copy remains unchanged until you execute a write command on the working copy; only then is the disk copy altered. In that sense the disk copy of a file is a permanent copy. It is not permanent in the sense of being unalterable, but it will remain unchanged on disk until you deliberately change or delete it.

Fig. 3.1   Buffer/Disk Relationship

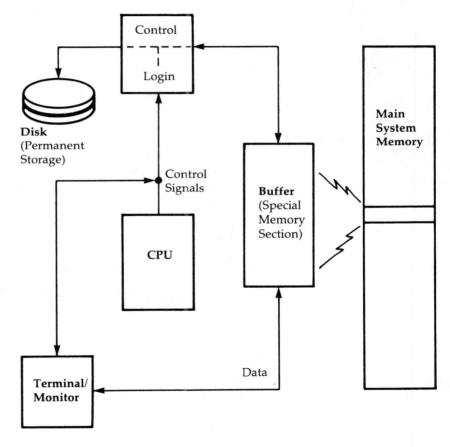

LESSON 3.1:	Command Mode and Text Entry Mode. Entering and Exiting **vi**. Inserting Text
NEW KNOWLEDGE:	The **vi** (filename), **i**, **w**, and **wq** commands
APPROXIMATE TIME:	30 minutes

If your system is not already up and running, bring it up and log in.

You enter **vi** by typing the letters **vi** followed by a space, a filename, and a ⟨**CR**⟩. Use the filename **jobreply**.

```
$ vi jobreply<CR>
```

Since there is no file called "**jobreply**" currently in existence, the UNIX system will respond by telling you. It assumes you wish to create a file by that name and allocates a working area for you labeled **jobreply**. Although the exact phrasing may vary—for example, some systems will display the message "jobreply" [new file]—the screen display should look like this:

```
□
~
~
~
"jobreply" No such file or directory
```

The squiggly lines on the left of the display are called *tildes*.

Command Mode and Text Entry Mode

Although **vi** is referred to as a single program, it is actually two subprograms. When you enter **vi**, either to create a new text file or to edit an existing file, you are in *command mode*, one of the two parts of **vi**. From command mode, you may manipulate a file by moving the cursor, delete unwanted text, or perform other editing functions. From command mode, you also save a file and leave **vi**.

To add new text to a file you must enter *text entry mode*, the other part of **vi**. The most common beginner's mistake is to forget the mode in which you are operating and either type characters into your file that should have been commands or type in text which is interpreted as commands.

The Insertion Command—i—Moves You to Text Entry Mode

You entered **vi** in command mode. To start putting text into the **jobreply** file, you move immediately into text entry mode by giving the **i**nsertion command. All keys struck from text entry mode are seen by **vi** as characters entered into your file.

The Escape Key—ESC— Moves You from Text Entry to Command Mode

Once you escape from insert mode by striking the ESC key, you return to command mode. In command mode, striking particular keys allows you to move through the text or to change the text. Keys struck in command mode do not add characters to the text.

Adding Line Numbers— The Colon : and set nu Commands

Now put some text into the **jobreply** file. The text will be used in the lessons throughout this chapter to demonstrate UNIX system operations. To make these demonstrations as clear as possible, we must be able to make exact reference to specific lines or words. Steps 1 and 2 make line numbers appear as you type text. Follow the instructions exactly. We will cover the command in more detail later.

Step 1

Press the colon (:) key to enter **ex**. Type the colon to enter **ex** and use some of its features to add line numbers. The main display remains the same except that the colon appears in the first column of the very last line of the display, and the cursor jumps down next to it, replacing the "jobreply" No such file or directory message.

~

~

~

: ▯

Step 2   Opposite the colon, type the command **set nu⟨CR⟩**.

```
  1   ☐
  ~
  ~
  ~
  ~
:set nu<CR>
```

The cursor returns to line 1 and the colon disappears. The numeral "1" appears in the first screen column, and the cursor is next to it, as shown below. In these first two steps you have commanded **vi** to add line numbers to your text for easy reference.

Step 3   Press the **i** (for insert) key. You have now left command mode and entered text entry mode. There is no apparent change in the display, but now any character you type will be treated as part of the text and will be placed in the file **jobreply**.

Step 4   Type each of the following lines exactly as shown in Table 3.1 below. After each line, press the carriage return (⟨CR⟩). If you make a mistake, do not try to make corrections at this time. Just go ahead and finish out the line. You can make all your corrections in the next lesson.

Table 3.1   Text of jobreply File

```
 1 Letter to Andrea Applicant<CR>
 2 from General Manufacturing Co. <CR>
 3 May 12, 1984<CR>
 4 Ms. Andrea Applicant<CR>
 5 1312 N. Main St.<CR>
 6 Oakland, CA 94612<CR>
 7 Dear Ms. Applicant:<CR>
 8 Thank you for expressing an interest<CR>
 9 in General Manufacturing Co.<CR>
10 After reviewing your application, <CR>
```

```
11 we find that we do not<CR>
12 have any openings suitable to<CR>
13 your qualifications at the<CR>
14 present time.<CR>
15 However, we will keep<CR>
16 your application on file<CR>
17 in the event that something<CR>
18 should become available<CR>
19 in the future.<CR>
20 We wish you the best of luck<CR>
21 in your job search, and once again,<CR>
22 thanks for your interest in<CR>
23 our organization.<CR>
24 Sincerely yours,<CR>
25 Mary Jones,<CR>
26 Manager, General Manufacturing Co.
```

Step 5   Press the **ESC** key. By pressing the ESC key, you "escape" from text entry mode and return to command mode. Now save the file and exit **vi** by following Steps 6 and 7.

Step 6   Press the colon (:) key. Observe that the main display remains unchanged except that the colon appears below the last line of text with the cursor opposite it.

Step 7   Type in the command **wq⟨CR⟩**. You have now saved the **jobreply** file and exited from **vi**. The UNIX system gives you a report on the file you just saved as shown in the display below:

```
:wq<CR>
"jobreply" 26 lines, 630 characters
$ ▯
```

Your own numbers may vary because the computer counts spaces and blanks as characters.

In the editor you can also enter the **write** command by itself without quitting by typing **:w⟨CR⟩**.

Important! When the **:w** command finishes, your cursor is returned to its original position on your screen. This command writes your **jobreply** file to a magnetic disk where it can be retrieved later for printing or further editing. If you make more changes to the file and issue another **w**rite command, the document on your screen will replace the corresponding file on the disk. Whenever you issue a write command, your file is permanently updated with your latest changes.

You should know that a computer failure would probably destroy the document you are currently editing (in the edit buffer). Fortunately, most computer failures will leave your disk files intact. If you do not want to lose many hard hours of typing in the twinkling of a power outage, a power surge, a software failure, or an accidentally yanked power cord, be sure to frequently update your work with the write command. You may issue the write command whenever you like. If you get into the habit of writing out a file about every 5–10 minutes, whether it needs it or not, you will never have to worry about losing a significant amount of text. Be sure to write out your file whenever you leave your terminal, since you never know who's going to come along and spill coffee on your keyboard while you are gone.

If your system's disk drive is damaged, you could lose your files, too. Even though your system manager should have copies of the disk, called *backups*, on hand, it is your responsibility to keep paper printouts of all your computerized text tucked away. The basic rule of computing is to never trust any system to always work the way it is supposed to.

Before going on to Lesson 3.2, practice entering and exiting **vi** several times by repeating Steps 1 and 7 above.

Summary

The first step in creating a file is usually to decide a name for the file and to run the **vi** program by typing **vi (filename)⟨CR⟩**. It is possible to "bring up" **vi** without assigning a filename, but that is not the usual procedure. In this case, the filename **jobreply** was chosen for you.

After executing, or at least initiating, **vi**, you began entering text and making preliminary edits. Several distinct operations/commands were involved in this editing:

- *You switched modes* as required, using the **i** command to put **vi** in the text entry mode and the **ESC** command to return **vi** to command mode.
- You also switched between line editing and visual editing commands. By pressing the colon (**:**) key, you set line numbers, wrote the file into storage and quit from **vi**. Commands given with the colon prompt are useful ex editor commands which are compatible with **vi**.
- You saved your file and exited from **vi** by the **wq** (**write/quit**) command.

The operations you performed and the sequence in which you performed them are the same operations you will always perform whenever you create text files in **vi**. You learn cursor motion, block moves and saves, string searches, and advanced cursor motion commands in the next lessons. However, with the minimum set of commands just learned, you have experienced the basic technique of text file creation.

In Lesson 3.2, you gain experience with cursor motion commands. You learn enough about fixing mistakes to edit the **jobreply** file. As you use the next few lessons on cursor motion, refer to Table 3.2, on page 83, for a summary of all the cursor commands.

LESSON 3.2:	Cursor Motion, Part 1
NEW KNOWLEDGE:	Use of the **h**, **j**, **k**, **l**, **G**, **(** and **)** cursor motion commands; deleting and replacing with the **x**, **dw**, **dd**, and **r** commands
APPROXIMATE TIME:	15 minutes

If you are not already up and running, bring up the system, log in, and access the **jobreply** file by typing **vi jobreply⟨CR⟩**. Set the line numbering by typing **:set nu⟨CR⟩**.

The easy way to move the cursor around is to use the keys on the terminal designed for cursor movement. Many terminals have four special keys with arrows printed on them; pressing these keys usually causes the cursor to move in the direction of the arrows. If your terminal has no arrow keys, use the **h**, **j**, **k**, and **l** keys while in **vi**. They perform exactly the same operations. Use the **h** key to move the cursor to the left, the **l** key to move it to the right. The **j** key moves the cursor down, and the **k** key moves it up.

The **l** (the letter l) key moves the cursor to the *right* one space at a time. Move the cursor three spaces to the right with the **l** key.

1 Letter...

1 Letter...

The **h** key does the opposite. It moves the cursor to the left, one space at a time. Use the **h** key to move the cursor back to the beginning of the line.

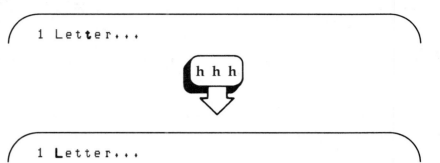

You are not limited to moving just one character at a time using these keys. If you wish to move five characters to the right, you precede the command by the numeral 5. Type **5l**, and observe that the cursor moves five spaces to the right.

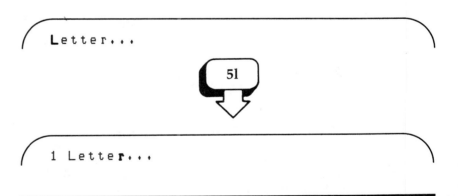

4h will move the cursor back to the left four spaces.

```
1 Letter...
```

The **j** key moves the cursor *down* one line at a time. Move the cursor down to line 5 with the **j** key.

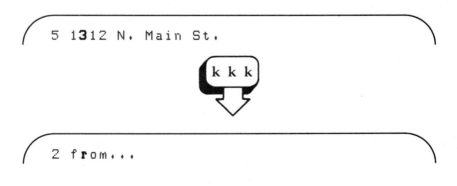

```
1 Letter...
```
jj j jj
```
5 1312 N. Main St.
```

Use the **k** key to move the cursor *up* one line at a time to line 2.

```
5 1312 N. Main St.
```
k k k
```
2 from...
```

Type **9j** to send the cursor down nine lines, to line 11.

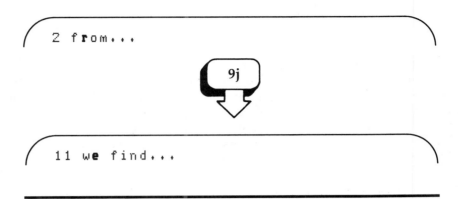

Send the cursor back up three lines, to line 8, by typing **3k.**

Capital Letters Count!

The **h**, **j**, **k**, and **l** keys perform entirely different functions in lowercase (No SHIFT) than they do in uppercase (SHIFT employed). For example, while the **j** key is used to move the cursor down a line, the same key in uppercase performs the special job of joining lines together. Unlike **h** and **l**, which move the cursor left and right, **capital H** sends the cursor to the beginning of the *first* line on the screen, while **capital L** sends it to the beginning of the *last* line on the screen. And although **k** moves the cursor up one line at a time, a capital **k** does nothing at all in **vi!** Whenever we refer to a key in a **vi** command, be sure to note whether it is uppercase or lowercase.

The **G** (**G**o) Command

The capital **G** (**G**o) command will move the cursor to any line when the **G** is preceded by a line number. For instance, **1G** moves the cursor to the beginning of line 1. Note that the numeral 1 must be pressed; the computer does not recognize the letter l as a number—typists may have to break an old habit here.

```
6
7 Dear Ms. Applicant:
8 Thank you...
```

1G

```
1 Letter to Andrea Applicant
```

The **G** command by itself moves the cursor to the beginning of the last line in the file. Type **G.**

```
1 Letter to Andrea Applicant
    .
    .
    .
22 thanks for your interest in
```

```
 4 Ms. Andrea Applicant
 .
 .
 .
26 Manager, General Manufacturing Co.
```

Moving to the Beginning or End of a Paragraph

The { (opening brace) key moves the cursor backward to the beginning of the paragraph in which you are currently working. Since **jobreply** is not broken down into paragraphs, **vi** treats the entire file as one paragraph, and the cursor is sent to the beginning of the file. The counterpart to "{" is the closing brace }, which moves the cursor forward to the next paragraph. Again, since **jobreply** is seen by the editor as a single paragraph, the } will place the cursor at the end of the file. Try it.

```
 4 Ms. Andrea Applicant
 .
 .
26 Manager, General Manufacturing Co.
```

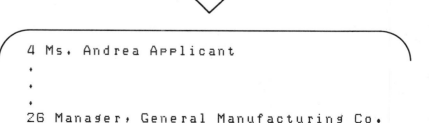

```
 4 Ms. Andrea Applicant
 .
 .
 .
26 Manager, General Manufacturing Co.
```

Tildes as Null Line Markers

In some cases, when you move to the last line of text, the line will appear in a location other than the last line in the window. When this occurs, the system fills out the remaining lines of the window with tildes. The tildes simply indicate that there are no more lines of text in the file. The display may look like the one below. These end lines are called *null lines*. You saw these lines when you first created the **jobreply** file. Send the cursor back to the beginning of the file with {.

```
19 in the future.
   ◆
   ◆
   ◆
26 Manager, General Manufacturing Co.
   ~
   ~
   ~
   ~
```

{

```
1 Letter to Andrea Applicant
   ◆
   ◆
   ◆
23 our organization.
```

Deleting and Replacing Characters

Deleting a character on the screen or replacing one character with another is basic to **vi**. Pressing the **x** key while in command mode will cause the character at the position of the cursor to disappear. When you actually do this you observe that the deletion does not leave a blank space. All the characters on the line to the right of the deleted position move one character to the left. For example, suppose the cursor was positioned over the **r** in the following line, as indicated by the boldface:

```
Please forward your new mailing
address.
```

The **x** key

If you press the **x** key, the line would appear as follows:

```
Please foward your new mailing address.
```

The cursor is still in the same column; however, it is now over the **w** in "forward." If the **x** key is pressed again, the display becomes:

```
Please foard your new mailing address.
```

Delete a Word—The **dw** Command

You will frequently need to delete an entire word or line. To delete a single word, place the cursor over the first letter of the word you wish to delete and press the **d** key, then the **w** key. For example, in the line above, suppose you wanted to delete the word "new." Position the cursor over the **n** and press **dw** (**d**elete **w**ord). The entire line moves to the left so that the cursor is now over the first letter of the word following "new," as shown below:

```
Please foard your mailing address.
```

Delete a Line—The **dd** Command

To delete an entire line, place the cursor anywhere on the line and press the **d** key twice, that is, **dd**. The entire line is deleted. Some terminals will mark the deleted line with an asterisk *. Other terminals will simply move the line below up to the position previously occupied by the deleted line.

Replace a Character—The **r** Command

You may want to replace one character with another, as when you have made a typographical error. For example:

```
Please farward your mailing address.
```

To correct the spelling of "farward," first assure yourself that you are in command mode (by pressing the **ESC**ape key). Then move the cursor over the "a" in "farward."

Finally, press the **r** key (for replace), followed immediately by the **o** key.

```
Please forward your mailing address.
```

The cursor is still over the "o."

Inserting Lines

If you have typed carefully, it is unlikely that you should have to delete and rewrite an entire line. However, if such is the case, and the line is not the last line, you will have to use a special command for inserting the lines.

Suppose, for example, you see that line 6 in the display below should be deleted and retyped:

```
5 1312 N. Main St.
6 Pslismf. Vstiogptmos 05362
7 Dear Ms. Applicant:
```

Perform the following steps:

Place the cursor anywhere on line 6 and press **dd**. Note that line 7 now becomes line 6 as shown below:

```
5 1312 N. Main St.
6 Pslismf. Vstiogptmos 05362
7 Dear Ms. Applicant:
```

```
5 1312 N. Main St.
6 Dear Ms. Applicant
```

The cursor is now over the "D" of "Dear."

NOTE: *Some terminals will leave a blank line with an @ symbol in the first column of the screen.*

Use the **k** key to move the cursor up to line 5.

Press the **o** key, used to insert lines. You are now back in text entry mode and anything you type will be entered as text. You have actually inserted a line just below the one on which your cursor was positioned. The display should appear as follows:

```
5 1312 N. Main St.
6 □
7 Dear Ms. Applicant
```

Now type in the correct line, "**Oakland, CA 94612,**" without pressing the carriage return. Pressing the carriage return causes another blank line to appear below line 6. Then, press the **ESC** key. You are again back in command mode, and the display should be correct.

Practice all of these commands as required to understand them fully. Then, proceed to Lesson 3.3, which covers other cursor motion commands.

LESSON 3.3:	Cursor Motion, Part 2
NEW KNOWLEDGE:	Use of the **w/W**, **b/B**, and **e** commands
APPROXIMATE	
TIME:	15 minutes

Moving the cursor left or right a few spaces with the **h** and **l** keys is adequate, but moving the cursor directly to the beginning or end of a word, or across many words is faster with other keys. Use the **w** (word), **b** (back), and **e** (end) keys to move quickly through lines of text.

Moving to the Next Word—The w Command

To move the cursor to the beginning of the next word, use the **w** command. With the cursor positioned over the *h* in *Thank*, as shown, press the **w** key.

```
8  Thank  you...
```

```
8  Thank  you...
```

Observe that the cursor moved to the beginning of the next word.

You are not limited with **w** to movements of a single word at a time. As with most cursor motion commands, you can precede the basic command with a number or quantifier to modify its range or scope. If you wish to move the cursor to the beginning of a word to the right, precede the **w** with a number. Type **3w** for the third word.

```
8 Thank you for expressing an...
```

```
8 Thank you for expressing an...
```

Observe that the cursor moved forward three words, to the *a* in *an*.

To **vi** commands, Punctuation Marks = Words

Note that the **w** stops the cursor at the beginning of words, and at punctuation marks as well. A punctuation mark is considered a word. To clarify this point, first move the cursor down to the next line by typing **j**.

```
8 Thank you for expressing an...
```

```
9 in General Manufacturing Co.
```

Now try to advance the cursor to the next word with a single tap of the **w** key.

9 in General Manufacturing **Co.**

9 in General Manufacturing Co.

Instead of moving on to the next word, the cursor stopped at the period.

In general, **vi** considers a sentence to be any set of successive words beginning with a capital letter and ending in final punctuation: period, question mark, or exclamation point. Another tap of the **w** key will send the cursor to the following word, on the next line.

9 in General Manufacturing Co.

10 **A**fter reviewing your application.

The **W** Command Ignores Punctuation

If you wish to ignore punctuation, use the **W** command. It moves the cursor to the beginning of the next word, but unlike the lowercase **w**, ignores punctuation. Move back to the beginning of the word *Co.* by typing **k3w** (up one line and over three words).

    10 **After** reviewing your application,

    9 in General Manufacturing **Co.**

Now advance to the next word, this time with the **W** command. Type **W**.

    9 in General Manufacturing **Co.**

    10 **After** reviewing your application,

Observe that the **W** ignored the period.

Moving Backward—The **b** Command

When editing, you often need to move back one or more words. The **b** key moves the cursor **b**ackward to the beginning of a word. Position the cursor back at the word *an* on line 8 with the sequence **kk4w**.

Now type **b**.

Observe that the cursor moved back (to the left) one word, from the beginning of *an* to the beginning of *expressing*.

As in the case of the **w** command, you may move any number of words by preceding the **b** with a number. Typing **2b** will move the cursor backward two words:

```
8 Thank you for expressing an...
```

```
8 Thank you for expressing an...
```

The B Command Ignores Punctuation

The same rule applies to punctuation marks as in the case of the **w**/**W** commands. The capital **B**, like capital **W**, ignores punctuation as it moves backward word by word.

Moving to the End of a Word—The e Command

Sometimes you want to move to the end of the word on which the cursor is located. To move the cursor to the end of a word, type **e**.

```
8 Thank you...
```

```
8 Thank you...
```

The **e** command can also be preceded with a number. Type **4e**.

```
8 Thank you for expressing an interest
```

8 Thank you for expressing an interest

The cursor moved to the end of the fourth word to the right. The capital **E** does the same as **e**, except that it acknowledges the punctuation as well as words.

In Lesson 3.4 you will learn advanced cursor motion commands. Before leaving this lesson, you should save the file you have just worked on by typing **:wq**⟨CR⟩. Although you have not made any actual changes in the text since the last time the file was saved, it is good practice to routinely save at the end of an editing session.

LESSON 3.4:	Advanced Cursor Motion, Part 1
NEW KNOWLEDGE:	Use of the ˆ (caret), **0** (zero), **$**, **M**, and **( )** (parentheses) commands; an additional use of the **G** command
APPROXIMATE TIME:	10–15 minutes

If your system is not already up and running, bring it up, log in, and gain access to the **jobreply** file in **vi** by typing **vi jobreply⟨CR⟩**. Then type **:set nu** to add line numbering.

Move the cursor to line 8 by typing **8G**. Use any sequence of keys you wish (w, w, w, . . .e for example) to move the cursor to the end of the line.

Moving to the Beginning of a Line—The Caret and Zero Commands

The caret (ˆ) and the **0** (zero) will both move the cursor back to the beginning of the line. Type ˆ.

```
8 Thank you for expressing an interest
```

```
8 Thank you for expressing an interest
```

Observe that the cursor "jumps" immediately to the beginning of the line.

Moving to the End of a Line—The $ Command

The **$** command will place the cursor at the end of the line. Press the **$** key.

8 Thank you...

8 Thank you for expressing an interest

Observe that the cursor jumps to its previous position at the end of the line.

Now use the **0** (zero) key to move the cursor back to the beginning of the line.

8 Thank you for expressing an interest

8 Thank you...

Observe that the cursor is once again at the beginning of the line.

Moving to the Beginning of a Line—The **G** and **M** Commands

In addition to moving the cursor from line to line, the capital **GB**, when preceded by a line number, will place the cursor at the beginning of that line. Type **12G**.

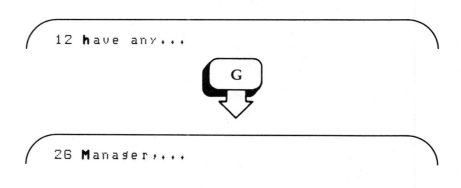

8 Thank you....

12G

12 have any...

Type **G** to send the cursor to the beginning of the last line.

12 have any...

G

26 Manager,...

Although it is a command not often used, the **M** command moves the cursor to the beginning of the middle line on the screen. Type **M**.

26 Manager,...

M

> 15 However...

Note that the actual destination line (15 in this case) may be different if your window size is different.

Moving to Beginnings and Ends of Sentences—The Parentheses Keys

Move the cursor a complete sentence at a time. The right parenthesis key,), moves the cursor forward to the beginning of the next sentence, and the left parenthesis key, (, moves it to the beginning of the sentence you are in, or to the beginning of the preceding sentence if you are already at the beginning of a sentence. Go back to line 7 by typing **7G**. Then type **)**.

> 7 Dear Ms. Applicant:

> 10 After reviewing your application,

Now go back to the previous sentence with the "(". Type **(**.

> 10 After reviewing your application,

8 Thank you for expressing ...

All of the cursor movement commands covered thus far are summarized in Table 3.2. Go over this chart and repeat any of the steps in the last three lessons until you feel confident and can move the cursor anyplace in the document with ease.

Table 3.2 Cursor Motion Chart

Key	Moves the cursor:
h	to the left one character
l	to the right one character
k	up one line
j	down one line
{	back to beginning of paragraph
}	forward to beginning of paragraph
w	forward to beginning of next word
b	back to beginning of word
e	forward to end of word
W	forward to beginning of next word, ignoring punctuation
B	back to beginning of word, ignoring punctuation
E	forward to end of word, including punctuation
^	to beginning of line
$	to end of line
0 (zero)	to beginning of line
G	by itself, to last line in the file; preceded by number, to that line
M	to beginning of middle line in screen
(	back to the beginning of sentence
)	forward to beginning of sentence
H	to the top of the screen
L	to the bottom of the screen

LESSON 3.5:	Text Editing with **vi**, Part 1
NEW KNOWLEDGE:	The **i** (**i**nsert), **a/A** (**a**ppend), and **o** (**o**pen) commands; the **u** (**u**ndo command)
APPROXIMATE TIME:	30 minutes

If your system is not already up and running, bring it up, log in, and gain access to **jobreply** in **vi** by typing **vi jobreply**⟨CR⟩. Type **:set nu**⟨CR⟩.

Now that you know how to move the cursor to any point in the file and can manipulate the file itself, you are ready for more advanced work with the **vi** program. By the end of this lesson, you will know how to make changes to the text in a file.

The lessons in the rest of the chapter build on each other. Do not make changes other than those given here. The accuracy of the text from one lesson to the next is very important. Because text processing requires practice, after you follow the lesson, create your own file of text to experiment with—make changes, make mistakes. But work through **jobreply** step by step with the lessons.

Inserting Words

The cursor should be positioned at the beginning of line 1 of the file. Now, let's change the first line by putting the word *Ms.* in front of Andrea's name.

Move the cursor to the beginning of *Andrea* by typing **2w**.

1 Letter to Andrea...

2w

1 Letter to Andrea...

Use the **i** command (insert) to insert *Ms.* Type **i**. By typing the "i" by itself, you have placed **vi** into the **i**nsert mode. Whatever you type next will be inserted directly in front of the current position of the cursor.

NOTE: *In some systems it may appear as though you are overwriting existing text. However, the full text is restored after the ESCape sequence.*

NOTE: *The symbol ⱡ means space or blank. When it is included in the directions, it means that you should press the space bar. When <u>underscored</u>, it indicates that the blank space is the location of the cursor.*

Type *Ms.* and a blank space.

1 Letter to **A**ndrea...

1 Letter to Ms, **A**ndrea...

The insertion is complete, so you will want to tell **vi** to abandon text insertion mode.

Press the **ESC** key.

1 Letter to Ms, **A**ndrea...

```
  1 Letter to Ms. ▮Andrea...
```

It is sometimes necessary to press **ESC** twice. If your terminal has a bell or beeper, it will sound on the second **ESC** to let you know you're in command mode. After pressing **ESC**, the cursor moves back to the left one space to the position of the last character (in this case, a space).

A Command You Will Use Often—The undo (**u**) **Command**

Move the cursor using cursor motion keys in any sequence you like to the beginning of the second word in line 10. Now press the **u** key and observe what happens to line 1.

```
 10 After reviewing...
```

```
  1 Letter to Andrea...
```

vi removed the *Ms.* you had just inserted. The **u** command (for "undo") completely negates your last operation. It works on the most recent command that *changed the contents of the buffer*. Moving the cursor around the screen does not affect the buffer's contents, so even after all that cursor motion, the **u** command was able to go back and undo the results of the insert. **vi** will let you undo a previous undo as many times as you like. Use it to restore your insert.

Again, press **u**.

```
  1 Letter to Andrea...
```

1 Letter to Ms, Andrea,,,

The line once again contains the *Ms.*

The Append—a Command

The **a** (append) works just like insert, except it appends text *after* the current position of the cursor. If the cursor is in column 20, the first character typed after the **a**ppend command appears in column 21. At first glance, it may seem unnecessary to have both the insert command and the **a**ppend command since the cursor can be moved to any position before issuing either one. However, as the name suggests, append is especially useful at the end of a line and need to add or **a**ppend text. The insert command will push the character beneath the cursor ahead of the inserted text. Place the word *The* in front of *General* on line 2.

First move the cursor to the blank space between *from* and *General* with the sequence **jel**.

1 **L**etter to Ms, Andrea,,,

2 from**ᵬ**General,,,

Now press **a** to append.

2 from**ᵬ**General

```
2 from General...
```

Finally, type **The␣**.

```
2 from General...
```

```
2 from The General...
```

You are now ready to end the **a**ppend and return to command mode.
Press **ESC**.

```
2 from The General
ESC
```

```
2 from The␣General
```

The word *The* was appended after the space occupied by the cursor when you save the **append** command. Once you **ESC**aped, the cursor was placed at the last character appended, in this case a blank space. To test the difference between the **append** and **insert** commands, **undo** your last operation by typing **u**. Repeat the last series of commands, positioning your cursor on the blank space between *from* and *General* on line 2. This time, rather than striking **a** to append the word *The*, strike **i** to insert the word *Theb* and press **ESC**. Type **u** and repeat the operation with the append command. Note the difference in the two operations.

Appending at the End of a Line—The A Command

You frequently want to append text at the end of a line. Assume that you wish to append the word *suitable* to the end of line 17.

Move the cursor to line 17 with **17G.**

    2 from The_General

    17 in the event that something

———————————————————————————

To append to the end of a line, use the capital **A** command. Type **A.**

    17 in the event that something

```
17 in the event that something▌
```

vi is now in the **Append** mode, ready to accept text input.

Type a blank space, followed by the word *suitable*. Press **ESC** to return to command mode.

```
17 in the event that something □
```

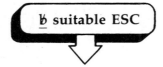
b̶ suitable ESC

```
17 in the event that something suitable
```

You have now appended the word *suitable* to line 17 and returned to command mode.

Inserting New Lines with the Open—o/O Commands

Opening up a new line above or below the cursor is the function of the **o/O** (open) commands.

First, move the cursor to line 5 with any sequence of commands you wish, for example, **5G**.

```
17 in the event that something suitable
```

5G

```
5 1312 N. Main St.
```

Now assume that you wish to insert a line after line 5. Type a lowercase **o**.

```
5 1312 N. Main St.
6 Oakland, CA 94612
7 Dear Ms. Applicant:
```

```
5 1312 N. Main St.
6 □
7 Oakland, CA 94612
```

Line 6 is now available for text input, and the old line 6 and all subsequent lines have been renumbered. Not only have you opened a new blank line, but you have switched to text entry mode. **vi** is now waiting for a new entry on line 6. Type **Apt. 205**.

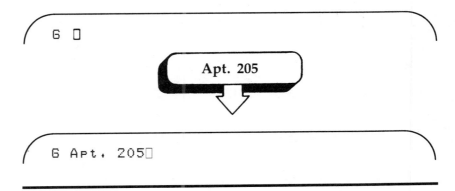

End text entry with **ESC**.

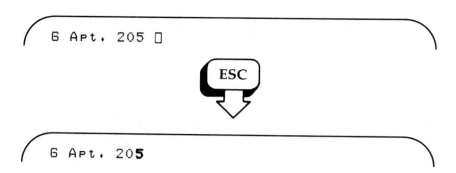

The position of the cursor indicates the last character typed.

The function of the capital **O** is similar to that of the small **o**, except that it opens up a line *above* the *current line* instead of below it. This lesson and the next should be completed at a single sitting. Proceed directly to Lesson 3.6 without quitting the file.

You have now seen the three basic text entry commands. Practice with them in another text file of your own creation until you are fully confident in their use.

LESSON 3.6:	Advanced Cursor Motion, Part 2
NEW KNOWLEDGE:	Pattern searches: the / (slash) and **n/N** commands; the **f/F** (find) command; the **q** and **q!** commands
APPROXIMATE TIME:	20 minutes

For this lesson, it is assumed that your system is still up, that you are in the **jobreply** file, and that your cursor is at the end of line 6. This lesson is a continuation of Lesson 3.5.

Searching for a Word or Phrase—The / (Slash) Command

Using the pattern searching capability of **vi** is one of the quickest ways to get to a point in a file; after you learn this capability, you will use it to move quickly to file locations when you do not have line numbers to refer to, or when the line numbers keep changing as you make editing changes. It is much easier to recall a unique phrase which remains the same regardless of line number changes than to use the **G** command and end up on the wrong line.

Suppose you wish to see every occurrence of the letter **e**. (Naturally, this particular exercise is not likely to be actually practiced, but will serve for purposes of demonstration.) First, type a slash (/). A slash will appear in the command area in the lower left-hand corner of the screen, as did the colon in Lesson 3.1.

Immediately after the slash, type the pattern you wish to find, say, lowercase **e**. No following slash is needed, but the search command must be terminated with a carriage return. The complete pattern is /e⟨CR⟩.

After the carriage return, the cursor will go to the first *e* following its current position.

Type **/e**⟨CR⟩.

6 Apt. 20**5**

```
8 Dear Ms. Applicant:
```

Slash Plus the n Command

Since the cursor was located at the end of line 6 when you typed the /, **vi** begins looking for the search pattern at the beginning of line 7, not at the beginning of the file. Once the cursor stops at the pattern, you may issue another command or perform a new operation. If you wish to find all occurrences of the pattern, press the **n** key to locate the next successive instances of the pattern. The **n** must be pressed each time the cursor finds the pattern and stops. Continue to press the **n** key until the cursor returns to the starting position. Then you will have located every *e* in the file. For the present exercise, just type **n** until the cursor is positioned at the first *e* of the word *interest* on line 9.

Press **n**.

```
8 Dear Ms. Applicant:
```

```
9 Thank you for expressing
```

Press **n**.

```
9 Thank you for expressing...
```

```
9 Thank you for expressing...
```

Press **n**.

```
9 Thank you for expressing...
```

```
9 Thank you for expressing an interest
```

Searching Backward
with the **N** Command

The lowercase **n** searches for the next instance of a pattern in the forward direction. If the pattern you wish to locate is behind (above) the cursor position, search "backward" by reversing the direction of the search with a capital **N**.

Type **N**.

```
9 Thank you for expressing an interest
```

```
9 Thank you for expressing an interest
```

The **f** (**f**ind) Command

Another way to move the cursor is with **f** (**find**). The **find** command can locate a single character on the same line as or to the right of the cursor. For instance, type **fg** to find the letter *g*.

```
9 Thank you for expressing...
```

```
9 Thank you for expressing...
```

The **f** command moved the cursor to the next occurrence of the letter *g*. If you try another **fg** at this point, the cursor will not move, indicating there are no more *g*s to the right of the cursor on that line. Your terminal may beep to indicate the command cannot be executed.

Like the relationship of **N** to **n**, pressing the **F** will move the cursor backward on a line to a specified character. Try it to find the letter *y*.

Type **Fy**.

```
9 Thank you for expressing...
```

```
9 Thank you for expressing...
```

The **q** (**q**uit) Command

Now leave the editor temporarily. Since none of the "practice" changes made in this or the previous lesson are needed, there is no point in saving them. Instead of writing the buffer contents onto the disk, simply abandon the work (**quit**). To "**quit**" the file without writing it, use the **q** command. Type **:q⟨CR⟩**. You receive a warning message of "No write since last change" (:quit! overrides). Since you do want to abandon this edited text, go ahead and type **q!⟨CR⟩**.

Type **:q!⟨CR⟩**.

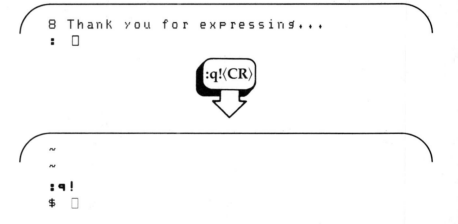

In the next lesson we will make some permanent changes to **jobreply**, learn a method of joining files, and learn new commands for **writing** and **quitting**.

LESSON 3.7:	Text Editing with **vi**, Part 2
NEW KNOWLEDGE:	Joining lines, the **J** command: moving text, the **y**/Yank and **p**/Put (**y** & **p**) commands
APPROXIMATE TIME:	20–25 minutes

If your system is not already up and running, bring it up, log in, and gain access to the **jobreply** file in **vi**. Type **:set nu⟨CR⟩**.

The J (Join) Command

Whenever changes are made in text files, especially large-scale insertions and deletions, it causes an unbalanced appearance. Some lines fold over on the screen; words appear to the left of column zero; others run off the page to the right past column 80, and still others are often only a word or two long. The **nroff** program is used to format and justify all of this unbalanced text on paper, but you usually want to straighten out the text before you run the **nroff** program to printout. The **J** or **J**oin command is used to even out the way text looks on the screen.

To demonstrate the **J** command, **J**oin lines 15 and 16 of **jobreply** to consolidate them into one line. The **J**oin command is executed by typing **J** with the cursor on the first line of the text to be joined. Move the cursor to line 15 (anywhere on the line will do), and type **J**. Fig. 3.2 shows the text before and after joining.

```
    15 However, we will keep
```

```
    15 However, we will keep your application on file
    16 in the event that something
    17 should become available.
```

NOTE: *There will be an extra file in your directory at the end of this lesson. We will remove it later.*

Fig. 3.2 Join Command Functions

BEFORE

```
15 However, we will keep
16 your application on file
17 in the event that something
18 should become available
19 in the future
```

AFTER

```
15 However, we will keep your application on file
16 file in the event that something
17 should become available
18 in the future.
```

Lines 15 and 16 were joined and all subsequent lines were renumbered. The Join command will connect any number of lines, beginning at the line where the cursor is located when the command is given. To join more than two lines, simply specify the number of lines to be joined, followed by a J; thus, the command **5J** joins five lines together.

The y (yank) and p (put) Commands

If you had joined a lot of lines, one might be too long. For practice, shorten line 15. The "yank" command in **vi** lets you move the word *file* from the end of line 15 and put it at the beginning of line 16. Note that in an ordinary editing session, the simplest procedure would be to delete the word *file* and retype it at the appropriate place. Alternately, you could delete the word and **p**ut it back in the appropriate line using the same **p** command that you will use with yank.

The system will yank a copy of the word *file* from the end of line 15 and put it at the beginning of line 16. The yank command makes a copy of a character, group of characters, line, or range of lines, and stores the copy in a temporary buffer. If you wish to use the "yanked" material elsewhere in the file, place the cursor at the desired position and execute the **p**ut command. This feature lets you copy rather than retype a segment of text, and you can repeat the process as many times as you want.

Move the cursor to the beginning of the word file. Type **3w**.

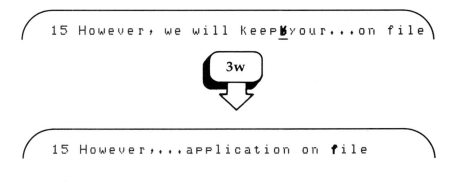

Yank Requires a Specifier

There are two forms of the yank command, **y** and **Y**, and neither form is ever used alone. Each requires a *specifier* that tells **vi** exactly how much text is to be yanked. The specifier for yanking a single word is the letter **w**. Thus, **yw** causes one word to be yanked; **y5w** would yank five words, and so on. Table 3.3 shows the specifiers used with the lowercase form of yank and what they mean.

The uppercase form of yank, **Y** is used to yank a number of lines *including* the one on which the cursor is located. Thus, if the cursor is on line 10 and the command **5Y** is typed, the system will yank lines 10 through 14.

Yanking makes a *copy* of the lines or text specified and writes the copy into a memory location for future use. These memory locations are called *buffers*. The text yanked is left where it is in the file—a copy is made. The text is not deleted. If you wish to delete the text you are "yanking," you must either use the **d**elete command, **d/D**, or yank first and then go back and delete the yanked text. (The delete command **d** was demonstrated in the elementary command

Table 3.3 Specifiers for the Yank Command

[(n)]y(specifier)

yanks n number of specified elements
if no number is specified, 1 is assumed

Specifiers:

l	letters (actually characters) to the right of the cursor
w	words to the right of the cursor
b	words to the left (behind) the cursor
$	all text from the cursor position to the end of the current line
o	all text from the beginning of the current line to the cursor position
k	lines above and in addition to the current line
j	lines below and in addition to the current line

Examples:

3yj	yank the current line and 3 lines underneath it
yk	yank the current line, and 1 line above it
y$	yank all text from the cursor position to the end of the current line
2yw	yank 2 words to the right of the cursor.

section in this chapter. The uppercase form of **d**elete is discussed in the next lesson.)

When the delete command (**d/D**) is executed, the system copies the "deleted text" into a buffer from which it can be recovered. Unlike the yank commands, deleted text is removed from the file. Both yanked and **d**eleted text can be recovered, but with the **d**elete command there are fewer available buffers. Since we won't be learning to recover from any but the last delete buffer, the last deleted text must be recovered *before* another insert, delete, or a simple yank is executed. In the case of the yank command, up to 26 different blocks of text can be saved in named buffers and recovered *prior to exiting* **vi**. If you yank blocks of text, delete the text at the original location, and then exit **vi** before copying the named buffers into your document, the text is lost. If you want them back, you will have to reenter them at the terminal.

Saving paragraphs in buffers and using them later is a common task for writers using **vi**. If you write a paragraph but decide it is not in the right place, buffers are convenient files for the text until you reach the appropriate place to use it.

You can specify up to 26 separate *named buffers* for yanked text, plus one unnamed buffer. The specified buffers are designated A through Z (either uppercase or lowercase is permissible). To specify a buffer you precede the yank command with " (double quotation marks) and a *letter*. For example, to yank four lines of text and save them in buffer M, type "M4Y. To recover this text, use the **put** command, which is demonstrated in the next section.

If no buffer is specified, the **yank** command saves your material in an unnamed buffer. If you inadvertently perform another yank or delete on a different block of text and fail to specify a buffer, the system will *overwrite* the first block with the second in the unnamed buffer.

We now return to the example of this exercise. yank the word *file* by typing **yw** (yank **w**ord).

```
15 However, ...application on file
```

```
15 However,...application on file
```

Observe that there has been no change in the display. However, the word *file* has now been copied into the un-named buffer.

The **p**ut Command

The **p**ut command is executed by typing **p**. The system will take whatever is in the unnamed buffer and print it beginning at the position of the cursor.

If you immediately try to **p**ut the word *file* at the beginning of line 16, the words *file* and *in* will be merged. To see this, move the cursor to the beginning of line 16 by pressing a carriage return, ⟨**CR**⟩.

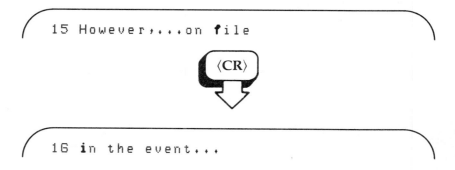

Then **p**ut the contents of the buffer in the line by typing **p**:

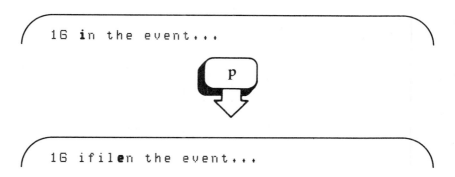

The word *file* was put at the position following the cursor—not what was intended. You want to place *file* in front of *in*. So, try again. First, **u**ndo the **p**ut command. Type **u** (isn't **u**ndo a useful command!).

```
1G file█n the event....
```

```
in the event....
```

Back the cursor up to the beginning of the line using the **0** (zero) or **^** (caret) command.

```
1G in the event....
```

```
1G in the event....
```

Now execute the uppercase form of the put command capital-P inserts the contents of the buffer in front of the cursor.

Type **P**.

```
1G █in the event....
```

```
16 file in the event...
```

The word file is now in the correct position.

If you had stored the word *file* in a named buffer, M for instance, you would retrieve it by typing **"MP**.

You have just completed a fairly complex yank and **put** procedure. Don't worry if you feel as though you're not sure exactly what took place; after practice you will master the operation. The same results could have been achieved by using simpler commands you already know, but this example illustrates some of the powers of **yank** and **put**.

Note that the word *file* now appears on both line 15 from which you "yanked" it and on line 16 where you "put" it. You will delete the extra word in the next lesson.

LESSON 3.8:	Text Editing with **vi**, Part 3
NEW KNOWLEDGE:	Use of the **c** (change command); more on the **x**, **d/D**, and **r/R**, commands
APPROXIMATE TIME:	30 minutes

If your system is not already up and running, bring it up, log in, and gain access to the **jobreply** file in **vi**. Since the exercises in this lesson begin on line 3 of the file, move the cursor to that line by any command or sequence of commands you wish.

Except for the change command (**c**), uppercase **R** and uppercase **D**, you have already used all of the commands discussed in this lesson: this lesson discusses refinements to them. More importantly, you will see that they are somewhat redundant. They provide several ways of doing the same thing: delete, delete and replace individual characters, or delete strings of characters.

The **c** (change)
Command

The change command is in one sense an extension of the replace **r/R** command. It lets you delete a string of characters and replace the string with another. Suppose you find that since you typed the letter **jobreply** the month has changed, and you are now in June. You could place your cursor on the first letter, M, delete the entire word, issue an insert command, and then type in June. That process uses more steps than actually needed. The change command lets you change the word directly.

Type **cw**.

```
3 May 12, 1984
```

```
3 Ma$ 12, 1984
```

vi replaced the last letter of the word to be changed with a dollar sign ($), which means that everything from the cursor to the **$** will be replaced by whatever you type in.

Type **June**.

```
3 Ma$ 12, 1984
```

```
3 June 12, 1984
```

The word *May* was replaced by the word *June*.

─────────────────────────────────────

NOTE: *After executing the c command, **vi** is in* text entry mode, *whereas after executing the r command, the system is still in* command mode. *Before moving the cursor after a c command, you must **ESCape**. Wouldn't you like to sit down whoever wrote **vi** and give them a talking to about all this mode changing?*

Press **ESC**.

```
3 June█12, 1984
```

```
3 June 12, 1984
```

The cursor moves back over the last character typed, in this case **w**, indicating that the change is completed.

The **c**hange Command Requires a Specifier

Note that the **c** command requires a specifier; you must specify **w** to change one word or c(n)w to change (n) number of words. Just for practice, change the data from June 12 to October 24. First move the cursor to the *J*.

Type **b** then **c2w**.

```
3  June 12, 1984
```

```
3  June 1$, 1984
```

Now type in the new date, **October♭24**, then **ESC**.

```
3  June 1$, 1984
```

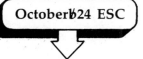

```
3 October⌷ 24, 1984
```

Return the line to its previous text using the undo command.
Type **u**.

```
3 October 24, 1984
```

```
3 June 12, 1984
```

Now change the word *application* on line 10 to *resume*.
Move the cursor with a simple search pattern. Type
/app⟨CR⟩.

```
3 June 12, 1984
```

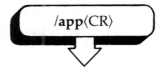

```
10 After reviewing your application,
```

Make the change by typing **cwresumeESC**.

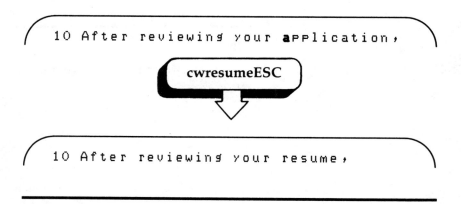

The x Command Again

To delete specific characters or a succession of characters, use the x command. Move the cursor again to line 3; type **3G**, and then move it over the 1 in 12 by typing **W**.
Type **W**.

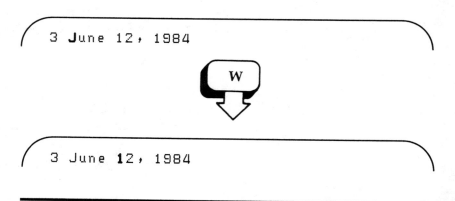

Now change the date from June 12 to June 2; to do so, the 1 must be deleted.

Type **x**.

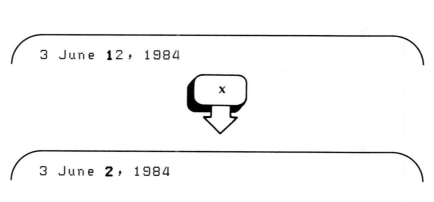

The **1** was deleted, and the rest of the line moved back one space. The **x** command is used to delete any number of characters specified. By itself, **x** deletes only the character under the cursor, as in the case of the 1 above. But as is often the case with **vi** commands, preceding **x** with a number will delete that number of characters, from left to right, beginning at the cursor.

Type **5x**.

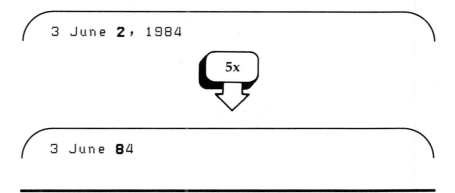

Note that the blank space before 1984 was counted as one of the characters deleted.

Undo the last command with **undo**. Type **u**.

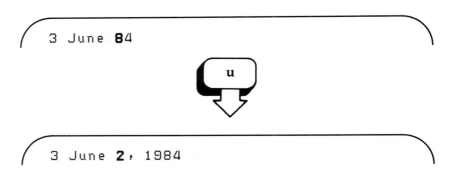

You will recall that in Lesson 3.7, after performing the Join command, you performed a yank operation to copy the word *file* and then **put** it at the beginning of line 16. However, the yank operation did not simultaneously delete the word *file* from line 15. You can use the **D** (Delete rest of line) command to delete the word file from line 15. First you must move the cursor to line 15, and then to the space before the word *file*. (Use any sequence of commands you wish.) Since there are no more needed words in the rest of the line, you can delete all remaining characters from the cursor position to the end of the line. To delete to the end of the line, use the **D** command.

Type **D**.

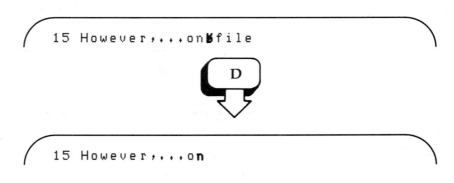

You probably would not use the **D** command when the deletion is just a single word. **vi** provides several methods to delete text. The next examples illustrate versions of the **delete** command.

Deleting Words—the **dw** Command

Use any sequence of commands to move your cursor to the beginning of line 17. Delete the word *should* from line 17 with the **delete word** command.

Type **dw**:

17 **s**hould become available

17 **b**ecome available

If you wish to reinsert the word *should* back into the text at another location, move the cursor to that position and use the **p** or **P** command to reinsert it. **P**utting words back into the text works with the **dw** command just as it did with yank's **yw** command. Single words, yanked or deleted from the text, are reinserted with **p** or **P**. Entire lines or groups of lines, put into a temporary buffer by yanking or **deleting** can also move back into text.

Append the letter *s* to the end of the word *become* and a period to the end of the line using the **a** and **A** commands. Move the cursor to the end of become with the **e** command and press **a** to append the *s*, followed by an **ESC**, **A**, the period and another **ESC**.

```
 17 become available


              easESCA.ESC

                  ↓


 17 becomes available.
```

Deleting Lines—the **dd** Command

Assume that you wish to delete line 18 (*in the future*) entirely. The command **dd** deletes an entire line. The cursor may be anywhere in the line when the command is given.
     Press the **j** key to move down to line 18.

```
 17 become available.

              j
              ↓


 18 in the future.
```

Type **dd**.

```
 18 in the future.

              dd
```

18 We wish you the best...

The **dd** command is used to delete a whole group of lines. For example, delete the next four lines by typing **4dd**:

18 We wish you the best of luck

18 Sincerely yours,

Whole lines or groups of lines can be yanked or deleted and **put** elsewhere in the text. You will find the **put** command most useful for blocks of text rather than individual words. To practice deleting and putting several lines, move now to line 1 of this text by typing **1G**.

18 Sincerely yours,

1 Letter to Andrea Appl...

Delete lines 1 through 3 by typing **3dd**. Type **3dd**.

```
1 Letter to Andrea...
2 from General Manuf...
3 June 2, 1984
4 Ms. Andrea Applicant
5 1312 N. Main St.
```

```
1 Ms Andrea Applicant
2 1312 N. Main St.
3 Oakland, CA 94612
4 Dear Ms. Applicant:
5 Thank you...
```

Move the cursor to the very last line of the file by typing **G**. Add the deleted lines onto the end of the file by typing **p**.

Type **Gp**.

```
1 Ms. Andrea Applicant
```

```
16 Mary Jones,
17 Manager, General...
18 Letter to Andrea...
19 from General Manuf...
20 June 2, 1984
```

You don't want these lines to remain permanently at the end of the file. Undo your **put** by typing **u**, return to the first line (**1G**) and **P**ut the three lines back above the cursor by typing capital **P**.

Type **u**.

```
16 Mary Jones,
17 Manager, General...
18 Letter to Andrea...
19 from General Manuf...
20 June 2, 1984
```

```
17 Manager, General...
~
~
~
```

Now type **1G**.

```
17 Manager, General...
```

```
1 Ms. Andrea Applicant
2 1312 N. Main St.
3 Oakland, CA 94612
```

Finally, type **P**.

```
1 Ms. Andrea Applicant
2 1312 N. Main St.
3 Oakland, CA 94612
```

```
1 Letter to Andrea...
2 from General Manuf...
3 June 2, 1984
4 Ms. Andrea Applicant
5 1312 N. Main St.
```

When editing a text file, you often only need to replace one or more single characters or some short string of characters. The basic replace commands are **r** and **R**. The remaining exercises in this lesson demonstrate these commands.

Replacing Characters—
The **r/R** Commands

Suppose that Andrea's street address should be 1412, not 1312. You can correct the error quickly with the replace command. Move the cursor to line 5 (**5G**) and then to the 3 of *1312* by striking l (the letter l).

Type **5G**.

```
18 Sincerely yours
```

```
5 1312 N. Main St.
```

Type **1**.

```
5 1312 N. Main St.
```

```
5 1312 N. Main St.
```

Press the **r** key. Nothing happens on the screen, but by typing **r**, you have placed **vi** in the character replace mode. You may now enter one character, and it will replace the 3.
Type **r4**.

```
5 1312 N. Main St.
```

```
5 1412 N. Main St.
```

Note that there is a difference between **r4** and **4r**! The **r** command lets you to replace only one character. If the **r** is preceded by a number, the replacement character will be used for that number of characters. For example, if you type **4r**, the next character you enter will replace four characters on the screen.

Type **4r1**.

```
5 1412 N. Main St.
```

```
5 11111 N. Main St.
```

Observe that *1412* becomes *11111*. However, since Andrea's street number is really 1412, **u**ndo this last change. Type **u**.

```
5 11111 N. Main St.
```

```
5 1412 N. Main St.
```

The **R** command is used to replace characters with any combination of new characters. Using any sequence of commands you wish, move the cursor down to the *6* in the zip code on line 6.

```
6 Oakland, CA 94612
```

If the zip code should really be 94759, only the last three digits need to be Replaced. Type **R**. Nothing happens, but just as with the **r** command, **vi** is now ready to accept Replacement characters.

Type **R759**.

```
6 Oakland, CA 94612
```

```
6 Oakland, CA 94759□
```

Now **ESC** to end the text entry.

```
6 Oakland, CA 94759 □
```

```
6 Oakland, CA 94759
```

Exit—**x** Command

Write these changes to disk and **q**uit for a while. Instead of issuing separate **w**rite and **q**uit commands, combine the two commands into one with the **x** (exit) command.

Type a colon to get the prompt; then type **x⟨CR⟩**.

```
6 Oakland, CA 94759
```

:x⟨CR⟩

```
"jobreply" 20 lines, 496 characters
$ ▯
```

Editing may be resumed by typing **vi jobreply⟨CR⟩**.

LESSON 3.9:	Advanced Editing
NEW KNOWLEDGE:	Escaping to the shell, reading and writing other files
APPROXIMATE	
TIME:	30 minutes

If the system is not already up and running, bring it up, log in, and gain access to **jobreply** in **vi**.

After you have acquired a basic knowledge of the UNIX system, you will perform many different tasks, text entry being just one. If you are working in the **vi** editor and need to perform another task or find out something about the status of the system, you leave **vi** and go to the *shell*. You may not always want to stop running the **vi** program, and you do not have to. The UNIX system provides a *shell escape*, a way to go temporarily to the shell. You can perform a UNIX operation while running your **vi** program in the *background*. When the shell operation is complete, you can return immediately to your document.

This chapter shows you how to reach the shell from **vi**. Subsequent chapters explain shell commands. To practice escaping to the shell, carry out the following steps.

Escaping with the Colon Plus Exclamation

You can "escape" to the shell in several ways, two of which are presented here. However, your system may not offer both. The first method allows you to execute a single command. From command mode, type the colon, **:**, followed by the exclamation point, **!**, the command name, and carriage return. To learn the date and time, type **:!date⟨CR⟩**.

```
$ 1 Letter to Andrea Applicant
~
~
~
: !date<CR>
Thu June 2 14:56:20 PDT 1984
[Hit return to continue]
```

Following the instruction which appears on the screen, pressing ⟨CR⟩ returns you immediately to the **jobreply** file.

Escaping with the Colon Plus sh (shell)

The second method creates a permanent *subshell* and you may perform as many operations as you like. Type the colon, :, followed by **sh** and the carriage return, **:sh⟨CR⟩**. The shell prompt, **$**, will now appear on your terminal. Execute the **date** command.

Type **:sh⟨CR⟩**.
Type **date⟨CR⟩** as shown.

```
1 Letter to Andrea Applicant
 ·
 ·
 ·
:sh
$ date<CR>
Nov 8 1984 03:10:22 PDT
$ ▯
```

You do not automatically return to the editor after the shell command has executed. You can continue to issue shell commands until you are ready to return to **vi**. When you type a control-d (**^d**), the screen will clear and return you to the **vi** editor.

Type **^d**.

```
1 Letter to Andrea Applicant
 ·
 ·
 ·
:sh<CR>
$ date<CR>
Nov 8 1984 03:10:22 PDT
$  ^d
```

```
1 Letter to Andrea Applicant
  .
  .
```

Finding and Merging Files with the Read (:r) Command

While editing a particular file, you might remember some text in another document that you would like to include in the present one. Using a shell escape, you can leave your current document, browse through your files in search of the text, then return to editing.

One of the most useful features of the UNIX system is its great capacity to manipulate and operate on files. In this lesson, you will practice merging two files: **jobreply** and a small seven-line file you will now create, called **jobreply.add**.

Create **jobreply.add** just as you created **jobreply**. Type **:vi jobreply.add⟨CR⟩**. When **vi** comes up, type **:set nu⟨CR⟩**. The screen will clear and show the familiar **vi** tildes, as seen below:

```
$ vi jobreply.add<CR>
     1 □
  ~
  ~
  ~
  ~
  ~
  ~
  ~
  ~
:vi jobreply.add<CR>
"jobreply.add" No such file or
directory
```

The cursor is waiting for you to add text, so give the command to begin insertion. Type **i**.

Now add the following text exactly as shown.

```
Please address any<CR>
future correspondence to:<CR>
Hiram Hardhart<CR>
Directory of Personnel<CR>
General Manufacturing Co.<CR>
1234 Jackson St.<CR>
San Francisco, CA 94112
```

Press the **ESC** key, write the file to disk and quit by typing **:wq⟨CR⟩**. The display should be approximately as shown below:

```
    .
    .
    .
    4 Directory of Personnel
    5 General Manufacturing Co.
    6 1234 Jackson St.
    7 San Francisco, CA 94112
~
~
~
  :wq<CR>
  "jobreply.add" [New file] 7 lines,
149 characters
```

To bring the original **jobreply** back up, issue another **vi** command. Type **vi jobreply⟨CR⟩**. Type **:set nu⟨CR⟩**.

You are now going to merge the two files using the **r** (read) command. Begin by moving the cursor to line 17 by any command or sequence of commands you wish.

Type **:r jobreply.add⟨CR⟩**.

```
17 becomes available.
18 Sincerely yours,
```

:r jobreply.add⟨CR⟩

```
17 becomes available.
18 Please address any
19 future correspondence to:
20 Hiram Hardhart
21 Directory of Personnel
22 General Manufacturing Co.
23 1234 Jackson St.
24 San Francisco, CA 94112
25 Sincerely yours,
```

Lines 18 through 24 now contain the text of **jobreply.add**.

Now join lines 17 and 18. Press the **k** key to move the cursor back up to line 17.

```
18 Please address any
```

```
17 becomes available
```

then Join lines 17 and 18 by typing **J**:

```
17 becomes available.
```

```
17 becomes available.□ Please...
```

Save these changes and exit to the shell by typing
:x⟨CR⟩.

[@On some systems, the same thing as **:x** be accomplished
by **ZZ**. Using **ZZ** is even easier than **:x** since it is not necessary to type a colon or a carriage return.@]

LESSON 3.10:	Printing a File
NEW KNOWLEDGE:	The **lpr** command with **-m** (**m**ail) option; the pipe command (¦), the **pr**int command (**pr**) with **-h** (**h**eader) option
APPROXIMATE TIME:	20 minutes

Regardless of the type of file you create—text, program, or other—you will usually want a printed or *hard* copy of it. Although the **print** commands are not part of **vi**, printing out a file you have just finished is the natural conclusion of an editing session.

Since the **jobreply** file is complete, you can practice printing out a copy on your system's printer. The command **lpr** (line **pr**inter) followed by a filename sends the text of the named file to the printer to produce a hard copy. You may not actually execute this command until you have read this whole lesson. However, if you have plenty of printer paper and wish to print the file each time with different options, proceed as shown.

Type **lpr jobreply⟨CR⟩**.

```
$ lpr jobreply<CR>
$ □
```

What Happens in the Computer When You Tell It to Print

The names of the files to be printed are retained in the *line printer queue*. They are printed on a first-in, first-out schedule. Even though several users ask to use the printer simultaneously, the files are printed in the order in which they reach the queue and as the printer becomes available. This process is commonly known as *spooling*.

If your printer is in a remote location, you may not know when your printing job is complete. The **m**ail option, **m**, is a signal to the spooler (or to the UNIX system via the spooler) that you wish to be notified of its completion. The command

```
lpr -m jobreply<CR>
```

will tell the system to notify you by electronic mail. A full discussion of the **mail** program is given in Chapter 7.

A printer is an output device attached either to a multiuser or to a stand-alone UNIX system. The contents of the edited file are sent to the printer directly with the **lpr** command or with a *pipe* command. The symbol for the pipe command is a vertical bar (on some machines the symbol actually looks like two short vertical dashes (¦)). The pipe command sends the output of one command to the input of another command.

For example, the command **pr jobreply ¦ lpr⟨CR⟩** tells the **print** (**pr**) command to pass its results to the printer spooler command, **lpr** (lineprint), which produced the printout. The print command, **pr**, adds a heading to your text file which includes the date, the name of the file, and a page number. The **pr** command without the pipe or any modifiers simply prints the file on the video display screen, not on paper.

The Header Option to the pr Command

Many memos and reports use *headers* on each page. Specify the header option **-h** and the **print** command interprets the words following the **-h** as a page header, or title. To print your letter with the header ''Job reply form letter'', type **pr -h ''Job reply form letter'' jobreply ¦ lpr**

```
$ pr -h "Job reply form letter" jobreply ¦ lpr
$ □
```

Note that if the title consists of more than one word, you must enclose the words in double quotation marks.

Your line printer may be either a hardcopy printer without a keyboard or a printing terminal with a keyboard. You can log in on a printing terminal, which is a self-sufficient terminal device. Unlike a video terminal, the printing terminal has no TV-screenlike display, but uses paper print out to communicate.

With a printing terminal, you use all system commands you learned on the video display terminal. A printing terminal is simply a different device for speaking to the UNIX system. You cannot use a screen editing program such as **vi**. Printing terminals were used several years ago when video terminals were priced prohibitively. Printing terminals, although slow electromechanical devices, are suitable for line-oriented editors.

EDITING OPTIONS The UNIX system contains many lists of editor options used to modify the format of a file or control its production. The function of an option is often indicated by its name. For instance, at the very beginning of this chapter you used the "number" option to show the line numbers in the file on the screen. The names of some options are not quite so closely related to their job.

All options are set in last-line mode by using the colon command, which appears on the last line below the text. To see a list of all options and their current values, bring up the **vi** editor with **vi jobreply**, then type a colon and **set all⟨CR⟩**.

Type **vi jobreply**⟨CR⟩.

Type **:set all**.

```
$ vi jobreply<CR>
$ :set all<CR>
noautoindent        open                noslowopen
autoprint           nooptimize          tabstop=8
noautowrite         paragraphs=         taglenth=0
nobeautify          prompt              ttytype=h19A
directory=/tmp      no readonly         term=h19A
noerrorbells        redraw              noterse
hardtabs=8          report=5            warn
noignorecase        scroll=8            window=16
nolisp              sections=           wrapscan
nolist              shell=/bin/sh       wrapmargin=10
magic               shiftwidth=8        nowriteany
number              noshowmatch
```

To see only those options that have been changed from their *default values*, type **:set**⟨CR⟩.

The most useful options are described in the following pages. Some of these, like the **window** option, are applicable to **vi** only. After typing a colon, you can set the options desired by **set {option} [= {value}⟨CR⟩**. You then return to full screen mode. If you are unable to change an option, it may have been arbitrarily set by the system manager.

The Window Option in vi

The window is the number of lines **vi** will display on the screen. The window size can range from 1 line to the maximum number of lines on the screen minus 1. Since most terminals display a maximum of 24 lines, the maximum window size is usually 23. The last line of the window is reserved for colon commands.

The syntax of the command is **set window = (n)⟨CR⟩**, where (n) is the number of lines you desire in your window. The command **set window = 16 ⟨CR⟩**, then, will set the window size to 16 lines.

Line Numbering (nu) in vi

This option determines whether line numbers will be displayed. To enable line numbering, give the command **set nu⟨CR⟩**. If you prefer to work without line numbers, **set nonu⟨CR⟩** will disable numbering.

The ignorecase (ic) Option in vi

ignorecase is an especially useful option. You can search for characters without noting their case. For example, with ignorecase set, the search pattern **/a** would find both lowercase a's and uppercase A's. The search pattern may also be expressed in uppercase characters, as in **/A**. To activate the ignorecase option, the command is **set ic⟨CR⟩**. To turn it off, use **set noic⟨CR⟩**, which is the default value.

The wrapmargin (wm) in vi

Examples in this chapter use short sentences and a carriage return at the end. If you wish to use longer line lengths and omit carriage returns, just continue typing. The **vi** editor will automatically move the cursor to the next line. However, wrapped lines without carriage returns make editing extremely difficult. **wrapmargin** determines the maximum length of lines for text entry. The default value of **wm = 0** lets you type all the way to the ends of lines (usually 64 characters) and wraps to the next line without a carriage return. For **vi** to insert carriage returns when wrapping lines, you much change the default wrapmargin from zero. Specify to the **wrap**margin option the number of characters from the end of the line before a carriage return is automatically inserted. For example, **wm = 10⟨CR⟩** will allow you 64 minus 10, or 54 characters per line. The syntax of the command is **set wm = {n}⟨CR⟩**, where {n} is any number from 0 to 64.

Several options can be set at one time with a single command:

```
: set nu ic wm=10
```

Now move on to Chapter 4 to learn about the powerful file manipulation and "electronic file cabinet" of the UNIX system.

4

THE UNIX* FILE AND DIRECTORY SYSTEM

This chapter describes the UNIX system's built-in filing system and gives directions for working with files and directories, so that you can build an "electronic filing cabinet" for your work.

* UNIX™ is a trademark of Bell Laboratories.

In this chapter you will learn to build, manipulate, and manage "electronic file cabinets" in the UNIX system. Most personal computer files are managed by separating them into groups, perhaps on different floppy disks or different surfaces of a hard disk. In most operating systems, combining pieces of documents or searching through them requires clumsy and limited commands. The UNIX system, as an integral part of its structure, contains program commands for very powerful file manipulation.

Before starting the interactive lessons in this chapter, we will discuss the characteristics of files and directories. The definitions of files and directories are quite simple and not very different from the ordinary English language definitions of the terms. The main topic of these chapters, however, and one which is a little more complicated is the *interaction* between you and the file and directory system; specifically, the method by which you gain access to and perform operations on files and directories in the UNIX system. When you learn to use the procedures in this chapter, you will be able to build your own electronic file systems.

Most of the interactive lessons in this chapter and the next cover commands used to handle whole files and directories, rather than commands to make changes inside files. Displaying, moving, creating, and deleting files and directories are explained here.

DEFINITION OF A FILE

The file is the most elementary form of data organization to the computer operating system. Directories and subdirectories are sets of files, usually but not necessarily grouped logically. A directory can itself be a file within another directory and be handled by the system as a file. In earlier chapters, the file was described as analogous to the object of the command "sentence" and as conceptually equivalent to the ordinary office file in a manila folder. It is in this second sense that the file is considered in these chapters.

In its simplest terms, the UNIX *file system* is simply the system's main tool for organizing and storing all types of data. In the early days of computers, the main function of the operating system was to handle files. Although the concept and functions of an operating system have expanded a great deal, handling files so that they can be recalled easily and rapidly is still the operating system's principal task, and consumes most of its time.

The UNIX file system is very flexible and adaptable. Within the limits of the directory structure, you can organize files to suit the job at hand. For most applications, the UNIX system limits neither the length of files nor the number of files that can be created or kept on the system, nor does it limit the number of directories containing files.

HIERARCHICAL FILE ORGANIZATION

Files are handled by an operating system in either a horizontal (flat) or hierarchical organization. In the past, most microcomputers used floppy disks that held a small number of files and had a flat file system. In simple microcomputer operating systems, for example, typing "dir⟨CR⟩" gives a list of all the files on a floppy disk or surface of a hard disk. You cannot group files together and call them a common name. The UNIX plan, in contrast, is called hierarchical. Figs. 4.1 and 4.2 illustrate the two schemes.

In a flat system, you can access any file immediately and no file is located *within* another file. Grouping of files must be by floppy disk. Many owners of micro systems maintain an index filebox of floppies, and keep different kinds of files (letters, memos, proposals, etc.) on different diskettes.

The UNIX system automates the separation of file groups on different diskettes or surfaces of a hard disk. UNIX software handles the separation automatically, and gives you many powerful tools to manage the files and directories.

Fig. 4.1   A "Flat" File Organization System

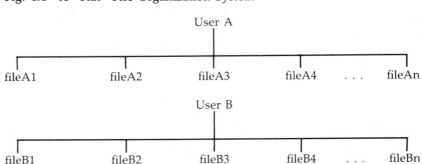

Fig. 4.2 A Hierarchical File Organization System

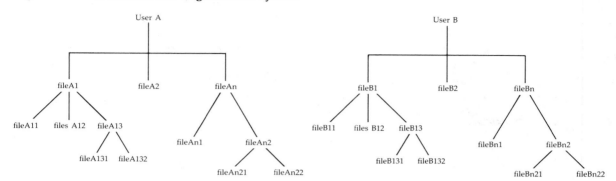

A hierarchical file system has a "vertical" orientation of files, and to reach a specific file you "go through" other files. Files can be nested within files, like an office filing cabinet.

Look at Fig. 4.3. Compare the "paper and metal" file cabinet with the representation of its electronic equivalent. First, compare and understand the way electronic files are diagrammed on paper, and in the lessons to follow, translate the drawings to what you see on the screen.

Your whole UNIX file system is like the metal cabinet. The drawers are major dividers, for example, Accounting, Documents, and Personnel, and can be compared to UNIX directories. "Pendaflex" folders, manila folders, and different groups of documents inside the folders represent the subdirectories and sub-subdirectories. The individual items in the paper folders become actual electronic UNIX files. Keep these ideas in mind as you continue.

THE FILENAME

When you create files, you first assign the new file a name, called a *filename*. The system stores the file under this name, and normally all references to the file are made using this name.

Choosing Filenames

A filename can be as many as 14 characters long, and may contain numbers, letters, punctuation, and special characters. You can name your files anything you choose. As a practical matter, certain characters have special meanings to the shell.

Fig. 4.3   Comparison of the UNIX File System with an Office Filing Cabinet

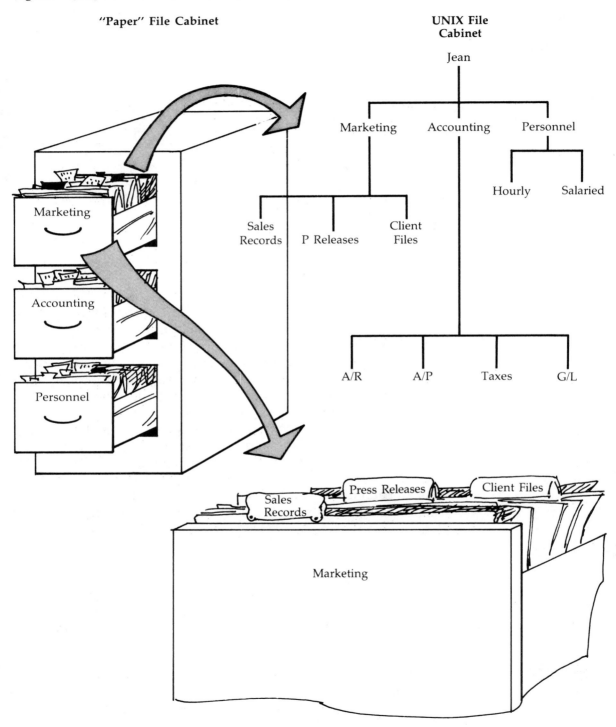

Although it is permissible to use these characters in filenames (by typing a special *escape* sequence, it is not recommended. For now, avoid using the following characters when naming your files:

```
&  *  "  [  ]  <  >  ;  :  /  '  ?  ^  -  and  the  blank
```

Restrict your filenames to letters (both uppercase and lowercase), numbers, periods, and underlines.

Filenames should be chosen thoughtfully. Computer files tend to accumulate rapidly. In no time at all your directory can be filled with files of unremembered origin. The careful selection of names that suggest the contents of the file will help you identify important files, remove unwanted files, and manipulate *groups* of files. Avoid using such filenames as

```
stuff  etc  things  people  accounts  tables
```

which might refer to anything. When you are trying to find that special file you created to hold all your clients' birthdays, you will wish you had used more descriptive filenames. The following names are more informative:

```
adjsmith.let      clients.bdays  accounts.rec
taxtable.sales    phone_nos.jly
```

Filename Extensions

In these examples, a period (.) breaks the file names into segments for easy identification. The part following the period is called the file type or filename *extension*. In the UNIX system, the total length of the filename is limited to 14 characters. Periods dividing the name count as a character.

UNIX commands let you manipulate more than one file at a time. The names of the files are separated by one or more spaces on the command line, so blanks cannot be used in filenames. Filenames without spaces may be hard to read. The filename phonenosjly in the example above is easier to understand with the underline (_) and period added.

Systematic File Naming

The following example illustrates the benefit of systematic file naming. Since you already know how to create text files using the UNIX **vi** text editor, create the file, **se_jc8aug.mem** to use as an example.

Type **vi se_jc8aus.mem**⟨**CR**⟩. Although this example is not part of an interactive lesson, carry out each operation as shown to practice using your system. This memo will be used in a later lesson.

```
$ vi se_jc8aus.mem<CR>
```

When you "come up" in **vi** as indicated by the screen display below,

```
▯
~
~
~
~
♦
♦
♦
```

```
"se_jc8aus.mem" No such file or directory
```

enter the following text.

```
8aus84

Sandy,

I have just read the rough draft of your
memo about the use of company vehicles.
I would like to add that the insurance
costs involved make it impossible for
employees to use their private vehicles
```

```
for company business. For the same
reason, employees are discouraged
from taking company vehicles home
at night.

Please add these items to your memo.

Chris
```

Now save the file to disk and exit from **vi**.

The filename **se_jc8aug.mem** is formatted for memo correspondence. It starts with the initials of the recipient and sender, separated by an underline and followed by the day and month the memo was written. Then, a filename extension (**.mem**) is added to identify the type of file it is (memo).

Suppose that after sending this memo to Sandy, several weeks pass and you forget about the subject of company vehicles. Then one day, another memo referring to the August 8th memo arrives via electronic mail from Sandy. You cannot remember exactly what the 8 August memo to Sandy was about, so you have to refresh your memory. Because you used a sensible file naming convention, you do not have a difficult search. You know it will be named something like **se_jc8aug.mem**. Thinking up your own conventions and standardizing them among all UNIX users in your company will increase efficiency and lessen the confusion.

DIRECTORIES

The UNIX system maintains a list of each user's files called a *directory*. When access to a particular file is requested, the system first looks at the directory to find out where the file is located on the disk or tape and then "goes out to the disk" and copies the requested file into a separate area of memory called the *buffer*. A directory is a file itself, and like a file, has a name.

When searching for a file, the UNIX system always starts at the "beginning" of the directory and searches until it finds the desired file. So far you have created just three files, **jobreply**, **jobreply.add**, and **se_jc8aug.mem**; your directory is not long, and you do not have to worry about keeping track of them.

Organizing Directories

Suppose that, a year from now, you have several thousand files, by no means an uncommon situation. Each time you want to see a file, the system checks through hundreds or even thousands of filenames before finding the right one. No one likes a list that is too long. It makes much more sense to divide your files into smaller groups and have a separate directory for each group. Now you will need a list for your lists; a directory for your directories.

The file system is logical and easily mastered. In fact, Bell's UNIX directory system is analogous to Bell's familiar telephone directory system. If there were just one telephone directory for the entire United States, the job of finding a particular Pete's Plumbing would be monumental. Fortunately, Bell has provided us with a different telephone directory for every city, town, and county in the country. So, if you know that the particular Pete's Plumbing you wish to talk to is in Seattle, you get a copy of the Seattle telephone book before you start looking. In that telephone book you will find further divisions of listings in even more specific sublists.

Guidelines for Working with Directories

Several rules about UNIX directory system management are important to know before starting the lessons. Turn back to this list if you get confused.

The rules:

- You can only "look" (operate) in one directory at a time.
- To gain access to a file, that file must be listed in the directory in which you are currently operating, or you must provide the appropriate directory name(s) when referring to the file.
- You cannot operate outside of a directory; you must be "in" some directory.
- A directory always exists within another directory and cannot be listed "by itself."

Other rules are explained as the need arises.

The Home Directory

When you first log in, you are assigned a specific workspace in the computer. Part of this workspace is a directory and is usually given your login name as its filename. It is your "default" directory. That is, it is the directory that you are automatically in when you login. It is called your *home directory*.

The three files you created during practice sessions with the **vi** editor are in your home directory. In addition, files created for you by your system manager are probably there, especially if you are working on a large, multiuser system. The purpose and content of these files are discussed in a later chapter.

Subdirectories

A directory contained within another directory is known as a *subdirectory*. The distinction between a directory and a sub-directory is an artificial one. *All* directories (except one, the *root*, or first, directory) are subdirectories; therefore, the term is just a way to show the relationships *between* directories.

Begin directory names with uppercase (capital) letters, and ordinary filenames with lowercase (small) letters. With this practice, you recognize directories at a glance. Because files named with capital letters are listed before those with lowercase letters when you ask for a listing of the files in your system, directories will be displayed first when using the **list** command (**ls**). (For a more detailed explanation of the precise order of listing, see *ASCII collating sequence* in the glossary.) The bigger your directory system grows, the more you will need naming conventions. This is not the only naming convention used today. Files outside of your own directory system may not follow this practice, and your company may decide on different filenaming conventions than suggested here.

The Inode Numbering System

A computer file is conceptually equivalent to an office file in a manila folder. (See the comparison diagram in Fig. 4.3.) Further, just as an office file has a name or identifying mark on it, so a computer file has a name. In big paper file systems, companies sometimes number files as well as name them. This practice introduces a higher level of security so files don't get lost, and makes them retrievable by a less vague title than "the accounts file" or other wordy descriptions. A computer file also has an identifing number called the *inode* number. The computer uses this number to locate the file.

Just as manila-folder files are arranged in file drawers and cabinets, so computer files are logically arranged. To locate a particular file quickly, many offices post the contents of a drawer or cabinet as a range of numbers and letters in a small bracket on the front of the drawer. A directory listing is comparable to this list, and the numbers are like the inode numbers.

The Current Directory

The UNIX system's directory contains the names of each file located "in the drawer," and the inode number. Whenever you go to your file cabinet to get out a file, you take the name of the file with you (maybe just in your head) and compare it against the names on the list. When you find the correct file cabinet and drawer, you open up the drawer and take out the file. Sometimes you leave the file drawer open or make note of the location so you know exactly where to put the file back. The idea of the "open drawer" is analogous to the idea of the UNIX *current directory*.

Now begin the interactive lessons and learn how to perform operations on files and directories.

LESSON 4.1:	Displaying Files, Part 1
NEW KNOWLEDGE:	The **cat** command
APPROXIMATE	
TIME:	30 minutes

If your system is not already up and running, bring it up and log in.

Suppose you wanted to reread the August 8 memo. You could summon the screen editor, **vi**, to read the memo. But that may be too much trouble just to look at a small memo, and you don't need to edit it; you just want to read it. There's a better way, the **cat** (**cat**enate) command. "Catenate" means to connect in a series.

cat (**cat**enate) also lets you take a quick look at the contents of files. To run **cat**, as with all UNIX system commands, you type the name of the command immediately after the prompt followed by any arguments and options. In this instance, the first argument is just the name of the file you wish to display.

```
$ cat se_jc8aug.mem<CR>
8aug84

Sandy:

I have just read the rough draft of your
memo about the use of company vehicles.
I would like to add that the insurance
costs involved make it impossible for
employees to use their private vehicles
for company business. For the same
reason, employees are discouraged from
taking company vehicles home at night.

Please add these items to your memo.

Chris
$ 
```

Error Messages

If you mistype a filename or request one that does not exist, you will get an error message. For example, try **cat**(ing) the file as follows:

```
$ cat se_jc8ag.mem<CR>
cat: can't open se_jc8ag.mem
$ ▯
```

You will get the error message: "cat: can't open se_jc8ag.mem." Although this indicates something went wrong with the command, the exact nature of the error is not stated. The same message is used to cover both the attempted **cat** of a nonexistent file (which is the same as a mistyped filename) and a request to **cat** a file without the proper *access permission*.

You may get a "permission denied" error message from the system. If you are certain that you have correctly typed the name of an existing file, but can't **cat** it, the file's *owner* has probably restricted public access to the file. The subject of access permissions is covered later; for now note that identical error messages can result from very different causes.

Catenating Files

Although the **cat** command is useful for quickly viewing short files, its main purpose is, as its name suggests, to join two files end-to-end. Suppose that you receive the following memo from Sandy.

```
From Sandy Wed Aug 25 09:56:52 1984

Chris:

Thanks for the 8aug84 reminder about
company vehicles. Whom shall I consult
concerning the particulars of our
insurance policies?

Sandy
```

You create the following file, using the **vi** editor, in reply to her request.

```
$ vi se_jc25aug.mem<CR>
~
~
~
.
.
.


"se_jc25aug.mem" No such file or directory
```

Enter the following text:

```
Sandy:

Contact either Hortense Boondoggle or
A. Philbert Nutt. If you want to contact
them by electronic mail, their user
names are boggle and pnutt.

Chris
```

Then write the file to disk and exit from **vi**.

Assume that you have sent this new memo and once again put the whole subject of company vehicles out of your mind. Later, the topic again arises and you want to look at both memos. You might type **cat se_jc8aug.mem**⟨CR⟩ and after reading that file, type **cat se_jc25aug.mem**⟨CR⟩. This would do the job. However, when the **cat** command is used with two filenames as arguments on the command line, separated by a space, it lets you view both files at the same time.

Type **cat se_jc8aug.mem se_jc25aug.mem⟨CR⟩**.

```
$ cat se_jc8aug.mem se_jc25aug.mem<CR>
8aug84

Sandy:

I have just read the rough draft of your
memo about the use of company vehicles.
I would like to add that the insurance
costs involved make it impossible for
employees to use their private vehicles
for company business. For the same
reason, employees are discouraged from
taking company vehicles home at night.
Please add these items to your memo.

Chris

Sandy:

Contact either Hortense Boondoggle or
A. Philbert Nutt. If you want to contact
them by electronic mail, their user
names are boggle and pnutt.

Chris
$ 
```

The files are joined end-to-end and displayed on the
screen.

There is no indicator of where the first file ends and
the second begins. You can add a row of asterisks or some
other attention-getting character at the end of your text to
make the boundaries between files more apparent.

LESSON 4.2:	Displaying Files, Part 2
NEW KNOWLEDGE:	The ^s and ^q commands
APPROXIMATE	
TIME:	5 minutes

When a file is **cat**ed whose length exceeds the capacity of the screen, the terminal will continue to scroll the text over the screen until it reaches the end of the file, making it difficult to read. To suspend scrolling temporarily, type ^s. Resume scrolling with ^q.

If your system is not already up and running, bring it up, log in, and **cat** the same two files as in the preceding lesson. Start and stop the display using the ^s and ^q commands.

```
$ cat se_jc8aug.mem se_jc25aug.mem<CR>
8aug84

Sandy:

I have just read ^s........................
...............^q the rough draft of
your memo about the use of company
vehicles. I would like to add that the
insurance costs involved make it
impossible for employees to use their
private vehicles for company business.
For the same reason, employees are
discouraged from taking company
vehicles home at night. Please add these
items to your memo.

Chris

Sandy:

You may contact ^s ...................
```

```
...............^q either Hortense
Boondoggle or A. Philbert Nutt. If you
want to contact them by electronic mail,
their user names are boggle and pnutt.

Chris
$ □
```

When using ^s and ^q, the display does not divide and produce the dotted lines as shown in the example. The dotted lines above show the passage of time.

The ^s and ^q commands can be used almost any time to control scrolling, not just when using the **cat** *command.*

LESSON 4.3:	Displaying Files, Part 3
NEW KNOWLEDGE:	The **more** command
APPROXIMATE	
TIME:	30 minutes

The start and stop commands, ^s and ^q, are used to browse through files. When you want to page through a text file carefully, the **more** command is used. It examines text files one screenful or one lineful at a time. After each screen (usually about 23 lines), **more** pauses and prints '--More--'. The use of the command is demonstrated with the on-line spelling dictionary.

If your system is not already up and running, bring it up, log in, and type **more /usr/dict/words⟨CR⟩**. The file specified here should be resident on your system. If you are using a small microcomputer, it may not be permanently installed on the system. Check with your computer manuals for how to install it.

NOTE: *Do not be concerned at this time with all of the parts of the command's argument. The filename is "words." To gain access to it, you must get into one of the UNIX system's library of directories. The "/usr/ dict/" does this for you.*

```
$ more /usr/dict/words<CR>
10th
1st
2nd
3rd
4th
5th
6th
7th
8th
9th
a
```

```
A&M
A&P
a's
AAA
AAAS
Aaron
AAU
ABA
Ababa
aback
abalone
--More--(0%) □
```

At the end of each screenful, **more** tells how far into the file you are, expressed as a percentage of the total file size. (In the example, the file viewed is so large that a single screenful is given as 0% of the total file length.) The cursor is now positioned after the '--More--' prompt. It will wait there until you are ready to see the next screen of text.

To display the next screen of text, press the space bar. To display only the next line of text, press carriage return. To quit from the **more** program and return to the shell, type **q**.

The **-d** Option to **more**

The **more** command has several options. If you want to be reminded to press the space bar, use the **-d** option when you invoke **more**. Remember, options are given after the command name and usually before the filename.

```
$ more -d /usr/dict/words<CR>
10th
1st
2nd
3rd
4th
5th
6th
7th
8th
```

```
9th
a
A&M
A&P
a's
AAA
AAAS
Aaron
AAU
ABA
Ababa
aback
abalone
--More--(0%) [Hit space to continue,
Rubout to abort]]]INTR
$ 
```

The system prints a message alongside the "more" prompt telling you to press the space bar to display a new screen or to press the "RUBOUT" key if you want to end (abort) the **more** command. **Rubout** stands for the **DEL** or **RUB** key. It returns you to the shell prompt. If the key on your terminal that produces the interrupt signal has been changed, use the new key. Consult your system manager or computer manuals if you have questions.

Other options in response to the '--More--' prompt are shown in Table 4.1.

Table 4.1   more Options

<CR>:	Print the next line of text.
d	reminds the user to press the space bar with a message at the bottom of the screen.
Q or q:	causes your exit from **more** (identical in effect to RUBOUT).
{n} space:	a number, {n}, followed by pressing the space bar, will print {n} more lines of text.
{n/expression} <CR>:	print the {n}th occurrence of the expression.
! **{shell-commandline}** <CR>	allows you to escape **more** temporarily to execute *one* {COMMANDLINE}.

V: puts your file into the vi editor, allowing you to make changes or move backward in the file. Quitting from the vi editor will return the file to the **more** program.

-{n} determines how many lines are printed with each press of the space bar.

Changing the Page Length of the **more** Command

The number of lines displayed on your screen at one time depends upon the type of terminal you are using. Sometimes you will want to use *a smaller page* length. To change the default size of a page, use the -{n} option where {n} is the number of lines printed after each press of the space bar.

The following exercises combine a small page of text with an escape to execute the shell command **who**. The use of a small screen prevents the **more** text from being scrolled away by the additional output from **who**. Use just ten lines of text in your display.

```
$ more -d10 /usr/dict/words<CR>
10th
1st
2nd
3rd
4th
5th
6th
7th
8th
9th
--More--(0%)[Hit space to continue,
Rubout to abort] ▯
```

In response to the "More" prompt, type ! to escape to the shell. The instant the ! is typed, the prompt line becomes a temporary command entry line; enter the command **who<CR>**.

```
           .
           .
           .
        6th
        7th
        8th
        9th
        !who<CR>
        root        console     Oct  17  13:55
        sabine      ttya0       Oct  17  13:01
        davida      ttya1       Oct  17  14:22
        chris       ttya2       Oct  17  12:03
        ------------------------------------------
        --More--(0%)[Hit space to continue,
        Rubout to abort] □
        space                    ←———————press space bar
        a
        A&M
        A&P
        a's
        AAA
        AAAS
        Aaron
        AAU
        ABA
        Ababa
        --More--(0%)[Hit space to continue,
        Rubout to abort] □
        ------------------------------------------
```

After executing the **who** command, the UNIX system returned immediately to **more**. When the space bar was pressed, the next ten lines were displayed.

Syntax and Summary of **more**

The complete syntax for **more** is

```
more [-d] [-n] [+{startline}] [+/{pattern}] {filename}...<CR>
```

Although this long command looks rather imposing, it is really not hard to understand. Recall from Chapter 2, any command in the UNIX system is like a sentence, and the first word usually implies a verb.

The word *more* is the verb here. The objects of the command sentence, or as we call them, the *argument*s and *option*s, all follow **more**. The items shown in brackets are options. The only argument that must be used with **more** is a filename. In its simplest form the **more** command is just **more filename**.

You have already seen the **d** and **n** options of **more** in the table (**d**—a reminder to press the space bar; **n**—the number of lines to display). The other two options, *startline* and */pattern* tell the UNIX system to start the display at a specific line or at the first occcurrence of some pattern (such as a word or group of characters). The plus (or minus) signs associated with these options tell the system to search forward or backward. Be careful of the syntax. These options *must* be preceded by **+** and **+/**, respectively.

In the following example, assume you want to locate the word, *intrepid* and display it with the 'Hit...' (**-d** option) prompt with a 10-line screen window.

```
$ more -10d +/intrepid /usr/dict/words<CR>
...skipping
intransigent
intransitive
intrepid
intricacy
intricate
intrigue
intrinsic
introduce
introduction
introductory
--More--(0%)[Hit space to continue, Rubout to abort] 
```

When a pattern is searched for and found, **more** starts two lines before the target pattern.

The following example displays the 11,659th entry in the dictionary using the 10-line window size, but does not require the **-d** option:

```
$ more -10 +11659 /usr/dict/words<CR>
intrepid
intricacy
intricate
intrigue
intrinsic
introduce
introduction
introductory
introit
introject
--More--(49%) 
```

Intrepid is the 11,695th word. Unlike the pattern search, **more** begins with a startline precisely on the specified line, not two lines before the requested line.

The **more** command, like **cat**, accepts multiple filenames on the command line. A header is printed at the beginning of each file. At the end of each file you will see the prompt ''—More— (Next file: {filename})''. At this prompt, press the space bar to display the next file.

```
$ more se_jc8aug.memse_jc25aug.mem<CR>
::::::::::::::
se_jc8aug.mem
::::::::::::::

8aug84

Sandy:

I have just read the rough draft of your
memo about the use of company vehicles.
I would like to add that the insurance
costs involved make it impossible for
employees to use their private vehicles
for company business. For the same
```

reason, employees are discouraged from
taking company vehicles home at night.

Please add these items to your memo.

Chris
--More--(Next file: se_jc25aug.mem)☐
space   ←————press space bar
::::::::::::::
se_jc25aug.mem
::::::::::::::
25 aug 84

Sandy:

Contact either Hortense Boondoggle or
A. Philbert Nutt. If you want to contact
them by electronic mail, their user
names are boggle and pnutt.

Chris
$ ☐

LESSON 4.4:   Displaying Files, Part 4
NEW KNOWLEDGE: The **head** and **tail** commands
APPROXIMATE
TIME: 20 minutes

The **head** command displays the first few lines of a file. The complete syntax for the **head** command is

head [-{count}] [{file}...]<CR>

where count is the number of lines displayed from the beginning of the file. If **count** is not specified, **head** defaults to 10 lines. The example below shows how to display the first seven entries in the dictionary.

Type **head -7 /usr/dict/words⟨CR⟩**.

```
$ head -7 /usr/dict/words<CR>
10th
1st
2nd
3rd
4th
5th
6th
$ ▯
```

[@Although **more** and **head** were originally part of the UC Berkeley UNIX system, they are often on computers whose manufacturers do not otherwise support the Berkeley software.@]

The **tail** command displays the "tail end" of text files. It is used to search text with easily recognized endings. The **tail** command is used when sending a file to someone via mail or telecommunications. Because it shows the end of a file, **tail** will confirm that an entire file reached its destination. The complete command syntax for the **tail** command is

tail [+/- {startline}] [bc] {filename}

where {startline} is the number of lines from the beginning (+) or end (-) of the file that display begins. The count is performed in lines, characters, or blocks of 512 characters. If **tail** is used without any options, the default display is the last ten lines. The example below shows how to display the **se_jc8aug.mem** file, starting eight lines from the end of the file.

Type **tail +81 se_jc8aug.mem**⟨CR⟩.

```
$ tail +81 se_jc8aug.mem<CR>
vehicles for company business. For the
same reason, employees are discouraged
from taking company vehicles home at
night.

Please add these items to your memo.

Chris
$ ▯
```

This command is an exception to the rule that all options must begin with a hyphen (-). Since a hyphen and a minus sign are the same symbol, a hyphen here would mean that you intended to display the last eight lines of the file. The + and - symbols, therefore, must be explicitly stated in the options.

Note that the + option does not cause the specified number of lines to be printed starting at the beginning of the file, but begins to display the text *after* the specified number of lines. The maximum number of lines from the **end** of the file specified with the + option is limited and depends on how many characters the lines contain.

The following example will display the last 40 characters of the same file.

Type **tail -40c se_jc8aug.mem**⟨CR⟩.

```
$ tail -40c se_jc8aus.mem<CR>
se add these items to your memo.

Chris
$ ▯
```

All spaces and carriage returns are counted as characters.

The command sentences of **head**, **more**, and **tail** suggest that filename arguments are *optional*. It is true that some commands work without an argument. If you type **head**, **more**, or **tail** without an argument, however, you will discover that either an error message results or nothing happens.

On some systems, you will get a "usage" line if you make a mistake in the command syntax. For instance, if you make a mistake in the **more** command, you might see

```
$ more<CR>
Usage: more [-dfln] [+linenum : +/pattern] name1 name2 ...
$ ▯
```

So far you have learned what files and directories are and how to name them. You have learned to display files separately and jointly with the **cat** command. You have seen how files are the basic unit of organization for characters and words. Files are organized into **directories**, the topic of the next lesson.

LESSON 4.5:   Listing Your Files and Directories
NEW KNOWLEDGE: The **ls** (**list**) command
APPROXIMATE
TIME: 5 minutes

Now that you are a more experienced UNIX user, begin each login session by checking your home directory to see what files it contains. Filenames tend to be abbreviations and it is easy to forget the abbreviations you've created. By listing all your files, you can remind yourself of the exact spelling of filenames. The command to list all the files in the current directory is **ls**.

If your system is not already up and running, bring it up and log in.

Type **ls⟨CR⟩**.

```
$ ls<CR>
jobreply
jobreply.add
se_jc25aug.mem
se_jc8aug.mem
$ 
```

ls generally prints the files in your directory in alphabetical order in a single column down the left side of the screen. Directories containing numerous files cannot be entirely displayed on one screen. Some systems offer the option to list your files in three or four columns.

We have created only two files so far in this chapter (**se_jc8aug.mem** and **se_jc25aug.mem**). The **jobreply** and **jobreply.add** files remain from the preceding chapter.

[@*NOTE:*   *It is not unusual to find old files in a newly assigned home directory. In most systems, the system manager copies these files onto tape in case the previous owner inquires about them. Should you ever encounter unknown files in your home directory, you should check with the system manager before removing them.*@]

LESSON 4.6:	Detailed List of Files
NEW KNOWLEDGE:	The -l (long) option for the ls command
APPROXIMATE	
TIME:	30 minutes

You often want to know more about your files than just their names. The UNIX system provides options to the **ls** command that give you more information. A list of some of these **ls** options appears in Table 4.2. One of the most useful options is **-l** (long). The syntax for *list long* is

```
ls -l {directory name}<CR>
```

Since you only have a few files and no directory in your account at present, we will use the files of a hypothetical user to show the full power of the long list. Assume that the user wishes to examine three directories, **Parts**, **Newstock**, and **Oldstock**.

Note that in the following hypothetical example the **ls** command accepts more than one argument on the command line, so you can view all the files at once. Remember, this is a hypothetical example!

Type **ls -l Parts Newstock Oldstock**⟨CR⟩.

```
$ ls -l Parts Newstock Oldstock<CR>

Parts:
total 5
-rw----rw-  1 polly     234 Sep 2 16:38 cylinders
-rw----rw-  1 polly     897 Sep 9 12:34 doors
-rw----rw-  1 polly     100 Sep 2 10:18 motors
-rw----rw-  1 polly     443 Sep 9 08:08 pumps
-rw----rw-  1 polly     388 Sep 3 18:10 screws

Newstock:
total 2
drwx---rwx  2 polly      46 Aug 8 12:04 Domestic
drwx---rwx  2 polly      96 Aug 8 12:04 Foreign
```

```
Oldstock:
total 2
drwx---rwx  2 polly    322 Aug 8 12:04 Domestic
drwx---rwx  2 polly     41 Aug 8 12:04 Foreign
$ ▯
```

Note that each directory name on the command line is automatically given a header in the display. The significance of each column or item in the display is summarized below from the directory **Newstock**. Observe that the display has been divided in four cateogires.

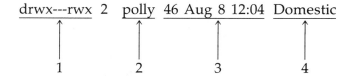

The first category of the display occupies the first ten columns. The first column in the display shows whether the file is an ordinary file or a directory. Directories are indicated by a *d*, ordinary files by an =.

Permission Bits

The remaining nine columns are further separated into three groups of three columns each, as shown below.

These items are called the "permission bits." The first set of three bits pertains to the owner of the file; the second set pertains to the group to which the owner belongs, and the third set pertains to the "public." The individual columns have the same significance for all three sets: from left to right, **r** (read), **w** (write), **x** (execute).

In the listing shown above, the *owner* (polly) has permission to read, write, and execute the file. The *group* is not permitted access at all (this usually means that there is no defined group). The *public* has the same permission as the owner to read, write, and execute the file.

The second category of the display is simply the name of the "owner" of the file, usually the login name of the creator of the file.

The third category of the display is a time and date stamp. It is a record of when the file was created or last modified. The numeral preceding the date gives the size of the file in characters.

The fourth category is the file or directory name. In this case it is the directory named **Domestic**.

NOTE: *The numeral between the permission bits and the owner indicates the number of links to the file. For the present, disregard this item. It will be discussed in a later chapter.*

Look now at another example, this time from the directory.

Parts

```
-rw----rw-  1 polly    234 Sep 2 16:38 cylinders
```

The hyphen in the first column shows that **cylinders** is an ordinary file. It is owned by **polly** and was created September 2 at 4:38 P.M. Both polly and the public have read and write permission.

When **ls** is used without an argument, its default argument is the current directory. If a subdirectory of the current directory is given as an argument, its files and subdirectories will be listed instead. See Table 4.2.

Table 4.2   list Options

l	gives more detailed information; "long" listing
t	lists in time order, beginning with most recently modified
a	lists all entries, including files
s	lists size in blocks
u	lists in time order, beginning with most recently accessed
r	lists in reverse order
d	reports directory status information

Analyzing Your Own Files

If your system is not already up and running, bring it up, log in, and execute the "list long" command.

Type **ls -l⟨CR⟩**.

```
$ ls -l<CR>
-rw-r-----       {your name}  648 date   jobreply
-rw-r-----       {your name}  151 date   jobreply.add
-rw-r-----       {your name}  375 date   se_jc25aug.mem
-rw-r-----       {your name}  163 date   se_jc8aug.mem
```

As your only exercise in this lesson, analyze the long listing for each of your files.

LESSON 4.7:	Establishing Your Own Directory System
NEW KNOWLEDGE:	Use of the **mkdir** (**make dir**ectory) and **cd** (**c**hange **d**irectory) commands
APPROXIMATE TIME:	60 minutes

You have learned to create files in your default or home directory. You could go on adding files to this directory until you run out of disk space. But usually you have files of different *kinds*, or files that contain different categories of information, such as names and addresses, accounting data, letters, and memos. It is much easier to keep track of files when they are grouped into separate directories according to a plan. Organizing by subject, for example, helps you to quickly access the group of files you need.

When you created files, you invoked the **vi** editor with a filename as an argument. Once you inserted text and wrote the file to disk, the file was created. To create a directory, however, the process is different. The command to create a directory is **mkdir** (**make dir**ectory). The complete syntax for the command is

```
mkdir {Dirname} {Dirname}...<CR>
```

Note that you may create more than one directory at a time.

Note also that after you create a directory, its name appears among the filenames when you list the current directory.

For the remaining lessons in this chapter and for the first few in the next chapter, we will need some typical files and directories to use as examples. We will begin by creating the directory **Account**.

If your system is not already up and running, bring it up, log in, and type **mkdir Account⟨CR⟩**.

```
$ mkdir Account<CR>
$ ls<CR>
Account
jobreply
jobreply.add
se_jc8aug.mem
se_jc25aug.mem
    "
    "
    "
```

The accounting directory, **Account**, is a good place to begin organizing a directory system. This directory will contain four basic accounting subdirectories **Genledger** (general ledger), **Inventory**, **Payable** (account payable), and **Receivable** (accounts receivable). In addition, five **taxtable** files are placed in a directory called **Taxtable**. The **Account** directory will ultimately contain the directories and files shown in Fig. 4.4 below.

Note that the filenames shown in this diagram all have extensions. The .prog extension means that the file is an *executable program file*. More will be said about this type of file in Chapter 6. Before creating the files and directories shown in this diagram, you must learn another command.

Fig. 4.4 Map of the Account Directory

Genledger	Inventory	Payable	Receivable	Taxtable
genledger.prog genledger.dat	inventory.prog	payable.prog	receivable.prog	taxtable.cty taxtable.exc taxtable.fed taxtable.sal taxtable.sta

Account

The Change Directory
(**cd**) Command

To access the directory **Account** use the **cd** (change directory) command. The complete syntax for the command is

cd {Dirname}<CR>

where {Dirname} is the name of a directory or a subdirectory that you wish to make your current directory. The
command really means "change current directory." When
cd is used without an argument, the home directory automatically becomes the current directory.

You are now ready to change directories. Use the **cd**
command to change the current directory to **Account**. Create your new directories with **mkdir**, then list the contents
of the current directory, **Account**. Multiple arguments may
be used on the command line.

Type **cd Account⟨CR⟩**.

Type **mkdir Genledger Inventory Payable Receivable
Taxtable⟨CR⟩ ls⟨CR⟩**

```
$ cd Account<CR>
$ mkdir Genledger Inventory Payable Receivable Taxtable<CR>
$ ls<CR>
Genledger Inventory Payable Receivable Taxtable
```

It may seem wasteful to create directories to hold only
one or two files, but important divisions such as these will
rapidly collect files and programs. For example, a file containing a list of habitually overdue accounts might be added
to the **Receivable** directory, and a new program to cross-
index the company's inventory could reside in **Inventory**.

A constraint or "rule" governing use of the **cd** command: with a single, noncomplex argument, the current directory can be changed one directory at a time, either to the
directory immediately "above" it or to one immediately "below" it. As you will see in the next chapter, it is possible to
move through several levels simultaneously with a single **cd**
command. For the present, we will restrict the command to
moving you down a single directory at a time. In any case,
all directory changes are "vertical." The idea of verticality is

Fig. 4.5   Directory System Created in Lesson 4.7

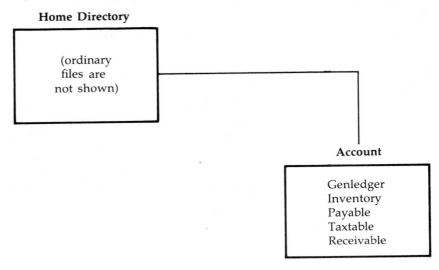

Home Directory

(ordinary
files are
not shown)

Account

Genledger
Inventory
Payable
Taxtable
Receivable

used in reference to the directory organization diagram in
Fig. 4.5.

You now have seven directories: **Account**, **Genledger**,
Inventory, **Payable**, **Receivable**, **Taxtable** and your **home
directory** organized as shown below in Fig. 4.5.

Practice changing directories.

**Creating Practice Files
and Directories**

Before proceeding to the next lesson, create the files listed
in Fig. 4.6, ''Map of the Account Directory.'' Be sure to
place each file in the appropriate directory as shown. Use **vi**
to create the files. Since you are currently in the **Account**
directory, you must change to each subdirectory as
required.

Type **cd Genledger⟨CR⟩
vi genledger.prog⟨CR⟩**.

```
$ cd Genledger<CR>
$ vi genledger.prog<CR>
~
~
~
~
~
genledger prog   No such file or directory □
```

No text is actually needed in these files at present. Just save the files with the **wq** command.
Type **:wq⟨CR⟩**.

```
  ~
  ~
  ~
  ~
:wq<CR>
"genledger.prog" [New file] 1 line 1 character
```

Repeat this procedure for the **genledger.dat** file, and again change directories to **Inventory**, **Payable**, **Receivable** and **Taxtable**. While you are in each directory, create the file or files for that directory in Fig. 4.6.

When you have finished creating all of the listed files, return to your home directory by typing **cd⟨CR⟩** without an argument. These files will be used in future lessons.

LESSON 4.8:	Deleting or Removing Files
NEW KNOWLEDGE:	Use of the **rm** (**rem**ove) command
APPROXIMATE	
TIME:	15 minutes

Most users have a tendency to keep files ("just in case") long after they have served their purpose. Generally, it is an uneconomical practice. Disk space, on microcomputers particularly, can rapidly become precious, and if you have dozens of files that you no longer need, you may be depriving yourself or someone else. Your system manager performs a periodic *backup* to tape or floppy disk of all files (usually called *archiving*). If you really must recover an old file, you can retrieve it from the backup tape. Files are removed by the **rm** (**rem**ove) command.

If your system is not already up and running, bring it up, log in, and execute an **ls** command to list the names of all the files in your home directory.

The **rm** command's arguments are the filenames you wish to remove from the current directory. Since you no longer need the **se_jc8aug.mem** and **se_jc25aug.mem** files, we can use them to demonstrate this command. Since the **rm** command does not print any message if the removal was successful, you should follow up an **rm** command with an **ls** command to verify that the operation removed the file as intended.

Type **rm se_jc8aug.mem⟨CR⟩**
    ls⟨CR⟩.

```
$ rm se_jc8aug.mem<CR>
$ ls<CR>
Account
Jobreply
Jobreply.add
se_jc25aug.mem
$ ▯
```

The **ls** command shows that the **se_jc8aug.mem** file is no longer in your home directory.

Repeat the above procedure for the **se_jc25aug.mem** file. Again, the **ls** command shows that the file has been deleted.

The **rm** command can be used with multiple arguments. The removal of the two files could have been accomplished in a single command as follows:

```
rm se_jc8aug.mem se_jc25aug.mem<CR>
```

If you wish to practice using this command with multiple files, you can change to the **Taxtable** directory and remove files. If you do remove any of the files, be sure to recreate them since they will be referred to in a later chapter.

One word of caution: the **rm** command is irreversible. The data in a removed file is irretrievably lost, so do not use the command casually. It is always a good idea to **cat**(enate) a file before you **rem**ove it to be sure of its contents.

When an invalid argument is given, as when a filename is misspelled, the **rm** command will execute all of the command that it can and issue an error message to inform you that all of the command was not executed. Suppose, for instance, you had typed "rm jbreply ....etc.," the UNIX system would respond with "rm: jbreply nonexistent" then proceed to the next item in the argument list.

LESSON 4.9:	Deleting or Removing Directories
NEW KNOWLEDGE:	Use of the **rmdir** (**rem**ove **dir**ectory)
APPROXIMATE	
TIME:	20 minutes

A directory cannot be removed with the same command (**rm**) that is used to remove an ordinary file. Directories require a special command **rmdir** (**rem**ove **dir**ectory). If you attempt to use **rm** to remove a directory, you will receive an error message: "{filename} nonexistent." This message does not mean that the *name* does not exist: it means that there is no *file* by that name. When you issued the **rm** command, you informed the UNIX system that you wanted to remove files, not directories.

There are one or two other differences between the removal of files and the removal of directories. The **rmdir** command with a simple filename argument can be successfully executed only if the directory is empty, that is, contains no files. This is a precaution so you don't lose files by mistake. If you attempt to remove a nonempty directory, you will receive an error message: "rmdir: {Dirname} not empty."

To remove the current directory you must first *ascend* to the next higher directory. This proscription is logical because a directory is not listed "in itself." The shell, which can only "see" the filenames listed in the current directory would not be able to find the directory name to remove it.

Removing Directories

We will now delete the directories you created in Lesson 4.6. You can recreate them before proceding to the next lesson. If your system is not up and running, bring it up, log in, and exeute an **ls** command.

First, attempt to remove the **Account** directory. Type **rmdir Account⟨CR⟩**

```
$ rmdir Account<CR>
rmdir: Account not empty
$ 
```

The directory **Account** contains nothing but other directories, but even if they were all empty, the shell does not check beyond the directory's list, and that is not empty. To delete the directory **Account**, move to the **Account** directory with the **cd** command. Then gain access to each of the subdirectories, again by the **cd** command, and **rm** the files in each of these. Then return to the **Account** directory by typing **cd Account⟨CR⟩**.

Type **cd Account⟨CR⟩**
   ls⟨CR⟩.

```
$ cd Account<CR>
$ ls<CR>
Genledger Inventory Payable Receivable Taxtable
$ ▯
```

Next, remove all the directories in **Account**.

Type **rmdir Genledger Inventory Payable Receivable Taxtable⟨CR⟩ ls⟨CR⟩**.

```
$ rmdir Genledger Inventory Payable Receivable Taxtable<CR>
$ ls<CR>
$ ▯
```

The absence of anything following the **ls** command verifies that all the directories have been removed.

Return again to your home directory with cd⟨CR⟩.

Type **cd⟨CR⟩** followed by an **ls** command.

```
$ cd<CR>
$ ls<CR>
Account      jobreply      jobreply.add
$ ▯
```

You are now ready to remove the **Account** directory. Type **rmdir Account⟨CR⟩** followed by the **ls** command.

```
$ rmdir Account<CR>
$ ls<CR>
Jobreply     Jobreply.add
$ ▯
```

The absence of **Account** shows that you successfully removed the **Account** directory.

Before going on to the next lesson, recreate the directories and files you just deleted.

LESSON 4.10:	Changing File and Directory Names
NEW KNOWLEDGE:	Use of the **mv** (**move**) command to rename a file or directory
APPROXIMATE TIME:	10 minutes

You will occasionally want to change the names of files. For example, you might realize that a different name better suggests the contents, or you may have typed the name incorrectly in the **mkdir** or **vi** command line.

Filenames are changed by using the **mv** (**move**) command. The **mv** command is also used to move files from one directory to another, and you use the command in the next chapter. For now, use it to change the name of a file. The complete syntax for the command is

```
mv {oldfilename} {newfilename}<CR>
```

If your system is not up and running, bring it up, log in, and execute the **ls** command.

For this exercise change the name of **Account** to **Accounts.n**. (It does not matter that **Account** is a directory; the command is the same.)

Type **mv Account Accounts.n**⟨CR⟩ followed by an **ls** command.

```
$ mvdir Account Accounts.n<CR>
$ ls<CR>
Accounts.n       jobreply        jobreply.add
$ 
```

The **ls** command shows that the **mv** command was successfully executed.

The commands and concepts learned in this chapter are very important foundations of knowledge about the UNIX system. It is a good idea to review the chapter before going on to Chapter 5. Chapter 5 contains continuing lessons on the commands used to manipulate files and directories.

5

THE UNIX* FILE AND DIRECTORY SYSTEM, PART 2

You can perform advanced file and directory management with the shell after learning the information in this chapter. This chapter gives the UNIX system user powerful office management tools.

* UNIX™ is a trademark of Bell Laboratories.

This chapter, a continuation of Chapter 4, teaches you advanced file and directory handling. Common office uses of the shell are explained. You will refine your knowledge from Chapter 4, and learn to apply it to your job.

LESSON 5.1:	Pathnames; The Double Dot (..) and Slash (/)
NEW KNOWLEDGE:	More on the **cd** (**c**hange **d**irectory) command and UNIX in directory organization
APPROXIMATE TIME:	15 minutes

In Lesson 4.6 you learned to change directories one at a time, and to move "vertically" through the directory system. In this lesson that concept is expanded to include the idea of a *pathname*. Pathnames are labels for the paths from one directory to another. Let's look at a command using this new concept. Suppose the following **cd** commands were executed. (Do not try to execute this command if you have just logged on. You are in your home directory and the display will be different.)

```
$ cd ../Accounts.n<CR>
$ ls<CR>
Genledger Inventory Payable Receivable Taxtable
$ ▯
```

The **cd** command's argument is in a new form, called a pathname or, more specifically, a *relative*, or *partial pathname*.

The **..** (Double Dot) and **/** (Slash) Commands to Change Directories

In the example, the pathname contains three separate elements, two directory names, the "double dot" (..) and **Accounts.n**. A forward slash (/) separates them. The two dot (..) symbol represents the directory one level above the current directory and is used in this command to tell the UNIX system to ascend one level in the directory structure. The / symbol means just the opposite. It is the command to descend one level to the directory whose name follows the /. The command **cd ../Accounts.n⟨CR⟩** in the sample screen above means "change directory to the directory immediately above the current directory, then *descend* one level to the directory **Accounts.n**." (Keep in mind that the UNIX file system is branched, not linear, so you can ascend, immediately descend, and be in a different subdirectory or file. Study Fig. 5.1 if you are still confused.)

Any number of ascend/descend instructions can be used as the argument of the **cd** command, as long as the instruction does not contain an impossible movement and the last element in the argument is the name of a directory. This is an efficient notation method and you will use it frequently when you build your own file/directory system.

If your system is not already up and running, bring it up, log in, and execute the following **mkdir** command from your home directory.

Type **mkdir Words⟨CR⟩**.

```
$ mkdir Words<CR>
$ ▯
```

Now change to the **Words** directory by giving the **cd** command. Type **cd Words⟨CR⟩**.

```
$ cd Words<CR>
$ ▯
```

For the following discussion, use Fig. 5.1's sample directory diagram, reproduced from Fig. 4.5, plus the newly created **Words** directory.

Fig. 5.1   Directory System Created in Lesson 5.1

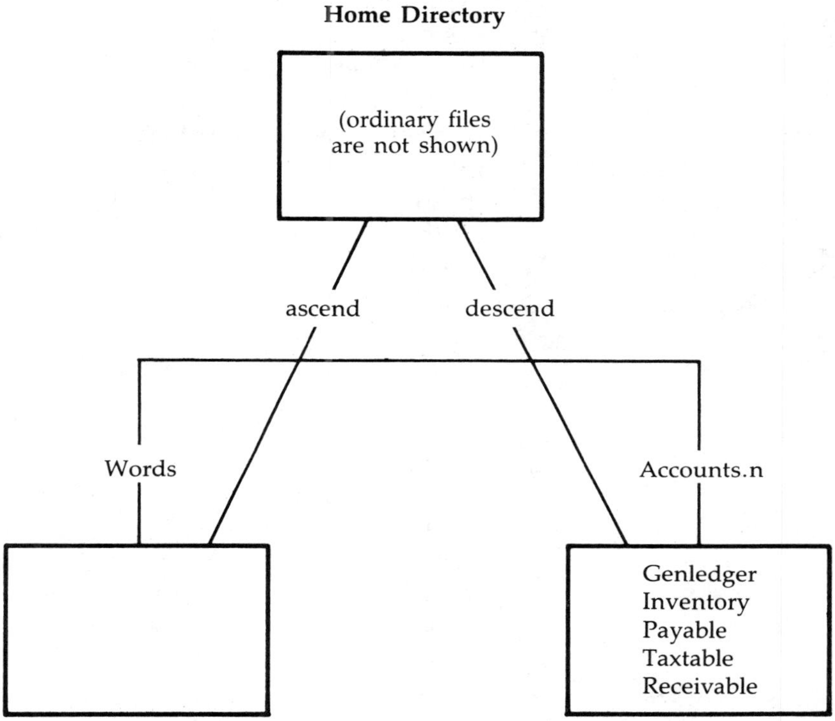

Home Directory

Your current directory is now **Words**. Suppose you
wish to make the directory **Taxtable** your current directory.
Consider the diagram. To reach **Taxtable** from **Words**, first
ascend to the home directory, then descend to **Accounts.n**,
and then descend to **Taxtable**. The complete pathname to
execute this move is

```
cd ../Accounts.n/Taxtable
```

which says "ascend one directory, descend one directory,
and descend yet another."
  Type **cd ../Accounts.n/Taxtable⟨CR⟩**.

```
$ cd ../Accounts.n/Taxtable<CR>
$ 
```

You have exhausted the directory moves within your own very small directory system. If you are on a multiuser system, you can carry out the following experiment for more experience.

First, return to your home directory by typing **cd⟨CR⟩**. Change directories to the one immediately above by executing a **cd ..⟨CR⟩**. This command will probably place you in the directory **usr**, which is often the UNIX directory holding all the users on the system. Then execute an **ls -l⟨CR⟩** on this directory.

Type **cd ..⟨CR⟩**
     ls -l⟨CR⟩.

```
$ cd ..<CR>
$ ls -l<CR>
total 6
-rwxr-xr-x 2  0    532 Feb 23 15:06 BACKUP
-rw-r----- 1  0    105 Jan 30 12:20 USERS
drwxrwxr-x 5  3    384 Jan  7 13:43 games
drwxr-x--- 3 30    444 Apr  9 12:50 brunhilde
drwxr-x--- 2 24    133 Mar 31 16:16 joanne
drwxr-x--- 9 25    576 Feb  9 14:00 vanilla
drwxr-xr-x 7 15    128 Nov 23 16:20 spool
$ ▯
```

The system response above is typical of what you see. Your system has different files and user names, but the format for your display should be the same.

You can see the names of other users and directories in this directory listing. Practice descending into other directories, executing the **ls** command as you go. Then trace the pathnames between your home directory and others in the system. Use pencil and paper to sketch out the directory structure. If you cannot access a directory, public access is probably restricted. Try another; most directories are accessible. Remember, you can always get back to your home directory by typing **cd⟨CR⟩**.

In the next lesson you will learn to ascertain the pathname from the UNIX system's **root** directory to the current directory. The root directory is the *first* directory on which the entire system is based. Fig. 5.2 demonstrates the root directory, and the overall map of a typical UNIX system. The terms for directories just below root are usually the same on all UNIX systems. Directory names before them are hypothetical.

Fig. 5.2 Overall Map of a Typical UNIX System

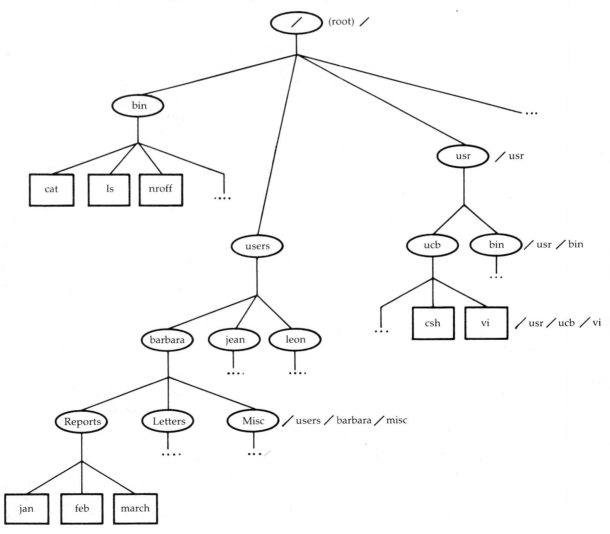

LESSON 5.2:	Ascertaining Your Current Directory
NEW KNOWLEDGE:	Use of the **pwd** (print **w**orking **d**irectory) command
APPROXIMATE	
TIME:	10 minutes

Although it may now seem unlikely to you that you could lose track of your current directory, it happens frequently in large directory systems. A directory system can become extremely complex, and instant access to current directory and pathname information is a valuable UNIX service. The **pwd** command names your current directory and displays the complete pathname to it.

If your system is not already up and running, bring it up, log in, and execute a **cd** command to make your current directory **Taxtable**. Type **cd Accounts.n/Taxtable⟨CR⟩**. The current directory is now **Taxtable**. Confirm this with the **pwd** command. Type **pwd⟨CR⟩**.

```
$ pwd<CR>
/usr/{home directory}/Accounts.n/Taxtable
$ 
```

The path from your home directory to **Taxtable** is a partial pathname, a pathname from a directory *relative* to the current directory. The **pwd** command, however, displays the whole or *absolute* pathname. You understand the partial pathname {**home directory**}/**Accounts.n/Taxtable**. It is the directory path from the home directory to the directory **Taxtable**. The /**usr**/ portion is the path from your home directory to the very top of the directory system known as **root** and symbolized by the solitary slash, /. Look at Fig. 5.2 to see the relationships. Your home directory is itself a subdirectory—in this instance, a subdirectory of **usr**, which is, in turn, a subdirectory of the **root** directory, /.

The UNIX system gives you the pathname of the directory immediately *above* the current directory with the .. command. The complete pathname of the *current* directory is handled by the single period, (.) command. Use the . command as the shorthand version of the pathname of the current directory, or /**usr**/{**current directory**}. If you must type the complete pathname from the **root** directory through your current directory to the last directory in the line, substitute the dot symbol, (.), for the initial portion of it and save the typing time. For instance, if your home directory is your current directory, the full pathname to **Taxtable** may be written

```
/usr/{home directory}/Accounts.n/Taxtable
```

or simply ./**Accounts**/**Taxtable**. /**usr**/{**home directory**} is handled by the period.

You have now learned two special symbols for shorthand notation:

- "." or dot, the current directory.
- ".." or double dot, the directory above the current directory.

If yours is a multiuser system, practice recording the pathnames to various directories in the system and moving to them. (Remember, you can always get back to your home directory by executing the **cd** command without arguments!)

LESSON 5.3:	"Wildcards" or Metacharacters
NEW KNOWLEDGE:	Use of the symbols *, ?, [,], and the -i option. Use of the **echo** command
APPROXIMATE TIME:	60 minutes to create files 60 minutes for the Lesson (in two 30-minute sections)

If your system is not already up and running, bring it up and log in.

To demonstrate the use of wildcards, you need files in each of your directories. The larger number of files will give you a more realistic experience of file manipulation in the next lessons.

Creating the files will take 45–60 minutes. Do this job in a separate session. It is a good idea to start this lesson's tutorial fresh, rather than after an hour of picky file creation.

Put all of the files you create in your home directory. You will move them to different directories as part of the exercises in this chapter. The files are empty because this chapter's lessons perform operations on entire files, not on their contents.

To create blank files, give the command **vi {file-name}⟨CR⟩**. When the bottom-line message "filename" No such file or directory appears, type **:wq** to save the file. Repeat this operation for every file named in the following list. **vi** will create only one file at a time.

Create the following files exactly as listed here.

access.m1.pam	ch2.sec2.om.m1	ch5.sec5.om.m1	pay.form
appl.m1.pam	ch2.sec3.om.m1	fri.diet.per	piano.per
bd_jc16may.mem	ch3.sec1.om.m1	jk_jc1jan.mem	resour.m1.pam
bozo	ch3.sec1.sm.m1	jk_jc1may.mem	rt_jc19may.mem
ch1.sec1.om.m1	ch3.sec2.om.m1	jk_jc7sep.mem	softball.per
ch1.sec1.sm.m1	ch3.sec2.sm.m1	jy_jc2jun.mem	sonofbozo
ch1.sec2.om.m1	ch4.sec1.om.m1	memo.form	ssi.form
ch1.sec2.sm.m1	ch4.sec1.sm.m1	mon.diet.per	thurs.diet.per
ch1.sec3.om.m1	ch4.sec2.om.m1	odds_ends.per	time.login
ch1.sec3.sm.m1	ch5.sec1.om.m1	order.form	time.logout
ch1.sec4.om.m1	ch5.sec2.om.m1	orthodont.per	tues.diet.per
ch2.sec1.om.m1	ch5.sec3.om.m1	outline.om.m2	wed.diet.per
ch2.sec1.sm.m1	ch5.sec4.om.m1	outline.sm.m2	wt_jc30jul.mem

The files beginning with the letters *ch* are chapters in hypothetical Service and Owner's Manuals.

Manipulating Files

When you begin day-to-day use of your UNIX system, you will quickly accumulate files and directories. You can replace lengthy typed commands and filenames on the command line with *single* characters that represent some or all of the long form of the command. The more you use the UNIX system, the more you will learn and appreciate its "shorthand" symbols. By the end of this lesson, you may start to agree with experienced UNIX users—the terse "shorthand" of UNIX takes some learning, but it sure speeds things up!

Characters with specific, larger meanings than normal when used in text are called *metacharacters*. When used as substitutes for other characters, these shorthand symbols are called *wildcards*.

The Star (*) Wildcard

Consider the star wildcard character (*). It is typical of UNIX wildcards. It replaces any set of characters and means "the whole set." You could type out

```
rm filename1 filename2 filename3 ...filename297<CR>
```

to remove files 1 through 297, or you could use the wildcard symbol * as follows:

```
rm -i * <CR>
```

Use the Interactive (-i) Option for Safety

Using the star wildcard character with the **remove** and other commands is both powerful and dangerous. You can guard against accidental misuse of a wildcard with the **-i** option. Whenever you use a powerful command like **rm** with a wildcard, you should include the **-i** (interactive) option on the command line. The **rm** command with the **-i** option and the wildcard to delete all files in the current directory is written **rm -i *⟨CR⟩**. The -i option makes the **rm** command pause before each removal to confirm your intentions. For each filename displayed, type **y⟨CR⟩** if you wish to delete the file, or **n⟨CR⟩** if you do not wish to delete it. (Actually, typing any character besides y is the same as typing **n**. You could, for example, simply ⟨**CR**⟩ to answer "no.")

You can use wildcards in the middle of a command line. The best way to understand wildcards in a command line is to use the **echo** command. **echo** expands and displays the wildcard arguments to preview exactly what the shell will do when it acts on a command with wildcard in the command line.

Start with another use of the star. To display the names of all files in Chapter 1 of the Owner's Manual, type **echo ch1.*.om.m1**⟨**CR**⟩.

```
$ echo ch1.*.om.m1<CR>
ch1.sec1.om.m1 ch1.sec2.om.m1 ch1.sec3.om.m1 ch1.sec4.om.m1
$ 
```

echo has shown you the filenames that have characters in the Chapter filename between the chapter (**ch1**) and the further categorization **.om**. By placing the * wildcard as a substitute for the section number part of the filename (**.sec{n}** becomes **.*.**), you can make commands act on all files with section numbering in the filename as shown. Note, however, that filenames with *other* text than "sec{n}" between the periods would also be deleted. You could limit the wildcard further by typing

```
echo ch1.sec*.om.m1<CR>.
```

then the **echo** command would work on only those files with any number of characters between "sec" and the ".om."

Be careful when the * is used to represent more than one character. It can cause problems. By making wildcards too broad, files that you may not want to include are acted on. To protect against this possibility, make your wildcard substitutions as specific as possible.

The Question Mark (**?**) Wildcard

In the example just shown, the more specific wildcard character **?**, could have been used. It only represents *one character at a time*. You can use the * to represent one character,

but you *know* that only one character will be "wildcarded" if
you use the **?**. Execute the **echo** command in the following
form.

Type **echo ch1.sec?.om.m1⟨CR⟩**.

```
$ echo ch1.sec?.om.m1<CR>
ch1.sec1.om.m1 ch1.sec2.om.m1 ch1.sec3.om.m1 ch1.sec4.om.m1
$ ▯
```

Although the wildcard used is different, there is no difference in the display.

Specifing the Range of a
Wildcard

The characters **[** and **]** (brackets) specify a range of characters that a wildcard is to match. For instance, the range of
all capital letters is A–Z. Thus, the command **echo
[A-Z]*⟨CR⟩** requires the *first* letter of any filename matched
by the wildcard to be a capital. Since your directory filenames all begin with capitals, this command can be used to
list all of the directories.

Type **echo [A-Z]*⟨CR⟩**.

```
$ echo [A-Z]*<CR>
Accounts.n Words
$ ▯
```

The system returns with your two directories, **Accounts.n**
and **Words**. If you have other capitalized files or directories
in your system, they show up as well.

Similar to capital letters, a numeric range may be specified. To preview all books with section numbers in the
range of 4–5, type **echo ch?.sec[4-5].?m.m1⟨CR⟩**.

```
$ echo ch?.sec[4-5].?m.m1<CR>
ch1.sec4.om.m1 ch5.sec4.om.m1 ch5.sec5.om.m1
$ ▯
```

Note the use of several metacharacters in the above example. The brackets allowed specification of a range of sections while the ?s guaranteed that every chapter and both the *om* and *sm* divisions would be included.

Study these examples very carefully. Wildcards are extremely powerful, but they can create *big problems* if used carelessly. You should always use **echo** to preview wildcard expansion, especially when removing files or directories.

Take a break now before continuing with this lesson.

LESSON 5.3

continued:	Building a Directory System
NEW KNOWLEDGE:	Organization skills
APPROXIMATE	
TIME:	30 minutes

Execute a **list** command from your home directory. Type
ls⟨CR⟩.

```
$ ls<CR>            ch2.sec1.sm.m1   fri.diet.per    piano.per
Account             ch2.sec2.om.m1   JK_jc1jan.mem   resour.m1.pam
Words               ch2.sec3.om.m1   JK_jc1may.mem   rt_jc19may.mem
access.m1.pam       ch3.sec1.om.m1   JK_jc7sep.mem   softball.per
app1.m1.pam         ch3.sec1.sm.m1   jobreply        sonofbozo
bd_jc16may.mem      ch3.sec2.om.m1   jobreply.add    ssi.form
bozo                ch3.sec2.sm.m1   jy_jc2jun.mem   thurs.diet.per
ch1.sec1.om.m1      ch4.sec1.om.m1   memo.form       time.login
ch1.sec1.sm.m1      ch4.sec1.sm.m1   mon.diet.per    time.logout
ch1.sec2.om.m1      ch4.sec2.om.m1   odds_ends.per   tues.diet.per
ch1.sec2.sm.m1      ch5.sec1.om.m1   order.form      wed.diet.per
ch1.sec3.om.m1      ch5.sec2.om.m1   orthodont.per   wt_jc30jul.mem
ch1.sec3.sm.m1      ch5.sec3.om.m1   outline.cm.m2   $ ▯
ch1.sec4.om.m1      ch5.sec4.om.m1   outline.sm.m2
ch2.sec1.om.m1      ch5.sec5.om.m1   pay.form
```

Note that there are nine files appended with the extension, **.per**. From their filenames, they appear to contain data of a personal nature—a schedule of softball games, a diet, and so on. Create a directory named **Personal** that contains a subdirectory named **Diet**.

As you build a directory structure from the list of files, start making your interactions with the system a bit more efficient by combining two or more steps or commands on a single line. Observe the sequences on the command lines in the following examples very closely.

Type **mkdir Personal Personal/Diet⟨CR⟩**.

```
$ mkdir Personal Personal/Diet<CR>
$ □
```

The directory **Personal** was created first; then *using the partial pathname* **Personal/Diet**, the second directory was created. If you want to create more subdirectories, the partial pathname is stated for *each* argument.

Move the personal files into their new directories, but use a different method. Instead of using your home directory as the current directory, use the *target directory* as the current directory. Practice using wildcards and pathnames by performing the entire move from **Personal**. Follow and execute the command sequences:

```
$ cd Personal<CR>
$ ls<CR>
Diet
$ mv /usr/{home directory}/*.????.per Diet<CR>
$ ls Diet
fri.diet.per thurs.diet.per tues.diet.per wed.diet.per
mon.diet.per
$ mv ../ob.per .<CR>
$ ls
Diet orthodont.per piano.per softball.per
odds_ends.per
$ □
```

The command **mv /usr/home directory/*.????.per Diet** is complicated, but you have the knowledge to unravel it. Note that a complete pathname /**usr/home directory/** is used. You could have used **../** instead to indicate the source of the **mv** as the directory above the current directory. The target directory on the command line is the current directory, indicated by the period (.). Alternatively, you could

have used the complete pathname **/usr/{home directory}/
Personal**.

Note the use of wildcards in the command line. The
command states, "match anything that ends in **.per**, and
has any four characters between periods." Only the **.diet**
files will match this description because they contain four
characters at this location.

If ***.per** alone was used, all nine **.per** files would have
gone into **Personal/Diet**. But now that the **.diet** files are no
longer in the home directory, **mv ../*.per .⟨CR⟩** will move
the remainder of the **.per** files into the current directory.
Change directories to your home directory and execute the
ls command to verify that the **.per** files are no longer there.

LESSON 5.4:	Organizing Files and Directories
NEW KNOWLEDGE:	The $HOME shorthand symbol; more file and directory organization
APPROXIMATE TIME:	60 minutes, in two 30-minute sessions

Carrying out the exercises in this lesson will complete the file and directory system started in Lesson 5.3 and give you more practice with the system. This lesson will take approximately one hour to complete, divided into two half-hour sessions.

Now that you have some practice with the **move** command and the use of pathnames, you can move some files into your **Words** directory. Create five subdirectories in **Words** and name them Memos, Books, Pamphlets, Outlines, and Letters. Change directories to **Words**. Create your subdirectories using the **mkdir** command: **mkdir Memos Books Pamphlets Letters Outlines⟨CR⟩**. Then verify that they were created in **Words** by typing the **ls** command.

```
$ cd Words<CR>
$ mkdir Memos Books Pamphlets Letters Outlines<CR>
$ ls<CR>
Books Letters Memos Outlines Pamphlets
$ ▯
```

Return to your home directory. Using the command **mv *.mem Words/Memos⟨CR⟩**, move the seven memos to the new subdirectory **Memos**, under the directory **Words**. Execute the **ls** command for verification.

Type **cd⟨CR⟩**. Type **mv *.mem Words/Memos⟨CR⟩**. Then, verify with an **ls** command.

```
$ cd
$ mv *.mem Words/Memos<CR>
$ ls Words/Memos<CR>
bd_jc16may.mem    jk_jc27sep.mem    rt_jc19may.mem
jk_jc1jan.mem     jy_jc2jun.mem     wt_jc30jul.mem
jk_jc1may.mem
$ 
```

Next, move the three pamphlets into their directory.

```
$ mv *.pam Words/Pamphlets<CR>
$ ls Words/Pamphlets<CR>
access.m1.pam appl.m1.pam resour.m1.pam
$ 
```

Finally, move the outline file and the letter files. Execute the **ls** command to list your home directory.

```
$ mv jobreply jobreply.add Words/Letters<CR>
$ ls Words/Letters<CR>
jobreply jobreply.add
$ mv outline.* Words/Outlines<CR>
$ ls Words/Outlines<CR>
outline.om.m2 outline.sm.m2
$ ls<CR>
Accounts.n        ch1.sec4.om.m1   ch3.sec2.sm.m1   memo.form
Personal          ch2.sec1.om.m1   ch4.sec1.om.m1   order.form
Words             ch2.sec2.om.m1   ch4.sec1.sm.m1   pay.form
bozo              ch2.sec3.om.m1   ch5.sec1.om.m1   sonofbozo
ch1.sec14.om.m1   ch3.sec1.om.m1   ch5.sec2.om.m1   ssi.formf
ch1.sec1.sm.m1    ch3.sec1.sm.m1   ch5.sec3.om.m1   time.login
ch1.sec2.om.m1    ch3.sec2.om.m1   ch5.sec4.om.m1   time.logout
ch1.sec2.sm.m1                     ch5.sec5.om.m1
ch1.sec3.om.m1
ch1.sec3.sm.m1
$ 
```

The breakdown of the **Words** directory and its subdirectories is shown in Fig. 5.3.

Fig. 5.3 Map of Sample Directory Words

```
                              Words
- - - - - - - - - - - - - - - - - - - - - - - - - - - - - - - - - - - - - - - - -
                               ¦ ¦
                               ¦ ¦
                               ¦ ¦
    Memos          Pamphlets  Books   Letters      Outlines
- - - - - - - - - - - - - - - - - - - - - - - - - - - - - - - - - - - - - - - - -
bd_jc16may.mem  access.m1.pam        jobreply     outline.om.m2
jk_jc1jan.mem   appl.m1.pam          jobreply.add outline.sm.m2
jk_jc1may.mem   resour.m1.pam
jk_jc27sep.mem
jy_jc2jun.mem
rt_jc19mar.mem
wt_jc30jul.mem
```

Organizing the Books Subdirectories

The greatest remaining number of files are the text files for two books, an Owner Manual for Model 1 and a Service Manual for Model 1. The filenames for the two books are divided into four sections, or fields:

1. chapter number (ch1., ch2.)

2. section number (sec4., sec1.)

3. owner manual or service manual (om., sm.)

4. model number (m1)

Organize the **Books** subdirectories according to the organization of the books themselves: chapters and sections. The presence of **.m2** in the **Outlines** directory suggests that a Model 2 is under development, so an empty directory should be created for it in advance. You will create all of the subdirectories under **Books**. The first subdirectories are **Model1** and **Model2**.

Model2 will remain empty; **Model1** will contain the subdirectories: **Owner** and **Service**.

Owner will contain the subdirectories: **Chapter1**, **Chapter2**, **Chapter3**, **Chapter4**, and **Chapter5**.

Service will contain the subdirectories: **Chapter1**, **Chapter2**, **Chapter3**, **Chapter4**.

After you have created the subdirectory structure, move the book files to their appropriate subdirectories under **Books**. The **Books** directory, when complete, should contain the subdirectories and files shown in Fig. 5.4.

Begin by returning to the home directory and creating the two subdirectories, **Model1** and **Model2**.

```
$ cd<CR>
$ mkdir Words/Books/Model1 Words/Books/Model12<CR>
$ ls Words/Books<CR>
Model1 Model2
$ 
```

Partial pathnames are used to give you additional practice. A shorter method would have been to **cd Words/Books**⟨CR⟩, then simply **mkdir Model1 Model2**⟨CR⟩. Alternatively, the complete pathname, starting with /, could have been used, but would have produced an even longer command line. Change directory to **Model1** and create the two subdirectories, **Owner** and **Service**:

```
$ cd Words/Books/Model1<CR>
$ mkdir Owner Service<CR>
$ ls<CR>
Owner Service
$ 
```

All that remains is to create the required chapter directories for each book. Create the **Service** directory first. It will be *much* easier if you make **Service** the current directory.

Fig. 5.4 Organization of Sample Directory Words/Books

```
                        Words

        Memos        Pamplets   Books   Letters        Outlines

bd_jc16may.mem  access.m1.pam                  jobreply      outline.om.m2
jk_jc1jan.mem   appl.m1.pam                     jobreply.add  outline.sm.m2
jk_jc1may.mem   resour.m1.pam
jk_jc27sep.mem
jy_jc2jun.mem
rt_jc19mar.mem
wt_jc30jul.mem

                  Model1                              Model2
```

```
Owner
                                                                            Service

           Chapter1         Chapter2         Chapter3         Chapter4
           --------         --------         --------         --------
           ch1.sec1.sm.ml   ch2.sec1.sm.ml   ch3.sec1.sm.ml   ch4.sec1.sm.ml
           ch1.sec2.sm.ml                    ch3.sec2.sm.ml
           ch1.sec3.sm.ml


Chapter1         Chapter2         Chapter3         Chapter4         Chapter5
--------         --------         --------         --------         --------
ch1.sec1.om.ml   ch2.sec1.om.ml   ch3.sec1.om.ml   ch4.sec1.om.ml   ch5.sec1.om.ml
ch1.sec2.om.ml   ch2.sec2.om.ml   ch3.sec2.om.ml   ch4.sec2.om.ml   ch5.sec2.om.ml
ch1.sec3.om.ml   ch2.sec3.om.ml                                     ch5.sec3.om.ml
ch1.sec4.om.ml                                                      ch5.sec4.om.ml
                                                                    ch5.sec5.om.ml
```

```
$ cd Service<CR>
$ mkdir Chapter1 Chapter2 Chapter3 Chapter4<CR>
$ ls<CR>
Chapter1 Chapter2 Chapter3 Chapter4
$ □
```

Now change directories to **Owner** and create the five chapter directories there. The quickest way to change to **Owner** is **cd ../Owner**⟨CR⟩, but for the sake of practice, use a complete pathname instead.

```
$ cd /usr/{home directory}/Words/Books/Model1/Owner<CR>
$ pwd<CR>
/usr/{home directory}/Words/Books/Model1/Owner
$ mkdir Chapter1 Chapter2 Chapter3 Chapter4 Chapter5<CR>
$ ls<CR>
Chapter1 Chapter2 Chapter3 Chapter4 Chapter5
$ □
```

The entire **Books** directory is now in place, and you can move files into it. Although it would be possible to move files into it from the current directory, **Owner**, be consistent by returning to the home directory and issuing the commands using relative pathnames. Remember, a **cd** ⟨CR⟩ returns you to your home directory. Use **pwd** (**p**rint **w**orking **d**irectory) to verify your current directory. Then list the current directory for a look at the rest of the files to be moved.

```
$ cd<CR>
$ pwd<CR>
/usr/{home directory}
$ ls<CR>

Accounts.n      ch1.sec3.sm.m1 ch3.sec2.sm.m1 memo.form
Personal        ch1.sec4.om.m1 ch4.sec1.om.m1 order.form
```

```
Words             ch2.sec1.om.m1  ch4.sec1.sm.m1  pay.form
bozo              ch2.sec1.sm.m1  ch4.sec2.om.m1  sonofbozo
ch1.sec1.om.m1    ch2.sec2.om.m1  ch5.sec1.om.m1  ssi.form
ch1.sec1.sm.m1    ch2.sec3.om.m1  ch5.sec2.om.m1  time.login
ch1.sec2.om.m1    ch3.sec1.om.m1  ch5.sec3.om.m1  time.logout
ch1.sec2.sm.m1    ch3.sec1.sm.m1  ch5.sec4.om.m1
ch1.sec3.om.m1    ch3.sec2.om.m1  ch5.sec5.om.m1
$ ▯
```

Moving Files into the Manual Subdirectories	Begin moving files into Owner Manual. Use the wildcard "?" to put all the sections of a particular chapter into place. Each chapter will require its own command line. Verify that the sections have been correctly moved.

```
$ mv ch1.sec?.om.m1 Words/Books/Model1/Owner/Chapter1<CR>
$ mv ch2.sec?.om.m1 Words/Books/Model1/Owner/Chapter2<CR>
$ mv ch3.sec?.om.m1 Words/Books/Model1/Owner/Chapter3<CR>
$ mv ch4.sec?.om.m1 Words/Books/Model1/Owner/Chapter4<CR>
$ mv ch5.sec?.om.m1 Words/Books/Model1/Owner/Chapter5<CR>
$ cd Words/Books/Model1/Owner<CR>
$ ls *<CR>
Chapter1:
ch1.sec1.om.m1 ch1.sec2.om.m1 ch1.sec3.om.m1
ch1.sec4.om.m1

Chapter2:
ch2.sec1.om.m1 ch2.sec2.om.m1 ch2.sec3.om.m1

Chapter3:
ch3.sec1.om.m1 ch3.sec2.om.m1

Chapter4:
ch4.sec1.om.m1 ch4.sec2.om.m1

Chapter5:
ch5.sec1.om.m1 ch5.sec2.om.m1 ch5.sec3.om.m1
ch5.sec2.om.m1 ch5.sec5.om.m1
$ ▯
```

Notice that **Model1/Owner** was made the current directory before the listing (**ls**).

The chapters for the Service Manual will be moved by the same method except commands will be issued form the directory **/usr/{home directory}/Words/Books/Model1/Service**. This time take the shortcut by changing directories from **Owner** to **Service**. To change from **Owner** to **Service**, type **cd ../Service**.

Now is a good time to take a break. You are about halfway through the lesson.

Shorthand Symbol:
$HOME

The following example contains another shorthand symbol, **$HOME**, to stand for the home directory. It can be used any place you would otherwise use the complete pathname to your home directory.

[@The UC Berkeley C shell uses the tilde (˜) to represent the home directory.@]

```
$ cd ../Service<CR>
$ pwd<CR>
/usr/{home
directory}/Words/Books/Model1/Service
$ mv $HOME/ch1.sec?.sm.m1 Chapter1<CR>
$ mv $HOME/ch2.sec?.sm.m1 Chapter2<CR>
$ mv $HOME/ch3.sec?.sm.m1 Chapter3<CR>
$ mv $HOME/ch4.sec?.sm.m1 Chapter4<CR>
$ ls Chapter1 Chapter2 Chapter3 Chapter4<CR>
Chapter1:
ch1.sec1.sm.m1 ch1.sec2.sm.m1 ch1.sec3.sm.m1

Chapter2:
ch2.sec1.sm.m1

Chapter3:
ch3.sec1.sm.m1    ch3.sec2.sm.m1

Chapter4:
ch4.sec1.sm.m1
$ 
```

Since the *destination directory* happens to be immediately below the current directory, the destination argument in the **mv** command requires only the directory name. Return to your home directory with **cd⟨CR⟩**, and **list** it.

```
$ cd<CR>
$ ls
                        order.form   ssi.form
Accounts.n   bozo       pay.form     time.login
Personal     memo.form  sonofbozo    time.logout
Words
$ 
```

Your home directory is now a manageable size. Your job is almost done. Before your home directory is fully organized you need to relocate the files with the **.form** extension and those beginning with the word **time**.

Organizing the Forms and Utilities Directories

The **.form** group of files contains forms you will probably need every day for memos, payroll, and ordering. Since the number of forms a company uses always seems to increase, you can benefit by creating a special directory to hold them. At the same time, create a directory named **Utilities** for the "time" files. Then move the appropriate files into these two directories.

```
$ mkdir Forms Utilities<CR>
$ mv *.form Forms<CR>
$ mv time.* Utilities<CR>
$ ls Forms Utilities<CR>
Forms:
memo.form order.form pay.form ssi.form

Utilities:
time.login time.logout
$ 
```

The **Utilities** directory will grow as your familiarity with the system increases. This is where you can store personal system tools. You will learn in the next chapter how to compose *command files* and *shell scripts*, files of commands grouped into powerful combinations to automate certain portions of your working environment. These shell scripts can be stored in your **Utilities** directory.

The current status of the home directory is shown below.

```
$ ls<CR>
Accounts.n     Utilities     bozo     sonofbozo
Forms          Words
Personal
$ ▯
```

We have now moved the contents of the entire home directory except for two miscellaneous files: **bozo** and **sonofbozo**. These files are included as general purpose personal files. Every person who works with a computer likes to experiment with its capabilities, test new commands, and try new programs. These activities frequently require "dummy files," like **bozo** and **sonofbozo**. The names you choose are purely arbitrary.

LESSON 5.5:	Copying Files
NEW KNOWLEDGE:	Use of the **cp** (**copy**) command
APPROXIMATE	
TIME:	15 minutes

The **cp** (**copy**) command files. The syntax of this command is

```
cp{source_file}{destination_file}<CR>
```

The source file must already exist. The destination file, however, will be created by the **cp** command and will be identical to the source file.

cp makes a copy of {**source_file**} and gives it the name {**destination_file**}. If {**destination_file**} already exists, the original version will be "overwritten" and the new version will be identical to the {source_file}. Take care not to confuse **cp** with the **mv** command. **mv** relocates a file. The **cp** command makes a duplicate of {source_file} but *leaves the original intact*. After a **cp** command is given, there are *two* identical files. The copy command can be used when you wish to experiment with a file, but do not want to risk damaging the original. For example, overwrite the file **bozo** with the **jobreply** file so you have a duplicate copy of **jobreply** to use for experimental changes. You will overwrite **bozo** by copying **jobreply** into **bozo**.

Since **jobreply** is now in the **Letters** directory, make **Letters** your current directory, then **cat**enate the **jobreply** file to check its contents.

Type **cat jobreply**⟨CR⟩.

```
$ cat jobreply<CR>
Letter to Andrea Applicant
from General Manufacturing Co.
June 2, 1984
Dear INTR
```

Since you wish to copy the **jobreply** file into **bozo**, which is in your home directory, use a pathname to get to the destination file. The quickest way is to use the **$HOME** shortcut. The complete command line then is **cp jobreply $HOME/bozo⟨CR⟩**.

One cautionary note: if the destination file already exists it will be overwritten by the **cp** command. If you do not want to lose what is currently in your file, assign a new filename for the destination file. The new file will be created by **cp** and will be a duplicate of the source file. If you fail to give a pathname, the destination fill will be created in your current directory. You would end up with a file named **bozo** in your home directory and a file **bozo** in your **Letters** directory. The file **bozo** in **Letters** would be identical to **jobreply**.

Execute the **cp** command followed by a **cat** of the **bozo** file to verify successful execution.

Type **cp jobreply $HOME/bozo⟨CR⟩**.

Type **cat $HOME/bozo⟨CR⟩**.

```
$ cp jobreply $HOME/bozo<CR>
$ cat $HOME/bozo<CR>
Letter to Andrea Applicant
from General Manufacturing Co.
June 2, 1984
Dear INTR
```

The cp Command Syntax Both the **move (mv)** command and **cp** can move or copy several files simultaneously. If the files do not already exist in the directory, they will be created. The syntax of the command is

```
cp {file1} {file2}... {Destinationdirname} <CR>
```

The syntax for the **mv** command is identical:

```
mv {file1} {file2}... {Destinationdirname} <CR>
```

NOTE: *You must take care that the last argument in the command line is a directory. The system can only copy or move multiple files into a directory.*

The **mv** and **cp** commands also allow use of metacharacters to move or copy several files simultaneously. For example, all of Chapter 1 of the Model 1 Owner's Manual could be copied into the current directory with the following command line:

```
cp $HOME/Words/Books/Model1/Owner/Chapter1/*.<CR>
```

Another example of **cp** command usage is seen in your **Accounts.n** directory. Most accounting program packages require the separate modules (in this case, **payable,prog**, **receivable,prog**, and **inventory.prog**) to share a common data file. The common data file is then used by the general ledger program (your **genledger.prog**) to create the monthly balance sheet. The file **genledger.dat** must simultaneously exist in each of the four accounting directories; further, because of the internal requirements of the separate programs, the name of the data files for **genledger.prog** must be different in each directory. The names **inventory.dat**, **payable.dat**, and **receivable.dat** might be used. When copying these files, the name of the file would be changed in the destination directory. If you were located in the **Genledger** directory and wanted to copy the file **genledger.prog** into the directory **Inventory** and rename it **inventory.prog**, you would type

```
cp genledger.prog ../Inventory/inventory.prog<CR>
```

Because **Inventory** and **Genledger** are both subdirectories of **Accounts.n**, the copy command had to specify the movement back up to **Accounts.n** and then down to **Inventory** by **../Inventory**. The existing file **inventory.prog** will be overwritten.

Copy and move files in your sample system. Try to keep track of the changes, and put it back in the same shape as you started before going on to the next lesson.

LESSON 5.6:	Linking Files
NEW KNOWLEDGE:	The **ln** (**link**) command, inodes, and the **i** option to the **ls** command
APPROXIMATE TIME:	30 minutes

A hierarchical file system is not the most useful file system when you want many people to read and update a central file like an inventory listing. Since UNIX restricts each user to their own directories, what can you do with such a universally requested file?

One solution is to put a separate copy of the file in each appropriate user's account. Unfortunately, changes made to one copy of the file will now show up in other people's copies. You would also run out of disk space soon, keeping many copies of the same file on the system. Another solution is to set up a special inventory account that contains the data file and is accessible to all concerned users. This is actually a good solution if you have many central files or a lot of inventory activity. Otherwise, it is wasteful to allocate an account for every central file that you have. It is also bothersome to log into different accounts to accomplish different tasks.

Fortunately, you can link different file names to the same body of information with the **ln** (**link**) command. For example, you could create an inventory file in one directory and then have everyone else create links, in the form of file names, that connect to that central file. It will appear to every user that the file is actually contained in their own directory, so that they can access it any way they want.

It is an illusion that a directory actually contains a file represented by a unique file name. In reality, file names point to bodies of information the same way that many street signs can point to the same building. When you edit a file by specifying a file name, you are really just telling UNIX where to find your file on the disk.

For a little insight into how linking works, use the **-i**(**i**-number) option to the **ls** (**list**) command. The i-number is printed just before each filename. Change your directory to

Accounts.n by using the **cp** command and verify that the command was properly executed with **pwd** (**p**rint **w**orking **d**irectory); then execute the **ls** command with the **i** option and the * to list each file.

```
$ cd Accounts.n<CR>
$ pwd<CR>
/usr/{home directory}/Accounts.n
$ ls -i *<CR>

Genledger:
7302 genledger.dat 7326 genledger.prog

Inventory:
7440 inventory.prog

Payable:
7439 payable.prog

Receivable:
7430 receivable.prog

Taxtable:
7268 taxtable.cty 7211 taxtable.fed 7106 taxtable.sta
7095 taxtable.exc 7219 taxtable.sal
$ ▯
```

The exact i-numbers will be different on your system.

Each disk file is associated with a unique *i-number* by the system. The "i" is short for *inodes*, which is the "identification" or "index number" for the file. You learned earlier that files are not actually "in" directories. The directories contain filenames and their associated i-numbers. The i-numbers tell the shell where the file is located on the disk.

When two or more files are linked—even if they have different names—all of the files are given the same i-number as the original file and are in all respects the same file. Any changes to the file made from any directory accessing the linked files will be apparent in all files that share the same i-number. This will become apparent as you link the files in your **Accounts.n** directory.

The **genledger.dat** file is the host file. At present, this file is empty, so you will have to put some experimental text in it. Use the **vi** editor to generate the following text.

```
$       Genledger/genledger.dat<CR>
        1 This file is a linked file.<CR>
        2 □
:wq
"Genledger/genledger.dat" 2 lines, 29 characters
$ □
```

Now use the **ln** (link) command to create links to this file in your other directories. The basic command syntax is

```
ln {original_filename} {newlink_filename}<CR>
```

Keeping in mind that the current directory is **Accounts.n**, link **inventory.dat** to **genledger.dat** first, followed by an **ls -i *** command.

```
$ ln Genledger/genledger.dat Inventory/inventory.dat<CR>
$ ls -i *<CR>
Genledger:
7302 genledger.dat
7326 genledger.prog

Inventory:
7302 inventory.dat
7440 inventory.prog

Payable:
7439 payable.prog

Receivable:
7430 accnt.rec.prog
```

```
Taxtable:
7268 taxtable.cty 7211 taxtable.fed 7106 taxtable.sta
7095 taxtable.exc 7219 taxtable.sal
$ ▯
```

The **ls -i *** display reveals that **Inventory/inventory.dat** and **Genledger/genledger.dat** now have the same i-number (7302). **cat** (**cat**enate) the linked file to verify that its contents are the same as the original.

```
$ cat Inventory/inventory.dat<CR>
This file is a linked file.
$ ▯
```

Both the i-numbers and the contents of the linked file demonstrate that the link exists. Now add linked files in the other two directories. You can now use **inventory.dat** as the source for a new link, or make another link from **genledger.dat**.

Type **ln Inventory/inventory.dat Payable/payable.dat⟨CR⟩**
ln Genledger/genledger.dat Receivable/receivable.dat⟨CR⟩
ls -i *⟨CR⟩

```
$ ln Inventory/inventory.dat Payable/payable.dat<CR>
$ ln Genledger/genledger.dat Receivable/receivable.dat<CR>
$ ls -i *<CR>
Genledger:
7302 genledger.dat 7326 genledger.prog

Inventory:
7302 inventory.dat 7440 inventory.prog

Payable:
7302 payable.dat 7439 accnt.pay.prog

Receivable:
7302 receivable.dat 7430 receivable.prog
```

```
Taxtable:
7268 taxtable.cty 7211 taxtable.fed 7106 taxtable.sta
7095 taxtable.exc 7219 taxtable.sal
$ ▯
```

Now **cat**enate the newly linked files to verify successful execution of the link.

Type **cat Payable/payable.dat Receivable/
receivable.dat⟨CR⟩**

```
$ cat Payable/payable.dat Receivable/receivable.dat<CR>
This file is a linked file.
This file is a linked file.
$ ▯
```

All four files are now associated with the same **i**-number, and all have the same content.

If the contents of any of the linked files are altered, the linked files in the other directories will also be altered. Although a modification to a linked file affects the other links, each linked file may be separately removed without affecting any of the others.

LESSON 5.7:	Classifying Files
NEW KNOWLEDGE:	Use of the **file** and **wc** (**w**ord **c**ount) commands
APPROXIMATE	
TIME:	20 minutes

After you have accumulated a large number of files, it is easy to forget what type of data is in each. You could bring up each file in **vi** or some other editor program and read its contents, but that procedure is time consuming. The UNIX system provides a means of classifying a file without gaining access to it. The command used to perform this operation is the **file** command. The command syntax is

```
file {filename} {filename}...<CR>
```

The command has no options, but it will accept multiple arguments. An entire directory can be classified by using the * wildcard: **file *⟨CR⟩**.

When you use the **file** command, it will probably return one of the following messages:

- **ascii text**: The file contains alphabetical and numerical characters; less than 20 percent of the punctuation characters are followed by a space or a newline.

- **cannot open**: The file exists, but access permission is denied.

- **cannot stat**: The file doesn't exist or is not accessible.

- **directory**: The file is a directory.

- **English text**: The file contains alphabetical and numerical characters with punctuation, but more than 20 percent of the punctuation is followed by a space or newline.

- **data**: Neither ascii nor English text, and not identifiable as program code.

```
$ cd<CR>
$ file *<CR>
Accounts.n directory
Forms:      directory
Personal: directory
Words:      directory
bozo:      English text
sonofbozo:      ascii text
$ ▯
```

It is possible that your display will differ from the above example since most of your files are empty, but you should see the correct message for the directories. The **file** command is not infallible. It may mistake text of files for program files written in the C programming language.

Determining the Size of Files with the Word Count (wc) Command

Occasionally you will not be concerned with the *contents* of a file so much as with its size of length. The **vi** text editor prints the number of lines and characters in a file when you bring it up for editing. Again, the invocation of an editor is a time-consuming way to determine file statistics.

This **wc** (**w**ord **c**ount) utility program provides a quick way to determine the number of lines (option **-l**), words (option **-w**), or characters (option **-c**) in a file. The command syntax is

wc [-lwc] {filename}...<CR>

When used without an option, **wc** reports the number of lines, followed by the number of words, and finally the number of characters in the file. For example, to analyze the **bozo** file, type **wc bozo⟨CR⟩**.

```
$ wc bozo<CR>
26    99    646 bozo
$ ▯
```

Your **bozo** data may be different.

When the **wc** argument is more than one file, the statistics for each file are printed with a summary total;

```
$ wc bozo sonofbozo [<CR>
      26 99 646 bozo
       1  0   1 sonofbozo
      27 99 647 total
$ ▯
```

Use of an option or options (**-lwc**) limits the reported statistics accordingly. In the example below, only the number of words and lines in a file are printed.

```
$ wc -wl bozo [<CR>
     99    26 bozo
$ ▯
```

When **wc** is used without options, the statistics are reported in **lwc** order. The option may be used in any order. The order in which the statistics are displayed will follow the option pattern.

There is one final point of interest on **wc**. Neither an option nor a filename is required. When invoked without a filename argument, **wc** will report statistics on the text entered from the keyboard. The end of the text is signaled by control-d.

Type **wc⟨CR⟩** and enter the text shown in the following display.

```
$ wc<CR>
The value of this feature<CR>
is questionable, since the text<CR>
entered is not sent to a file.<CR>
    ^d
     3  17  89
$ ▯
```

You can use **wc** when you want to count letters for a header, and you are calculating how many spaces to leave on either side so it is centered.

Now that you have the simple tools

```
cat     (catenate)
cd      (change directory)
cp      (copy)
echo    (display
file
ln      (link)
ls      (list)
mkdir   (make directory)
more    (view files)
mv      (move)
pwd     (print working directory)
rm      (remove)
rmdir   (remove directory)
vi      (visual editor)
wc      (word count)
```

you have the basics for creating, organizing, viewing, and removing files. The next step is to practice with the sample system. Review the lessons and consider the way that you will set up your own file and directory system.

ADVANCED FILE AND DIRECTORY MANIPULATION— REFERENCE SECTION

The remaining pages of this chapter will give you further information on the UNIX system. If you wish, execute the commands and make your own observations about the results, but the text goes faster and shows fewer examples in this "reference" section. The material is very useful; read it carefully and follow through the exercises mentally.

More about the ls Command

In the preceding chapter, you learned the meaning of **ls** (list) with the -l (long) and -i (i-number) options. A third option, **-a** is available. The function of **-a** is to add the "dot" (.) and "double dot" (..) indicators to the listing, as well as any other files that have names beginning with a dot.

The command **ls -ail** ⟨CR⟩ generates a long listing of all files contained in the current directory, including "dot" files and the i-numbers for each file and directory.

```
$ ls -ail<CR>
total 30                                            <======9
 8739 drwx------ 8 chris 1296 Sep 18 10:50 .
 8841 drwx------ 3 root   368 Sep 14 10:33 ..
 1004 drwx------ 4 chris  144 Sep 14 10:10 .profile
 3420 drwx------ 7 chris  128 Sep 18 19:21 Accounts.n
 8336 drwx------2 chris    96 Sep 16 16:04 Forms
 8371 drwx------ 3 chris  144 Sep 16 11:36 Personal
14984 drwx------ 7 chris  112 Sep 16 12:35 Words
 9351 -rw------- 1 chris   70 Sep 18 10:50 bozo
 9350 -rwx------ 2 chris  112 Sep 16 15:23 sonofbozo
$ □
```

```
/\   /\ /\       /\      /\     /\      /\          /\
| |  | | | |     | |     | |    | |     | |         | |
| |  | | | |     | |     | |    | |     | |         | |
| |  | | | |     | |     | |    | |     | |         | |
 5    1   8       7       2      6       3           4
```

1. The first character in the ten-character display describes the type of file. 'd' means directory, '-' ordinary file, and 'b' or 'c' denotes a special device file.

2. The "owner" of the file is the login name under which the file was created. To personalize the example, the owner has been given the name "chris."

3. Time and date are listed when the file was created or last *modified*. The -t option to ls will list the files in the order in which they were last modified, with the most recent files listed first. Similarly, the -u option will list the files in the order most recently *accessed*.

4. The file or directory name.

5. The i-number.

6. The total number of characters in the file.

7. The number of links to a file. If the file is a directory, this number is two greater than the number of subdirectories.

8. The access permissions which are described below.

9.   The total amount of disk storage space (in 512-character blocks) occupied by the directory. This information, by itself, can be obtained with the **-s** option to **ls**.

The directory listed has dot (.) files. If you had executed a simple **ls** command, they would have been hidden. You would not have been aware of their presence unless the **-a** option was used. You would not have been allowed to remove this directory without first removing the dot files. The existence of invisible files illustrates the flexibility of the directory structure. Invisible files allow a user to maintain uncluttered directory listings by hiding files that seldom or never change.

The **ls** command causes the files and directories to be listed in *ASCII collating sequence*, a type of listing which includes numbers, punctuation marks, and all other characters. If a reverse-ordered listing of the directory is desired, add the **-r** option.

Access Permissions

The nine-character field indicated by the number eight arrow in the display represents *access codes*. In any computer system handling sensitive data, personnel files, or confidential information, unlimited access to files must be denied to some employees. The amount of access granted is indicated by the access permission codes, which appear in three fields, each containing three characters.

```
        {rwx}  {rwx}  {rwx}
        /\     /\     /\
        | |    | |    | |
        | |    | |    | |
        | |    | |    | |
Fields:  1      2      3
```

Field 1 contains the permission codes for the owner of the file, field 2 for members of specified groups, and field 3 for the public (users not part of the group).

Each of the three fields consists of three characters, **rwx**, which stand, respectively, for **r**ead permission, **w**rite permission, and e**x**ecute permission. The presence of the letters **r**, **w**, and **x** indicates that the permission is granted; a '-' indicates that the permission is denied.

To illustrate these codes, look at the **ls -ail** display above. Notice that all files and directories contain identical permissions. The owner, **chris**, has full permission to read and write to all files, and the additional permission to execute—that is, to use the file as a program.

In the discussion of shell scripts in Chapter 6, you will learn that files can be written to perform as programs. In order to do so, they must be made executable. Permission for the group or the public to examine the same files may be granted or denied. All group permissions and all general public permissions are denied. Thus the owner may perform any UNIX command operation on his own files but no one else may. The owner of a file does not necessarily have permission to make changes to it. An owner may choose to deny write permission to himself to protect against accidental removal of the file.

Sometimes you have to remove files owned by another user. In most cases you will not be able to remove a file that belongs to someone else without having the system manager or superuser do it. Sometimes, however, the file has all of its permission bits enabled; permission is granted to anyone to read, write or execute the file. If this is true, you can remove the file in the same way you would any other file.

The default access permissions for files is determined by company policy. This is generally, but not necessarily,

`-rw------ for files, drwx------ for directories`

Access is often given only to the owner. Most files do not need execute (x) permission.

When the users on a system are divided into groups, such as departments in a company, the customary default permissions are

`-rw-rw---- for files, drwxrwx--- for directories`

In this situation, the owner retains full access to all files, and so do all members of the group to which the owner belongs.

Attempting to perform an operation on a file for which you do not have permission will result in an error message. The best way to illustrate the effects of different permission codes is to move your current directory around the system to look at other users' files. Since your home directory probably resides in the directory /**usr**, other users' home directories should also be in /**usr**. Execute a **cd** (change **directory**) to /**usr** followed by **ls- 1⟨CR⟩**. If your home directory does not reside in /**usr**, typing **cd ..** will bring you up one level to a directory which probably contains accounts other than yours. After changing to this directory, typing **ls -l⟨CR⟩** will allow you to see these other accounts.

```
$ cd /usr<CR>
$ ls -l<CR>
drwxr-xr-x   3 ags         1072 Sep 15 15:01 ags
drwx------  12 amyr         528 Sep 17 16:46 amyr
drwxr-xr-x   4 suzanne      176 Sep 18 00:06 suzanne
drwxrwxrwx  10 anderson    448 Aug 14 09:47 anderson

    INTR
$ []
```

Try to list the directory **amyr:**

```
$ ls amyr <CR>
amyr unreadable
$ cd amyr<CR>
amyr: Permission denied
$ []
```

This directory is completely denied to us. Without read permission, the directory cannot even be listed. Without execute permission, the directory may not become the current directory. Observe that the same error *condition* caused a different error message with each command.

The directory **ags** is more open. The owner has full permissions; a group (name still unknown to you) has permission to read, execute, but not write; the public also has permission to read, execute, but not write. Since the public has read and execute permission, we should be able to list it and to make it the current directory.

```
$ ls ags<CR>
alsafe          f10hdr      meadowvalley      pine.out
cartblone       test        paclow.table      site.spec
elk.int.pch mangroves
    INTR
$ cs ags<CR>
$ ls -l <CR>
total 482
-rw-------  1 ags 1239 Jul 14 22:02 cartblone
-rw-r--r--  1 ags  125 Sep 14 12:01 f122hdr
-rw----rw-  1 ags   10 Sep 01 12:00 test
-r-xr-xr-x  2 ags 4605 Feb 05 16:17 msmods
    INTR
$ cat cartblone<CR>
cat: can't open cartblone
$ cat f122hdr<CR>
To Whom It May Concern:

It has come to our attention that Ms.
    INTR
$ □
```

An attempt to **cat** (**catenate**) **cartblone** was unsuccessful because that file denies read permission to the public. The **f122hdr** file, however, does grant read permisison to the public, and was successfully **cat**ed.

Next, attempt to create a new file, **testfile**, in the directory using the **vi** editor.

```
$ vi testwrite<CR>
"testwrite" No such file or directory
     1 Can I create files in a directory
     2 without write permission?
:wq<CR>
"testwrite" Permission denied
:q!
$ □
```

When we attempted to **write** and quit the editor, the error message, "permission denied" resulted. Without **write** permission for a directory, new files can not be created or removed.

The file **msmods** grants execute permission to the public. This file may be in use as a UNIX command (depending on the contents of the file).

```
$ msmods<CR>
Monday, 20Sept84
There are 3 users on the system
$ □
```

Typing **msmods⟨CR⟩** on the command line caused the shell to attempt to execute a file by that name in the current directory. Because the file granted execute permission, the command was carried out; **msmods** is apparently a simple command file to display the date and time together with the number of users on the system. You will learn about command files in Chapter 6.

The file **test** is probably a personal file, like your **bozo**. The public is given **write** permission, so you are allowed to change the file as you please.

```
$ cat test<CR>
I guess I like this UNIX stuff.
It's complicated but if I figure it out,
I think I'll impress my boss.
$ vi test<CR>
Go
I guess I like this UNIX stuff.
It's complicated but if I figure it out,
I think I'll impress my boss.
She says "can't make heads or tails of
it."
I even know what UNIX "head"s and
"tail"s are!
:wq<CR>
```

```
"test" 5 lines, 193 characters
$ cat test<CR>
I guess I like this UNIX stuff.
It's complicated but if I figure it out,
I think I'll impress my boss.
She says "can't make heads or tails of
it."
I even know what UNIX "head"s and
"tail"s are!
$ ▯
```

Fig. 5.5 shows how each access permission affects both files and directories.

Fig. 5.5   File Permissions/Access Definitions

READ

Files: allows the user to examine (e.g., **cat**) that file.

Directory: allows the user to **ls** the directory, but not **ls -l**. Permission to read a directory does not automatically grant the right to read the files in a directory.

WRITE

Files: allows the user to alter a file (e.g., edit) or **rm** (**rem**ove) it.

Directory: allows the user to create new files and **rm** (**rem**ove) files.

EXECUTE

Files: allows the user to treat the file as a UNIX command. Execute permission does not assure that the file will actually function properly as a command; only that the shell will *attempt* to execute it.

Directory: allows the directory to be searched, and to become the user's current directory using **cd** (**c**hange **d**irectory). Execute permission is sometimes called "search" permission. This permission also is required to perform a **ls -l**.

It is impossible to give examples of all the circumstances under which denied permission will cause error messages. Even though an error message may be caused by the lack of an access permission, the error message seldom mentions it. Whenever you are prevented from performing some operation to a file or directory and there is no apparent reason for your failure, check the access permissions on the associated files and directories.

This completes the discussion on the file and directory system. It is time for you to begin to explore the directory structure on your own computer. In the process, you will soon get back to first or **root** directory.

A Quick Glance at the root Directory

Begin with **cd** /⟨**CR**⟩ to get to the **root** directory (/). Since UNIX directory systems evolve and change so rapidly, it is not possible to guide you through yours. The locations of certain files, however, are *almost* universal. The following list shows some of the most common directories found in a UNIX system.

/bin	Directory of UNIX commands.
/dev	Directory of special devices such as printers, terminals, etc.
/etc	Directory of system maintenance programs and data files.
/lib	Directory of library routines used in "C" programming language.
/tmp	Directory of temporary files. Many UNIX programs, such as editors and **mail**, use temporary files.
/usr	Many of the seldom-used commands reside here or in the /**usr/ bin** directory. User files systems generally are placed here.
/usr/games	System games directory.
/usr/man	The on-line UNIX Programmer's Guide directory.
[@/usr/mail	The system post office directory.@]
/usr/pub	Directory containing useful data files such as the ASCII character set, Greek alphabet, etc.

Interesting Files to Investigate

Here are some of the files you may want to inspect:

/etc/passwd	The password file (list of all system accounts (users)).

`[@/etc/profile`	System login command script (Bell System III and newer).@]
`/etc/group`	A list of the groups.
`/etc/motd`	The message-of-the-day.
`/etc/termcap`	A list of supported terminals and their characteristics. The information in this file allows UNIX to function with a variety of terminals.
`/etc/utmp`	Contains the names of the users currently logged in. Used by the **who** command.
`/usr/dict/words`	The on-line spelling dictionary.

Touring or examining directories and files and generally poking around in the corners of the system is an excellent way to develop a sense for the dimensions of the UNIX system. Be careful not to remove, move, or disturb other users' files especially if you are logged in as superuser. Go to it!

6 MAKING THE SHELL WORK FOR YOU

The UNIX* shell programs can do a great deal more for you than just interpret simple commands. Once you know how to make the shells work for you, you can have the system perform routine tasks automatically, which leaves you free to concentrate on more challenging work. Moreover, you can custom-tailor your UNIX system for the specific equipment you have in your office.

* UNIX™ is a trademark of Bell Laboratories.

In this chapter you will learn to use a group of special commands called shell functions, or shell commands. The UNIX system lets you combine groups of software tools to create simple programs. You will learn to build powerful sets of shell commands to automate frequently performed tasks. There are two types of shell commands, *interactive* and *programmed*. In the previous chapters you have used the interactive type of command. When you use an interactive command like **cp**, **rm**, or **cat**, you type the command line and receive an immediate response from the system. In this chapter, you will learn to use the programmed type of command.

Programming the shell involves writing a collection of commands, such as **date**, **who**, **cat**, etc., into a file, and, when desired, having the shell execute them, which it does sequentially without user interaction. Regular commands may also be combined with commands written in the *shell command language*, in order to create what is known as a *shell script*, or, more generally, as a *shell procedure*. However, most of these latter operations are beyond the scope of this book. If you wish to obtain information on these advanced shell operations, consult the *Programmers' Guide to UNIX*.

INSTRUCTIONS AND COMMANDS

The definition of the "command" must be explicitly understood before using programmed type commands. The first step is to distinguish between the terms *instruction* and *command*. They are used interchangeably in some software program manuals but for our purposes, the term *instruction* means machine instruction. A machine instruction can be one of many specific operations or functions built into the hardware of a particular machine. The CPU can carry out a specific discrete set of elementary operations, and only the instructions in that set. Machine instructions are usually quite basic, and for the most part bear little resemblance to the more elaborate concept of a command.

Many instructions in machine language are executed for every command that you type. The shell takes the one- or two-command word and interprets the words as lists of instructions. It sends the instructions to the right parts of the computer hardware to execute the instructions and perform the command. In a strictly literal sense, a computer does not execute commands at all. It only executes instructions. To carry out some defined operation by performing a sequence of machine instructions is equivalent to executing a command.

A program is nothing more than a set of instructions carried out one at a time for the purpose of performing some specific function. The same definition fits the term *command*. The commands that you will learn in this chapter, and the majority of all commands you will use in the UNIX system are "executed" by running a program. Even the "built-in" shell commands in this chapter are programs incorporated into the operating system.

All text and data in a UNIX system, including programs, are organized into files. When the shell reads a command line, it assumes the command name is a file containing the instructions to execute the command. The shell searches through the current directory for a file of that name. If it does not find the file in the current directory, it looks in several system directories. If no executable file by the name is found, the shell assumes it is one of its built-in commands. Finally, if it cannot find the command name in its list of built-in commands, it returns the message "No match" or "Command not found."

SHELL FUNDAMENTALS

When you first log in, the system puts a copy of the shell program into your home directory. In effect, this is your own shell, called your *login shell*. The shell is a program that interprets your commands and acts as a liaison between you and the individual programs and kernel of the system. Its primary function is to call or "turn on" other programs. When you type the command to edit a file, for example, the shell's first action is to go and get the edit program and all other relevant programs needed for and by the editor and copy them into your working space in main memory.

While you are using the editor, the shell has turned control of the system over to the edit program. It does not resume control again, nor will it prompt you until you exit (or use a shell escape from) the editor. Once you leave the editor, the shell resumes its functions of interpreting your commands and fetching system programs.

[@More than one shell may be available with your UNIX implementation. Many systems support two shell programs, the Bell Labs or Bourne shell, and the UC Berkeley or C shell. The

Bourne shell is designated **sh**, and the UC Berkeley C shell is designated **csh**. The Bourne shell's usual prompt is a dollar sign (**$**); the C shell's usual prompt is a percent sign (**%**). Systems that provide the C shell usually have other Berkeley software, like **ex** and **vi**. If your system includes the C shell (%), it may also have the Bourne shell ($), and you may use either. Systems which do not have the UC Berkeley utility programs usually provide only the Bourne shell.@]

MICROCOMPUTER MENU SHELLS

Many microcomputer systems feature "menu" shells that simplify interaction with the UNIX system. Menus consist of a list of commands from which you make a selection. The operation selected is implemented by a combination of commands hidden from you. Menu selections perform a specific task, such as file sorting or list printing. These *menu driven* shells help inexperienced users understand and perform computer jobs without understanding the underlying operating system. Since no special knowledge of command names and command syntax is required, menus are more friendly than the standard UNIX shells. A menu shell is a shell over (hiding) the UNIX shell. Each menu item stands for a series of shell commands that users would otherwise have to type in. Menu shells are easy to learn but limited in power. The standard shell must be used to gain the full powers of UNIX software.

THE SHELL COMMAND, (sh) OR (csh)

Since the shell is a program, you may command the UNIX system to "run a shell program" just as you can command it to run any other program. The shell program is invoked by the command **sh** for the Bourne shell of **csh** for the C shell. Your login shell is a *subshell* of the main shell program. Shell programs that run under the login shell are also subshells. You can have sub-subshells too, several levels deep.

Just as you are always "in" a directory, so are you always "in" some shell. If you are in a shell other than your login shell, you must return to your login shell before the UNIX system will permit you to log out. A shell, unlike a directory, is a program that you are running. If you logged out of the system while in a subshell, all subshells above your current one would still be running, and there would be no way to get them stopped short of consulting the system manager or shutting down the system. To exit from a shell, you use the ^**d** (control-d) command. You must exit from each shell you have created using ^**d** until you reach your login shell.

STANDARD INPUT AND OUTPUT

Just about every function performed by the UNIX system involves file handling. Even printers, tape drives, and your video terminal are treated as files. This idea is not as unusual as it may seem when you put yourself in the system's position. When the system directs the output of a command to appear on your video terminal, as far as the system is concerned, it is *writing* (sending output) to a *file*. This is as if you are sending a letter to an address without knowing or caring who lives at that address—the *form* of letter and the manner of sending are the same whether or not you know the addressee.

When the shell accepts input from your keyboard, it is *reading* (getting input) from a file. Terminals, printers, magnetic card readers, modems, disk drives, tape drives, and all other peripheral devices are treated by the system as files. (The special characteristics of these files will be discussed later.) In short, the UNIX system sees little *functional* difference between displaying the contents of a file on your video terminal or writing it to a disk file. All input/output (usually abbreviated I/O) is handled through files.

REDIRECTION OF INPUT AND OUTPUT

The keyboard and video display are the normal input and output for the shell and are called *standard input* and *standard output*. Whenever a command is executed by the shell, it takes its input data from the keyboard and sends any output to the terminal screen. To change either the source of input or the receiver of output, you have to name a new file for that purpose. Changing input and output from the standard is called *redirection*. The symbols to redirect input and output are

```
> for redirecting output
< for redirecting input
```

The command syntax for redirection is

```
Out: {command} {options} {argument} >new_output_file
 In: {command} {options} {argument} <new_input_file
```

Do not put a space between a redirection symbol and its associated filename.

You may combine redirection of input and output on the same command line. In fact, you may specify the "new input file" and "new output file" in any order on the command line as shown below

```
{command} [ {option}... ] <{new_input_file} >{new_output_file}
{command} [ {option}... ] >{new_output_file} <{new_input_file}
```

In the next few interactive lessons you will use the redirection commands. Since most of your files are empty, take a few minutes to create some lines of text in each of the **.mem** files.

LESSON 6.1:	Redirecting Output
NEW KNOWLEDGE:	Use of the) command; another use of the **cat** command
APPROXIMATE TIME:	10 minutes

Redirection is often used to save otherwise transient data. You can avoid memorizing the results of an operation by saving it. The output of a command may be redirected into a disk file for examination or editing at your leisure.

Suppose you wanted to consolidate all your memos from the **Memos** directory into a single master file. You could use an editor, but it is more efficient to use the **cat** command first to link all the memo files together. Then, instead of permitting the output of **cat** to be sent to your screen, redirect it into a new file named **memolist**. Finally, **cat** the file **memolist** to verify its contents.

```
$ cd Words/Memos<CR>
$ cat *.mem >memolist<CR>
$ cat memolist<CR>

16May84

Bob:

Would you please send me a printout of
current inventory. We're going to spot-
check physical inventory against the
computer files. By Thursday PM if
possible. Thanks.

Joe
.
.
.
Joan
```

```
Please check with Production on the
status of the Manuals, Can you meet with
Sylvia on Monday to discuss the format
of the screens? The deadline is fast
approaching,

Joe

Sandy:

I have just read the rough draft of your
memo about INTR
$ 
```

cat was interrupted with **INTR**.

Use Wildcards Carefully with Redirection

Since every file in this directory is assumed to be a memo, you may be wondering why we did not use the star wildcard, **cat *)memolist⟨CR⟩**. The redirection symbol, because of the order it reads the command line, would interpret **memolist** as *both* the input and output file, and give you an error message. Even though the shell *reads* a command line sequentially left-to-right, it does not necessarily execute the separate parts of a command in that order.

Before the **cat** command even begins to execute, the shell creates the new file **memolist** or, *if it already exists, erases its contents*. Right here, you run into problems. The wildcard in the argument is then expanded and the **cat** command takes the resulting filenames as its argument list. Therefore, **memolist** exists in the current directory *before* **cat** commences and will itself become a file to be **cat**ed, just like the other files in the current directory when the command line was entered. When **cat** attempts to redirect **memolist** into itself—a logical impossibility—an error message will occur: "cat: input memolist is output."

A file cannot simultaneously be the input and output of a command. Although in this case the command may succeed in spite of the error message, you can lose an existing file if you try to redirect its contents into a file of the same name. If you need to **cat** *everything* in a directory to a new file, place the new file in a different directory, for example,

cat *)$HOME/memolist⟨CR⟩. memolist will no longer be included in the **cat** of the current directory, but will be placed in your home ($HOME) directory instead.

Avoid Accidental File Loss with Redirection

An even worse problem occurs when trying to *redirect* the contents of a file or files to one of the same name, as in the example below. (*Note*: Do not try to execute these commands.)

```
$ cat se_jc8aug.mem memolist >memolist<CR>
cat: input memolist is output
$ cat memolist<CR>
8Aug84

Sandy

I have just read the rough draft of your memo INTR
$
```

In the above example, using redirection, the existing contents of the input file **memolist** were lost because the contents of **memolist** were erased before the **cat** began. The contents of **se_jc8aug.mem** were written into a newly emptied **memolist**. When the shell was called upon to redirect **memolist** into itself, the operation was terminated and the error message was issued. **memolist** now contains only **se_jc8aug.mem**.

Using Redirection and cat to Make Small Text Files

You can use redirection with the **cat** command to quickly make a small text file. Keyboard input to the **cat** command is normally echoed to the screen while its output is simultaneously redirected to a file. The UNIX kernel program automatically echoes whatever you type at the keyboard (the standard input) to the terminal (the standard output). However, the shell program can be instructed to redirect the output of the **cat** command to a disk file. To have whatever you enter at the keyboard go automatically into a file called **memo dash**, type **cat)memo_dash⟨CR⟩**. Then type the text shown in the example.

```
$ cat >memo_dash<CR>
This is a quick way to dash off a memo<CR>
without using a text editor. Its<CR>
biggest limitation is that there<CR>
is no way to correct mistakes<CR>
after a carriage return.<CR>
    ^d
$ []
```

After the ⟨**CR**⟩ on the command line, the shell accepts more input from the keyboard. When the standard end-of-text signal, control-d, is typed, the accumulated text is stored in **memo_dash**. If **memo_dash** had not existed, **cat** would have created it. Using the usual syntax, **memo_dash** can now be **cat**ed to demonstrate the existence of new text.

```
$ cat memo_dash<CR>
This is a quick way to dash off a memo
without using a text editor. Its biggest
limitation is that there is no way to
correct mistakes after a carriage
return.
$ []
```

There is one minor inconvenience to using **cat** this way. A single ^**d** will terminate text entry only if it is the first character typed after a carriage return; otherwise, two must be used, ^**d**^**d** and the double control-d can cause some problems. Until you become more experienced, use the ^**d** as the first character on the line to end text entry.

LESSON 6.2:	Appending Output
NEW KNOWLEDGE:	Use of the ⟩⟩ command
APPROXIMATE	
TIME:	10 minutes

In the preceding lesson you used the **cat** command together with the wildcard and the redirected output commands to create a single new file containing all of the **cat**(ted) files. If you had tried to redirect all the **cat**(ted) files into a file that already existed, the data in the existing file would be over-written. You may want to append one file to another and preserve both. The command to append one file to another is a *double redirection symbol, ⟩⟩*.

If you wish to append the current date and time to the file **memolist** created in the preceding lesson, type **date ⟩⟩memolist⟨CR⟩**. Then, **cat** the **memolist** file to verify execution, **cat memolist⟨CR⟩**.

```
$ date >>memolist<CR>
  cat memolist<CR>

16May84

Bob:

Would you please send me a printout of
current inventory. We're going to spot-
check physical inventory against the
computer files. By Thursday PM if
possible. Thanks.

Joe
.
.
.
Sandy:
```

```
I have just read the rough draft of your
memo about the use of company vehicles.
I would like
    .
    .
    .
Wed May 5 13:09:06 PST 1984
$ ▯
```

The append symbol, >>, can also be used with the **cat** command to append lines to an existing file without an editor. Suppose you wish to add the few lines shown below to the **memo_dash** file. You could use **cat >>memo_dash⟨CR⟩**. Begin typing the lines to be added. Having entered all the text you wish, type **^d** on a line by itself to return to the shell.

```
$ cat >>memo_dash<CR>
However, using >> will add<CR>
text to the file.<CR>
   ^d
$ cat memo_dash<CR>
       .
       .
       .
is no way to correct mistakes
after a carriage return.
However, using >> will add
text to the file.
$ ▯
```

LESSON 6.3:	Redirecting Input
NEW KNOWLEDGE:	Use of the ⟨ command
APPROXIMATE TIME:	20 minutes

The redirect command is most frequently used to execute a program that requires commands, data, or both from a file. Suppose you have a program called **win.races** that computes the most favorable odds on each horse in a group of horses running at a particular track. There is another file, called **feedbag.info** that is updated periodically with information on each horse. When the time comes to run the **win.races** program, it obtains data from the **feedbag.info** file. The redirect input command is used to get the information from the file. The complete command syntax in this example is **win.races ⟨feedbag.info⟨CR⟩**. If you wanted the computed information to be placed in a third file, you could use either the redirect output, ⟩, or the append command ⟩⟩. The syntax for the former is

```
win.races <feedbag.info >thirdfile<CR>
```

The redirect input command can direct text into a command file containing a specific series of editing commands to be carried out on the text file. For example, the input to a command could be

```
ed_file <commandfile<CR>
```

commandfile contains a series of editing commands that automatically edit the file as if you were editing from the keyboard. Redirection of standard input is most useful when used to read commands from other files, a topic covered later in this chapter.

Before continuing with the interactive lessons, several commands and terms are explained. They are used in shell programming in this chapter.

COMMAND LISTS

The shell can execute more than one command in sequence on a single command line. A command and its arguments are separated from other commands by a semicolon (;), and the command line is terminated as usual with ⟨**CR**⟩. Command sequences like these are called *command lists*.

If a single command line extends past the screen limit, it may be continued by typing until the line wraps around. For visual clarity you may "escape" the carriage return by typing a backslash and then a carriage return: \⟨**CR**⟩. The cursor returns to the beginning of the next line but, because the carriage return is escaped, does not execute the command sentence. Instead, the shell signals that it is expecting *more* command input by displaying the *secondary prompt* symbol, ⟩. Do not confuse this symbol, shown in normal type in this book, with the redirect symbol shown in boldface.

The four command sequence shown below **lists** a directory to a file in the home directory, copies that file (changing its name in the process) to another directory (**Words**), renames the file, and finally appends a copy of the file to our experimental file **memo_dash**.

[@Systems using the C shell will not display a secondary prompt. The ⟩ shown in the example display below will not appear if you have the C shell. If you type it in you will receive an error message.@]

```
$ cd<CR>
$ ls /bin > binlist; cp binlist Words/binlist2;mv /<CR>
> binlist newbinlist; cat newbinlist >>memo_dash<CR>
$ cat memo_dash
 .
 .
 .
text to the file.
ac
```

```
adb
 •
 •
 •
write
yacc
yes
$ ▯
```

Command lists can be very efficient. As your repertoire of commands grows, stringing commands together will become a standard procedure.

PIPELINES

The *pipeline* is another way to string commands together. Without really understanding the significance of the symbol (¦), you used a pipe in Chapter 3 to send text files to a line printer. Pipes redirect the output of one command to the input of another *command*. By contrast, redirection sends the output of a command to another *file*. Using pipes can greatly compress command sequences and make the command line more efficient.

To illustrate the effectiveness of pipelines, consider the following sequence of commands separated by semicolons. (Note that your number may differ.)

```
$ ls /bin >binlist; wc -w <binlist<CR>
     150
$ ▯
```

This command sequence lists the /**bin** directory and redirects the list to a file named **binlist**. It then performs a **wc** (word count) of the words (names) in **binlist** by using the -**w** (word) option of the **wc** command by redirecting the input. The number of words in **binlist** is equal to the number of files in the /**bin** directory, which usually contains files for command programs. Thus, with some difficulty, we have counted the command file names in /**bin** using command sequences with semicolons.

By piping the output of one command directly into the input of the next, the number of operations can be greatly reduced.

```
$ ls /bin | wc -w<CR>
       150
$ ▯
```

The mechanics of the pipeline operation can be conveniently expressed in a diagram. See Fig. 6.1.

Fig. 6.1 Pipeline Operation, Functional Block Diagram

l s	list
/bin	the **/bin** directory
¦	and pipe the list (the output of **ls**)
wc	through the word count program
-w	option to report only words counted

If you require a permanent record of the count, you can redirect the output to a file.

```
$ ls /bin | wc -w >bincount<CR>
$ cat bincount
       150
$ ▯
```

Another advantage of pipelines over command lists is the time savings. In command lists, temporary files *must* be created to hold the intermediate results of each command; these intermediate files then become the arguments of the next command. Temporary output files are not needed when pipes are employed. The pipe bypasses the need for a temporary file by sending the output of one command directly to the input of the next.

Pipelines and Redirection

When a pipeline is used, execution is started on all of the commands *simultaneously*. Redirection can, therefore, be used only for the final output of a pipeline or for its first input. Once redirection has been requested, no more pipes are permitted.

Input to a pipe may come from a file but this must be the *first* operation on the command line, such as:

```
ed filename< commandfile ¦ lpr<CR>
```

Filters

A pipeline is often used with *filter programs* such as **cat** or **more**. Filter programs are those commands which can take their input from the standard input, *perform some transformation*, and direct their output to the standard output. The UNIX utility programs that meet this definition can be used as filters. However, a command such as **ls**, which takes its input not from standard input but from a *directory*, may not be used as a successful filter between one command and another. Some examples of the utility programs we have discussed which are filters include **cat**, **echo**, **more**, and **wc**. Filter programs are discussed in greater detail later in the chapter.

Take care to arrange pipes, filters, and redirection in a logical order. When commands are logically composed, they can usually be used successfully as filters between commands that are surrounded by pipelines. As with command sequences that use semicolons, a single command line may include several pipes.

The tee Command

Pipes, filters, and redirection have one annoying drawback. Because these functions reroute information destined for the standard output to another command, the user may be deprived of the video display of that command. The **tee** or "pipe fitting" command solves this problem. With **tee**, command output may be redirected to a file *and* be displayed simultaneously on the terminal screen. You can think of the **tee** feature as a road sign being read simultaneously by two or more motorists as shown in Fig. 6.2 below.

The **tee** function can be used either as a filter or as a command. If you entered **ls /bin ┆ wc -w : tee bincount⟨CR⟩**, the number of filenames in /**bin** will be sent not only to the file **bincount**, but also to your terminal screen. Note that the target filename comes at the end of the command; since a **tee** is itself a form of redirection, no explicit redirection symbol is required.

```
$ ls /bin : wc -w : tee bincount<CR>
   150
$ cat bincount<CR>
   150
$ ▯
```

Fig. 6.2   The tee Command, Functional Block Diagram

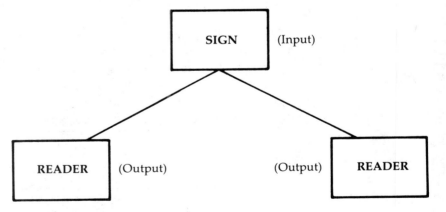

LESSON 6.4:	Command Files
NEW KNOWLEDGE:	Creating customized commands; the **.profile** file
APPROXIMATE TIME:	30 minutes

Because a command is usually executed by the running of an executable file, a sequence of UNIX commands can be placed in an ordinary file which then becomes a "custom-built" UNIX command that can be executed by anyone having read and execute permission for the file. In a command file, command lines are usually on separate lines, separated by ordinary carriage returns.

Automating Login with .profile

The use of a command file can be illustrated by a special file called **.profile** file in your home directory. When you log in, the shell searches your home directory for **.profile** and executes it as a command.

NOTE: [@*The equivalent to* **.profile** *when using the C-shell system is a file named* **.login**. *The same commands described in the following paragraphs may be put into* **.login** *if you are running the C shell.*@]

A command file can be quite simple. Use the redirected version of **cat** to create **.profile** in your home directory and put two familiar commands in the file.

NOTE: *If* **.profile** *already exists, use two redirection symbols,* 〉〉, *to append the following commands, rather than recreating the file.*

```
$ cat >>.profile<CR>
date<CR>
who<CR>
    ^d
$ 
```

It is possible that you do not actually have read and execute permission on the newly created **.profile** file, even though you are the author. If such is the case, when you try to execute this file from the command line by typing **.profile**⟨CR⟩, you may get some error message, such as ".profile: "Cannot execute" if you lack *execute* permission, or "-sh: .profile: cannot open" if you lack *read* permission. If this occurs, examine the access permissions on your home directory with ls - l **.profile**⟨CR⟩. If you do not have both execute and read permission (at least **r-x** in the leftmost column), log out and log in again. The default permission will allow you to read, write and execute on all files in your home directory. Then, at logout the necessary permissions will be set. At login the output from the **who** and **date** commands will be displayed.

```
login: {your username}<CR>
password: {your password}

GENERAL MANUFACTURING COMPANY UNIX SYSTEM

[your company's messages here]

Wed Oct 6 16:22:11 PDT 1984

root    console Oct 6 14:10
chris   ttya1   Oct 6 16:22
sandy   ttya2   Oct 6 09:23
  .
  .
  .
$ 
```

If you do not wish to know *who* is on the system, only *how many*, you can execute the **wc** command with **-l** option (number of lines) in the output of **who**. First, delete the **who** command from the **.profile** file using the **vi** editor.

Then, the **.profile** file should be changed as shown below.

```
$ cat>>.profile<CR>

who | wc -1
     ^d
$ ▯
```

By piping the output of **who** through **wc** with the line option, the number of users on the system is printed when you log in.

```
login: {your username}<CR>
password: {your password}

GENERAL MANUFACTURING COMPANY UNIX SYSTEM

[your company's messages of the day here]

Wed Oct 6 16:22:11 PDT 1984
        3
$ ▯
```

Making Command Output a Part of Other Commands

In the display above, the 3, showing the number of users is not very noticeable. Unlike the **date** output above it, there is nothing to tell what the 3 refers to. If you wish to include enhancing information, you can do so by using the **echo** command. **echo** sends any argument to the standard output. For example, type **echo I hear an echo**⟨CR⟩, the screen display would appear as below.

```
$ echo I hear an echo<CR>
I hear an echo
$ ▯
```

To include the output of a command within an **echo** message, enclose the command in grave accents (`` ` ``), or back quotation marks. The output of the command will appear on the screen, the command enclosed in grave accents will execute, and its output will form part of an argument to another command.

Type

```
$ echo There are `who | wc -l` users on the system.
There are 3 users on the system.
$ □
```

Now edit **.profile** using **vi** to include the line **echo There are `who | wc -l` users on the system**. Then log out and log back in again. Your login would now appear as shown below.

```
login: your username<CR>
password: your password<CR>

GENERAL MANUFACTURING COMPANY UNIX

[your company's messages on the day here]

Wed Oct 6 16:22:11 PDT 1984
There are 3 users on the system.
$ □
```

Escapes

You will sometimes include wildcard characters in your message text. You could draw a banner of *'s across the screen to separate your login messages from the company's messages. However, the * is the wildcard symbol from universal substitution. Whenever **echo** encounters a wildcard character on the command line, it will print every file in the current directory that matches the wildcard definition. Since the '*' matches everything, a directory listing is printed.

Force the shell to ignore the special meanings of such characters by *escaping*. A character's special meaning is escaped by putting it inside either double or single quotation marks. Thus, to ensure that the system actually prints a row of *'s, you enclose the symbols in quotation marks.

Type **echo** *''***********''*⟨**CR**⟩.

```
$ echo "**********" <CR>
**********
$ echo '**********'<CR>
**********
$ □
```

Double quotation marks are usually preferable for echo messages. Using double instead of single quotation marks gives you certain benefits which become important in advanced shell use, such as expansion of variables.

Whether single or double quotation marks are used, note that the quotation marks themselves are not printed. The question naturally arises, ''how could quotation marks themselves be included in the argument to **echo?**'' The shell's general-purpose *single character* escape is the backslash \. Whether the backslash is used in a command argument, the character following it is treated as its regular symbol. Thus \'' follows the '' to be printed.

Type **echo** \''**I hear an echo**\''⟨**CR**⟩.

```
$ echo \"I hear an echo\"<CR>
"I hear an echo"
$ echo now is the time for\<CR>
  all good men to...<CR>
now is the time for all good men to...
$ □
```

As you have seen before when typing long command lines, the second command shows that even nonprinting characters like carriage returns and control characters can be escaped using the backslash.

Command File Programs In the remaining pages of this chapter we are going to return to the concept discussed in the opening pages: the idea of a program or sequence of steps being equivalent to a command. More than any other system, the UNIX operating system makes use of this command concept. More than 200 command programs are available on fully implemented UNIX systems. Each of the commands you will be using is executable as a simple entry on the command line. Each performs a specific function. There are two principal advantages to such a system.

First, the main procedures in the operating system are much simpler. Shell, for example, consists of relatively few lines of code when compared with similar programs in other operating systems. This economy results from the fact that shell's main function is to call other programs to execute the command. The shell simply acts as a command interpreter, passing it on to the right program.

Second, once you have learned the basic strategies for catenating commands, you can put sequences of commands into files, which can be run as "custom commands" using the names of the files to invoke them. As your range and knowledge of commands increase, writing command files will become an essential first step for all but the smallest jobs. The usual procedure is to test each line to be placed in a command file by executing it first before putting it in the file.

Command files save a great deal of time since to repeat a set of commands, you do not have to rethink tasks and retype the commands. The more commands you know, the easier it is to write command files. The scope of this book does not permit discussion of all known UNIX commands, nor does it permit an exhaustive explanation. Examples of a few of the more frequently used commands will demonstrate common functions that such commands perform. Explanations are limited to a brief discussion of a command and its options. A few example screens are included. Because of the lack of content in the files created in the interactive lessons, the examples given will not necessarily match your text.

LESSON 6.5:   Command File Programs, **grep**
NEW KNOWLEDGE: Use of the **grep** command/program
APPROXIMATE
TIME: 20 minutes

The **grep** command finds specific patterns of text in files. It searches for patterns and expressions in exactly the same way that editors do. Consider a document from which you must delete a particular phrase or reference that occurs in several places. You can invoke **grep**, specify the pattern, and the command will take you, interactively, to each occurrence of it. The **grep** command will place the cursor on the first occurrence. You may note it, delete it, or do whatever you wish, and then proceed to the next occurrence and so on through the entire file until you have dealt with all occurrences of the pattern.

The syntax for **grep** is as follows:

`grep [ {option} ...] {pattern} [ {file}... ]<CR>`

grep options are shown in Table 6.1.

Table 6.1   grep Options

- **-v**   Only those lines that *do not* contain the *pattern* are printed.
- **-c**   Only a count of matching lines is printed.
- **-l**   The names of files with matching lines are listed (once) separated by newlines.
- **-n**   Each line is preceded by its line number in the file.
- **-y**   Lowercase letters in the pattern will also match uppercase letters in the input.
- **-h**   Suppresses header display
- **-e**   {pattern}
         Used in the case of the pattern beginning with "-"

The rules for the expansion of matching characters are similar. They are given in Table 6.2.

Table 6.2   Rules for Expansion of Matching Characters with grep

1. A backslash \ followed by a single character matches that character. The \ must be used when requesting **grep** or **egrep** to find 'special characters' such as \ . **$ * [ ] ? ^ ' ( )**. For best results, enclose the **expression** between single quotation marks (' ').

2. The character ^ precedes a patten at the beginning of a line. The character **$** follows a pattern at the end of a line.

3. A . matches any character.

4. Any ordinary character matches itself.

5. A string enclosed in brackets **[ ]** matches any single character from the string. Brackets are often used to enclose ranges of possibilities. For example, the expression **[A-Z]** will find all capital letters. Ranges may also be juxtaposed. The expression **[A-Za-z]** finds all capital and lowercase letters.

6. * matches 0 or more repetitions of the preceding character. The **+** character is more precise. It matches one or more repetitions of the preceding character. The interrogation mark, **?**, matches any single character.

The **grep** utility (command program) finds lines from the input file that contain the specified pattern. It will print those lines on the standard or other designated output. For example, execute a **who** command and **pipe** the output through **grep** using your own username as the pattern.
Type **who** ¦ **grep {yourusername}⟨CR⟩**.

```
$ who ¦ grep {yourusername}<CR>
yourusername ttya3 Sep 21:21:23
$ ▯
```

In this example, **grep** has passed the line containing the pattern 'yourusername' from the output of the **who** command to the standard output.

In the following example, find all the lines beginning with the word *The* in all files with a **.mem** extension. Find the line number in each case. First, change directory of **Words/Memos**, then type **grep -n "^The" *.mem**⟨CR⟩. The **-n** option specifies that the line numbers will be printed, and the ^ specifies the first word in the line. The display shows the paths to the files and the names of the files with their associated line numbers. You may not have any content in your **.mem** files that contain the specified pattern; if you do, the display should be in the format of the sample below.

```
$ cd Words/Memos
$ grep -n "^The" *.mem<CR>
xx.mem:2:The lazy dog.
xx.mem:5:The log.
xx.mem:1:The rolling moon.
xx.mem:3:The lost horizon.
$ □
```

LESSON 6.6:	Command File Programs, **sort**
NEW KNOWLEDGE:	Use of the **sort** command/program
APPROXIMATE	
TIME:	30 minutes

The **sort** command can rearrange lines of files into alphabetic or numeric order, by field. Each word or number on the line is one field. A field is a string of characters separated by blanks. Field numbers begin with 0, and are read left to right. For example, a list of names and addresses could be sorted by first name, last name, or zip code depending on which field was specified to **sort**.

Create a file named **list** with the text shown in the following display. The **cat list⟨CR⟩**.

```
$ cat list<CR>

Mary Sams, 1427 The Alameda, Berkeley, CA 94705
James Armstrong, 133 Tarragon Way, Saratoga, CA 94204
Charles Williams, 704 Castro St., San_Francisco, CA 94117
Laurie Benitez, 885 10th Ave., San_Francisco, CA 94122
Frank Crawford, 917 Irving St., San_Francisco, CA 94122
$ 
```

Consider this list of names and addresses. In the first line

```
"Mary" is field 0
"Sams," is field 1
"94705" is field 7
```

Notice that "San_Francisco" has its two words joined with an underline (_) to make them into a single "field." Without the underline, **sort** would consider San Francisco to be two fields. This mailing list must have a fixed number of fields, in a fixed order, for **sort** to function properly.

To sort alphabetically by last name, use **sort +1 list⟨CR⟩**. This means, sort on the second field, counting from 0. (0,1,2,3. . .).

```
$ sort +1 list<CR>

James Armstrong, 133 Tarragon Way, Saratoga, CA 94204
Laurie Benitez, 885 10th Ave., San_Francisco, CA 94122
Frank Crawford, 917 Irving St., San_Francisco, CA 94122
Mary Sams, 1427 The Alameda, Berkeley, CA 94705
Charles Williams, 704 Castro St., San_Francisco, CA 94117
$ []
```

Getting **sort** to operate correctly on the zip code field is more complicated. **sort** considers blanks to be spaces. The **-b** option forces **sort** to ignore blanks, usually with better results.

sort may not operate correctly on numbers unless the **n** option is added to the number of the field to be sorted. Since all zip codes have the same number of digits (unless someone has switched to the 9-digit postal code), the **n** option is not strictly necessary here.

```
$ sort -b +7n list
Charles Williams, 704 Castro St., San_Francisco, CA 94117
Frank Crawford, 917 Irving St., San_Francisco, CA 94122
Laurie Benitez, 885 10th Ave., San_Francisco, CA 94122
James Armstrong, 133 Tarragon Way, Saratoga, CA 94204
Mary Sams, 1427 The Alameda, Berkeley, CA 94705
$ []
```

Note that **sort** did not make any distinction between the two lines bearing the same zip code, 94122. They are not arranged in any specified order.

The importance of adding the **n** to the sort field may be seen if you try to sort the list above according to street number.

```
$ sort -b +2 list
James Armstrong, 133 Tarragon Way, Saratoga, CA 94204
Mary Sams, 1427 The Alameda, Berkeley, CA 94705
Charles Williams, 704 Castro St., San_Francisco, CA 94117
Laurie Benitez, 885 10th Ave., San_Francisco, CA 94122
Frank Crawford, 917 Irving St., San_Francisco, CA 94122
$ ▯
```

The street numbers are not sorted in numerical order, but in ASCII order. If you add the **n** option to the sort field, the sort program knows to handle the address numerals as numbers.

```
$ sort -b +2n list
James Armstrong, 133 Tarragon Way, Saratoga, CA 94204
Charles Williams, 704 Castro St., San_Francisco, CA 94117
Laurie Benitez, 885 10th Ave., San_Francisco, CA 94122
Frank Crawford, 917 Irving St., San_Francisco, CA 94122
Mary Sams, 1427 The Alameda, Berkeley, CA 94705
$ ▯
```

Now the output is sorted in numerical order as desired. The **sort** utility is a filter program. The following sequence sorts users according to their tty number.

```
$ who : sort -b +1 <CR>
albert  ttya0 Dec 20 15:22
bret    ttya1 Dec 20 12:12
chris   ttya3 Dec 20 14:13
```

The meaning of this command is diagrammed in Fig. 6.3.

Fig. 6.3   Command who : sort -b +1 Diagram

who   execute the **who** command

¡   and pipe the output

sort through the **sort** filter

-b   **sort** option to ignore blanks

+1   sort on field 1

There are many useful options to **sort**. Notice that in the example above the only thing that is sorted is the list that appeared on your screen. Your file **list** remains unchanged. The **-o** (output) option tells sort where to put the sorted material if you want it somewhere other than on your screen. The command

```
sort +1 list -o newlist<CR>
```

sorts your file **list** by last name and puts the sorted list into a new file called **newlist**. You can have your file **list** sorted and returned to a file also named **list** by typing the command

```
sort +1 list -o list<CR>
```

Table 6.3   Sort Options

-o   output: puts sorted material into a filename following the **-o.**

-r   reverse: sorts by specified field but in reverse order.

-c   check: sends to output only those lines that are out of sort.

-m   merge: merges files but they must already be sorted.

-i   ignore: ignores characters outside ascii range 040-0176. Those include spaces, alphanumeric characters and punctuation — i.e., basically the standard typewriter keyboard.

-d   dictionary order: sorts only on letters, digits, and blanks.

-t x   tab: 'tab character' separating fields is an **x**.

-n :   numeric: sorts by arithmetic value rather than ASCII.

LESSON 6.7:	Command File Programs, **uniq**
NEW KNOWLEDGE:	Use of the **uniq** command/program
APPROXIMATE	
TIME:	30 minutes

The **uniq** command is an alternative to **sort -u** for removing repeated lines in a file. It is especially useful after you have merged several files of lists and as a result have more than one entry for the same item.

The syntax of **uniq** is

```
uniq {inputfile} {outputfile}<CR>
```

This command will remove duplicate lines that are adjacent to each other and place the remaining lines into an output file. No redirection is necessary to specify an output file when **uniq** is used as a direct command. The input file must be sorted first so that duplicate lines are adjacent to each other. **uniq** then removes all duplicates. The **uniq** command is also a filter program.

Create two files, **list1** and **list2** as shown in the following display. Type the names in a different order than shown! They will be rearranged into this order by the sort command. **list1** and **list2** are in the same format as **list** which was used to illustrate **sort**. The lists could be sorted in zip code order and alphabetically within zip codes, then merged into one list with duplicate names removed. These sample lists are named **list**, **list1**, and **list2**. Since we are interested in an ordered version of each name and address list, first sort each list on the zip code field, then on the last name field, to produce the three different ordered lists shown below.

```
$ sort -b +7n +1 list >list.sort<CR>
$ sort -b +7n +1 list1 >list1.sort<CR>
$ sort -b +7n +1 list2 >list2.sort<CR>
$ cat list.sort<CR>
```

```
Charles Williams, 704 Castro St., San_Francisco, CA 94117
Laurie Benitez, 885 10th Ave., San_Francisco, CA 94122
Frank Crawford, 917 Irving St., San_Francisco, CA 94122
James Armstrong, 133 Tarragon Way, Saratoga, CA 94204
Mary Sams, 1427 The Alameda, Berkeley, CA 94705

$ cat list1.sort<CR>
Charles Williams, 704 Castro St., San_Francisco, CA 94117
Laurie Benitez, 885 10th Ave., San_Francisco, CA 94122
James Armstrong, 133 Tarragon Way, Saratoga, CA 94204
Cindy Melsen, 456 Berkeley Way, Berkeley, CA 94703
Mary Sams, 1427 The Alameda, Berkeley, CA 94705

$ cat list2.sort<CR>
Mary Green, 809 Castro St., San_Francisco, CA 94117
Charles Williams, 704 Castro St., San_Francisco, CA 94117
Laurie Benitez, 885 10th Ave., San_Francisco, CA 94122
James Armstrong, 133 Tarragon Way, Saratoga, CA 94204
Mary Sams, 1427 The Alameda, Berkeley, CA 94705
$
```

The sorted lists show the zip codes in order, and the names in alphabetical order within a given zip code group. There are many duplicate names among the three lists.

After repeating the above **sort** command for each list, you would end up with several sorted lists named (for example) **list.sort**, **list1.sort**, **list2.sort**, and so forth. These lists could then be merged, using the same sort criteria, and duplicate lines removed, with the command

```
sort -bm +7n +1 *.sort | uniq >cleanlist<CR>
```

```
$ sort -bm +7n +1 *.sort | uniq >cleanlist<CR>
$ cat cleanlist<CR>
Mary Green, 809 Castro St., San_Francisco, CA 94117
Charles Williams, 704 Castro St., San_Francisco, CA 94117
Laurie Benitez, 885 10th Ave., San_Francisco, CA 94122
Frank Crawford, 917 Irving St., San_Francisco, CA 94122
```

```
James Armstrong, 133 Tarragon Way, Saratoga, CA 94204
Cindy Melsen, 456 Berkeley Way, Berkeley, CA 94703
Mary Sams, 1427 The Alameda, Berkeley, CA 94705
```

This last **sort** command line means "sort on the **7th** field in numerical order and then sort on the last name (**1**) field, ignoring blanks, and merge all lists ending in **.sort**, pipe the result through **uniq** and place the output in a file named **cleanlist**." When **uniq** is used as a filter, redirection is necessary to specify the output file.

uniq is generally used without options; however, several options are available. See Table 6.4.

Table 6.4 Uniq Options

- **-u** generates output *only* of lines for which no duplicates were found. Any lines that did have duplicates are not output.

- **-d** generates output (once) only of lines that did have duplicates.

- **-c** gives a count, before each line output, of the number of times it occurred in the input.

uniq can also work with fields and characters in the lines of sorted files, say, to skip over fields in order to make one particular field "unique." For example, a unique representative of each zip code may be drawn from **cleanlist**, which contains names and addresses that have been sorted by zip code, and alphabetically within zip code, with duplicate names removed. The command is

uniq -6 cleanlist uniquelist <CR>

This command skips over the first seven fields (numbers 0 through 6) and outputs the first name and address in each different zip code area.

```
$ uniq -6 cleanlist uniquelist; cat uniquelist<CR>
Mary Green, 809 Castro St., San_Francisco, CA 94117
Laurie Benitez, 885 10th Ave., San_Francisco, CA 94122
James Armstrong, 133 Tarrason Way, Saratoga, CA 94204
Cindy Melsen, 456 Berkeley Way, Berkeley, CA 94703
Mary Sams, 1427 The Alameda, Berkeley, CA 94705
$ □
```

After the last two lessons, it may seem that the command lines are beginning to get a little complicated. They are. Yet part of the beauty and efficiency of the UNIX system is its *brevity* (or *terseness*, as it is sometimes called). You now have sufficient familiarity with the command line procedures to analyze each item on the line and absorb its meaning. Read and study each example methodically and what appears as complicated at first glance will become clearer with each example.

LESSON 6.8:	Command File Programs, **awk**
NEW KNOWLEDGE:	Use of the **awk** command/program
APPROXIMATE TIME:	20 minutes

The **awk** command, like **uniq**, works with 'fields.' **awk** selects patterns from fields that meet certain conditions, and performs specified operations on them. This command is not particularly easy to use, but it can handle several fields at one time, performing comparisons and computations. The program is frequently used to operate on fields containing numeric data.

The syntax of the **awk** command is

`awk {pattern}{action}{filename}...<CR>`

Pay close attention to the order and meaning of each item on the command line and make reference to it whenever needed.

A missing action statement simply causes the selected lines to be printed on the standard output (terminal).

awk's concept of field is different from that of **sort** and **uniq**. The first field on a line is understood as "Field 1." Field 0 is a special case, and refers to the whole line. As before, fields are strings of nonblank characters separated by blanks. When fields are referred to in patterns, they are preceded by a dollar sign. The symbol **$1** refers to field 1, **$5** to field 5, and so forth.

Each line (separated by a new line) is one record. The **awk** program automatically keeps track of the number of records selected in the **NR** (**N**umber of **R**ecords) variable. **NR** may be used to report the number of records selected, or to compute averages, totals, etc.

As a simple example, use **awk** to select from the combined mailing list produced in the preceding lesson all names and addresses with zip code numbers larger than 94117. The zip code numbers are in field 8, (for **awk**). The full command line then is

`awk '$8 > 94117' cleanlist<CR>`

This command prints lines in which the zip code number is larger than 94117. The symbol ⟩ is the mathematical symbol for "greater than." Enclose the pattern for **awk** in single quotes to avoid confusing the shell.

The display resulting from this command is shown below.

```
$ awk $8 > 94117' cleanlist<CR>
Laurie Benitez, 885 10th Ave., San_Francisco, CA 94122
Frank Crawford, 917 Irving St., San_Francisco, CA 94122
James Armstrong, 133 Tarragon Way, Saratoga, CA 94204
Cindy Melsen, 456 Berkeley Way, Berkeley, CA 94703
Mary Sams, 1427 The Alameda, Berkeley, CA 94705
$
```

If an action statement is missing, the selected lines would simply be displayed on the terminal; they could also be redirected to a file. If a pattern statement is missing, the action is performed on every line in the file. The **awk** command can operate on several files and perform several operations on each one.

As an example of an action statement in **awk**, change the previous example to print out the names of people in **cleanlist** in reverse order, last name first. Note that the action statement should also be enclosed in single quotation marks to not confuse the shell.

Type **awk '(print $2, $1)' cleanlist ⟨CR⟩**.

```
$ awk '(print $2, $1)' cleanlist<CR>
Green,Mary
Williams,Charles
Benitez,Laurie
Crawford,Frank
Armstrong,James
Melsen,Cindy
Sams,Mary
$
```

If **awk** proves a bit difficult to handle and you find that you are getting error messages instead of the desired results, do not be discouraged. Go on to the next lesson; when time permits, you can return to this lesson, consult with your system manager, or obtain and study the references shown in the bibliography.

LESSON 6.9:	Command File Programs, **comm**
NEW KNOWLEDGE:	Use of the **comm** (**comm**on) command/program
APPROXIMATE	
TIME:	10 minutes

The **comm** (**comm**on) command compares two *sorted* files. It is used to produce a listing of lines identical in both files, and of the lines unique to each input file. Its chief usefulness is in checking and producing cross references.

The syntax of the **comm** command is

```
comm {file1} {file2}<CR>
```

Use **comm** to redirect output to a file, for example, **comm file1 file2 ⟩ commfile⟨CR⟩**. Then **commfile** will have three columns: The first column of the **comm** report contains lines found only in the first file, the second column prints lines found only in the second file, and the third column prints lines found in both files. If the files are identical, only the third column will be printed, and **commfile** will contain one copy of the text of the identical files.

For comparison purposes, **list** and **list1** must be sorted in ASCII collating order. This is the order that results when **sort** is used on lists without specifying any fields or options. To not disturb the original lists, **sort** them into two files with extension **.ascii**. Note that ASCII collating order is not useful for numeric data.

To sort the **list** file into ASCII collating order, type **sort list ⟩sort.ascii⟨CR⟩**; to do the same for **list1**, simply substitute **list1** for **list** in the command line. Then **cat**enate both files to display the contents.

```
$ sort list >sort.ascii;
  cat sort.ascii<CR>
Charles Williams, 704 Castro St., San_Francisco, CA 94117
Frank Crawford, 917 Irving St., San_Francisco, CA 94122
James Armstrong, 133 Tarragon Way, Saratosa, CA 94204
```

```
Laurie Benitez, 885 10th Ave,, San_Francisco, CA 94122
Mary Sams, 1427 The Alameda, Berkeley, CA 94705
$ sort list1 >sort1.ascii; cat sort1.ascii<CR>
Charles Williams, 704 Castro St., San_Francisco, CA 94117
Cindy Melsen, 456 Berkeley Way, Berkeley, CA 94703
James Armstrong, 133 Tarragon Way, Saratoga, CA 94204
Laurie Benitez, 885 10th Ave,, San_Francisco, CA 94122
Mary Sams, 1427 The Alameda, Berkeley, CA 94705
$ ▯
```

After both lists have been sorted, the comparison may be made using the following command line:

comm sort.ascii sort1.ascii<CR>

A look at **commsort** shows lines found only in **sort.ascii** in the left column; lines found only in **sort1.ascii** in the center column, and lines shared by both files in the third column. **comm**'s output is sometimes a bit crowded, but it is a quick way of comparing two sorted lists.

If you do a **comm** on two radically different files, or if you compare lists which have not been sorted, the **comm** report may contain no third column, since the files would have no lines in common.

Fig. 6.4 Diagram of commsort Display

```
$ comm sort.ascii sort1.ascii >commsort<CR>
$ cat commsort<CR>
                Charles Williams, 704 Castro St., San_Francisco, CA  94117
        Cindy Melsen, 456 Berkeley Way, Berkeley, CA 94703
Frank   Crawford, 917 Irving St., San_Francisco, CA 94122
                James Armstrong, 133 Tarragon Way, Saratoga, CA 94204
                Laurie Benitez, 885 10th Ave., San_Francisco, CA 94122
        Mary Sams, 1427 The Alameda, Berkeley, CA 94705
--              V
--      --
V       --      --
column1         column2         column3
```

LESSON 6.10:	Command File Programs, **cmp** and **diff**
NEW KNOWLEDGE:	Use of the **cmp** (**comp**are) and **diff** (**diff**erence) commands/programs
APPROXIMATE TIME:	30 minutes

The **cmp** (**comp**are) command reports whether two files differ, and at what point (with reference to the first file named) the first difference occurs. That's all **cmp** does, but it does it quickly and accurately.

The syntax of **cmp** is

```
cmp {file1} {file2}<CR>
```

If the files are the same, **cmp** doesn't report anything. If the files are different, **cmp** reports the character (including tabs and spaces) and line number at which the first difference is noted, with reference to the first file named. Files need not already be sorted, but the output of **cmp** is normally more useful if used on sorted lists. To demonstrate the command, type **cmp list.sort list1.sort⟨CR⟩.**

```
$ cmp list.sort list1.sort<CR>
list.sort list1.sort differ: char 114,
line 3
$ 
```

The **diff** Command

The **diff** (**diff**erence) command is more complex than **cmp**. It tells you not only if the files differ, but also how to change one into the other. It provides you with a list of editor commands you can use to make the files identical. The **diff** program is used to show where two files differ, and for updating documents or to show how a document has changed over a period of time.

To compare two slightly different versions of a long document, **diff** speeds the task and shows you exactly where they differ. It saves you the laborious task of manual comparison.

As a quick example, first change directory to **Words/Letters**, the location of the **jobreply** file. Make a copy of **jobreply**, and call it **jobreply.new**. Then edit **jobreply.new** as if Andrea's home address had changed. Suppose her new home address is 29 Palms Harbor Vista, Sleek Suburb, California 94714. Now the new copy of the letter will have a different home address.

The **diff** command will report which lines in the first file named on the command line are different than the second file. The screen will list all required changes as editing commands (add, change, or delete) with line numbers. Follow the editing commands in the order listed, starting with the numerically largest line number, since the line numbers referred to are otherwise incorrect. Adding or deleting lines changes all subsequent line numbers.

Type **cp jobreply jobreply.new⟨CR⟩**. Enter **vi** and change the address by typing **vi jobreply.new**, etc. After your edit is complete, execute the **diff** command. Type **diff jobreply jobreply.new⟨CR⟩**.

```
$ cd Words/Memos
$ cp jobreply jobreply.new<CR>
$ vi jobreply.new   <-----[put in new address]
$ :w9
$ diff jobreply jobreply.new<CR>
5,6c5,6
< 1412 N. Main St.
< Oakland, California 94612
- - -
> 29 Palms Harbor Vista
> Sleek Suburb, California 94714
$ □
```

The **diff** report indicates that lines 5 and 6 in the first file need to be changed according to the information in lines 5 and 6 of the second file.

diff with the **-e** option will produce an editing script which can be used to make the first file identical with the second file automatically.

First, use **diff -e** on the two slightly different files and redirect the result to a new file called **diffscript**.

Type **diff -e jobreply jobreply.new >diffscript⟨CR⟩**.

Type **cat diffscript⟨CR⟩**.

```
$ diff -e jobreply jobreply.new >diffscript<CR>
$ cat diffscript
5,6c
29 Palms Harbor Vista
Sleek Suburb, California 94714
.
$
```

If this script is used with **vi** to edit **jobreply**, it will behave just as though you were editing **jobreply** from the keyboard. To invoke this script, invoke **vi** in the normal fashion, and then quit from visual mode using the capital Q command to put the system into the **ex** mode. (The capital Q command is used rather than the colon because it is a more fully implemented form of entering the **ex** command mode than just typing colon (:) from **vi**.) This action will cause the familiar colon to appear. Instruct the editor to use **diffscript** as the source of command input, then reenter **vi** mode. The entire sequence is shown below.

Type **vi jobreply⟨CR⟩** followed by **Q**. At the colon prompt, type **source diffscript⟨CR⟩**.

```
$ vi jobreply<CR>
1 Letter to Andrea Applicant
.
.
.
4 Ms. Andrea Applicant
5 1412 N. Main St.
6 Oakland, CA 94759
.
.
.
```

```
Q<CR>
:source diffscript<CR>
6 Sleek Suburb, California 94714
:vi<CR>
1 Letter to Andrea Applicant
 .
 .
 .
4 Ms. Andrea Applicant
5 29 Palms Harbor Vista
6 Sleek Suburb, California 94714
```

LESSON 6.11:   Command File Programs, **spell**
NEW KNOWLEDGE: The **spell** command
APPROXIMATE
TIME: 10 minutes

One of the most useful programs available on a UNIX-based system, especially in an office environment where many long text files are produced, is its **spell** program. When this program is executed it checks the spelling of every word in the text file against a 24,000-word, built-in dictionary. When the program finds a misspelled word it prints it on the monitor screen. The syntax of the command is simply

```
spell (filename)<CR>
```

Suppose you wish to check the spelling of the **jobreply** file. First, ensure that you are in the correct directory (**Words/Letters**), then type **spell jobreply⟨CR⟩**.

```
$ spell jobreply
CA
Co
Hardhart
$ 
```

Although **jobreply** contains no spelling errors, **spell** did not find the two abbreviations CA and Co in its dictionary. You will notice, however, that some other abbreviations were accepted: Ms, N (for north) and St (street) were all accepted as were some names, including Andrea and Hiram. The dictionary includes a list of proper names.

You can create a customized dictionary. The **spell** program allows you to add to the dictionary, a useful feature if your files contain a large number of abbreviations, jargon, mnemonics, and job-specific terms. After such a word has been added, it will not be flagged as an error.

The **spell** program may be used during an escape from an editor. For example, after you have entered text to a new file and have written the new file to disk, you could run a spelling check then immediately return to the file for corrections. Note that multiple filenames may be given on the command line; however, **spell** will not indicate in which file each misspelled word was found. Try running the **spell** program on the file you created for text editing practice.

LESSON 6.12:	Command File Programs, Running Programs in the Background
NEW KNOWLEDGE:	The **&** (ampersand) command
APPROXIMATE TIME:	15 minutes

You often run programs that take some time to execute. When a program is run that requires a large (by computer standards) number of instructions or that has large amounts of data to process, it can take an appreciable and significant amount of time to complete, especially when there are many other users on the system. The result of this situation is that if you run a lengthy program (for example, **spell**, on a text file that contains thousands of words), you could be sitting in front of your terminal for perhaps half an hour. The UNIX system has provided a way to run such a program in the background and free the terminal for use in running other programs.

The command to run a program in the background is the **&** (ampersand) symbol placed at the end of the command line. The compete syntax of the **cat** command for five files redirected to a new file and run in the background is

```
cat file1 file2 file3 file4 file5 >newfile &<CR>
```

```
$ cat file1 file2 file3 file4 file5 >newfile &<CR>
304                          <-----[sample PID number]
$ □
```

As soon as the command is executed with the **&**, a number appears on the next line, and the shell prompt appears on the line after that. The number is the *PID* or *process identification* number assigned to the program that you are running. A PID number is always assigned a running program; however, in the interactive mode, it is not reported. When the shell prompt returns, proceed as normal.

It is standard practice to redirect the output of the program running in the background. This action prevents the background program from writing all over your terminal when it has finished executing.

An excellent demonstration of the use of the "background" command can be seen by running the **spell** program on the **memo_dash** file in the background and then executing vi on the **memolist** file.

First, ensure that you are in the directory containing **memolist** and **memo_dash**. Then type

```
spell memo_dash >memo_dash.errs &<CR>
```

followed by **vi memolist⟨CR⟩**.

```
$ spell memo_dash >memo_dash.errs &<CR>
746
$ vi memolist
16May84
Bob:
Would you please send me a printout of
current inventory. We're going to spot-
check physical inventory against the
computer files. By Thursday PM if
possible. Thanks.
Joe
.
.
.
:w9
```

After about two minutes, exit from **vi** and execute a list (**ls**) command to verify that you have the newly created **memo_dash.errs** file. This file will contain all the words which did not match the UNIX dictionary. You should remove the file before continuing. Type **rm memo_dash.errs⟨CR⟩**.

It will be an amusing (and enlightening) experience to perform the above operating without redirecting the output.

Type **spell memo_dash &⟨CR⟩** followed by **vi memolist⟨CR⟩**.

```
$ spell memo_dash &<CR>
307
$ vi memolist<CR>
16May84
Bob:
Would you please send me a printout of
current inventory. We're going to spot-
check physical inventory against the
computer files. By Thursday PM if
possible. Thanks.
Joe
  .
  .
  .
```

Do not take any action. Just sit and wait. Observe that all at once your screen is "clobbered" by the list of misspelled words reported by the **spell** program regardless of the fact that you are in another program.

As a final note, it should be mentioned that certain programs, for example **vi**, cannot be run in the background. If you should attempt to do so you will receive an error message.

7

COMMUNICATING WITH YOURSELF AND OTHER USERS

Sending messages, notes, routine memos, and meeting notices using the UNIX* system's electronic mail programs can save you time and steps. You get a permanent copy for your files at the same time that you send messages, and you can communicate with people in your office and across the country. The UNIX system will also keep an appointments calendar and send you "reminder messages."

Electronic Mail
The Commands **write** and **mesg**
over and out
Do Not Disturb
write and Redirection

Communicating with Other Users by mail
Composing and Sending **mail**
mail and Input Redirection
Setting up a **mail** directory

Calendar and Reminder Service
cal
calendar, The UNIX System's Reminder Service
Reminders in Your Mail

---

* UNIX™ is a trademark of Bell Laboratories.

The communications capabilities on your UNIX system are a valuable, cost-effective business tool. You will reduce the stacks of paperwork on your desk by using the **mail** and **write** commands to send memos, messages, and routine office correspondence to other users on your system. The message "you have mail" will greet you at login. The items in your mailbox may be backup notices from the system manager, invitations to lunch from another user, or daily reminders that you have posted to yourself the evening before. You can communicate immediately with other users via the **write** command. The message will appear on the receiver's screen as soon as you send it. If the person is using their terminal, they can send a reply directly back to you for quick response.

You can use the **calendar** function to set up a detailed "tickler" file for daily, weekly, and monthly schedules of appointments, flags of "hot" items, and timekeeping chores. The **cal** program is an on-line perpetual calendar for any month or year in the range 1 to 9999 A.D.

If you have several UNIX systems you will be able to "network" them together for electronic mail and file transfer by using the UNIX-to-UNIX (**uucp**) functions. The community of UNIX users grows every day. If you do business with other companies that use the UNIX system, or if your company has more than one UNIX-based computer, the need inevitably will arise to transfer data between systems. The system program **uucp** (**u**nix-to-**u**nix **c**opy) allows the transfer of files between participating UNIX installations. Similarly, **uux** (**u**nix-to-**u**nix execute) enables the users of one UNIX system to execute commands on another. The **mail** program will call up the **uucp** program automatically.

At the end of this chapter, we will discuss ways the UNIX system communicates with you about itself. The system documentation is both printed and on-line, and the **learn** program offers interactive tutorials on the editing programs and file management utilities.

ELECTRONIC MAIL

The Commands write and mesg

The **write** program connects two logged-in users so that one user's standard input is sent to the other user's standard output. Simply stated, what is typed on one keyboard shows up on the other screen. The syntax for the **write** command is

```
write {username} [{ttyname}]<CR>
```

The easiest way to practice **write** is to write to yourself.

If you wish to carry out these examples, substitute your own login or username for chris.

```
$ who am i<CR>
chris ttya4
$ write chris<CR>
Message from chris ttya4...
This is a message to myself.<CR>
This is a message to myself.
^d
EOF
$ □
```

Before typing the **write** command, **who am i⟨CR⟩** identifies your terminal (**ttya4**) and your login name (**chris**). After **write chris⟨CR⟩**, the announcement "Message from chris...ttya4" is printed on your screen. If more than one terminal had been logged in under your name, it would be necessary to state your terminal name in the command **write chris ttya4⟨CR⟩** to differentiate between terminals. "This is a message to myself" is typed; when you press return, the message is transmitted. Since you are writing to your own terminal, the message returns to your terminal almost immediately. The actual delay between issuing the carriage return and the printing of the message will depend upon the system's current load. To end the **write** session type ^d, the standard end-of-file character. The **write** program acknowledges your request by printing "EOF" (end-of-file). Finally, the shell prompt, $, indicates that you have exited **write** and returned to the shell.

A sample exchange between two users is shown below. For clarity, both users' screens are shown adjacent to each other. Again, if you can find another user to practice with, the experience with the command will be helpful. Your message to **root** (a system manager, Brunhilde) is transmitted line by line after each carriage return. The leading periods (dots) before the received transmission indicate the passage of time between the reception of lines. The example shows messages *sent* from a user in boldface on the sender's screen. Messages received by the user are shown in normal type.

```
$ write root<CR>                  $ Message from chris ttya4...
Hello, Bruny, I can't<CR>          ...Hello, Bruny, I can't
seem to make the 'sort'<CR>        ...seem to make the 'sort'
command work at all.<CR>           ...command work at all.
It was fine on Friday.<CR>         ...It was fine on Friday.
Any ideas?<CR>                     ...Any ideas?
-o-<CR>                            ...-o-
Message from root console...       $ write chris ttya4<CR>
...I wasn't here this weekend,     I wasn't here this weekend,<CR>
...but I understand some           but I understand some<CR>
...programs were moved.            programs were moved.<CR>
...I'll check it out and get       I'll check it out and get<CR>
...back to you.                    back to you.<CR>
...-o-                             -o-<CR>
thanks<CR>                         ...thanks
-oo-                               -oo-
...you're welcome                  you're welcome<CR>
...-oo-                            -oo-<CR>
^d                                 ...EOF
...EOF                             ^d
$ []                               $ []
```

over and out

You use radio transmission protocol, "-o-" ("over"), to signal that you are ready to receive. Notice that when Brunhilde (root) receives your message, she cannot immediately return a message. She must first enter **write** by typing **write chris ttya4⟨CR⟩**. When both have entered **write** in this manner, the two terminals are linked. **root**'s reply is sent line by line to your screen and is ended with "-o-". Both users communicate that they are ready to end the session by signaling "-oo-" ("out"). You await **root**'s agreement to sign off, and upon receiving "-oo-", type control-d. The letters EOF then appear on **root**'s screen. She responds to the EOF by also typing control-d. The return of the shell prompt to both screens indicates that the two terminals are disengaged.

Do Not Disturb

Sometimes you may not want to be disturbed by incoming messages, especially when running the screen editor, **vi**. The spontaneous appearance of messages on your screen can be disconcerting, and if you are not careful, can cause you to lose the overwritten text if your reaction inadvertently purges the buffer. If a message should burst in on your screen, don't panic and don't retype your text. Only the screen copy is disfigured. Both the working **copy** (the edit buffer) and the disk copy are still unchanged. On some systems, typing a control-l (^l) will redraw the screen. When you are reviewing formatted text, the arrival of a message could be annoying.

The UNIX system allows incoming messages to be locked out. To prevent them from coming in, type **mesg n⟨CR⟩**. To permit messages again, type **mesg y**⟨CR⟩. To check which way your "do not disturb" sign is flipped, type **mesg⟨CR⟩**.

The example below shows the results of an attempt to write to **root** with messages locked out.

your account

```
  "
  "
  "
$ write root<CR>
Permission denied
$ 
```

root's account

```
$ mesg n<CR>
$ []
 "
 "
```

To gain some insight into how the UNIX system treats your terminal as a *file*, examine the entry for your terminal in the special character file /**dev/tty**. A long listing of your terminal's file before and after **mesg n⟨CR⟩** will reveal that the lockout is accomplished simply by removing public **write** permission for your terminal. You might note also, that the first column contains a *c*, which shows that the terminal is neither an ordinary file (–) nor a directory *d*.

```
$ who am i<CR>
chris ttya4 10 Oct 82
$ mesg y<CR>
$ ls -l /dev/ttya4<CR>
crw--w--w- 1 chris 4 10 Oct 82 /dev/ttya4
$ mesg n<CR>
$ ls -l /dev/ttya4<CR>
crw------- 1 chris 4 10 Oct 82 /dev/ttya4
$ []
```

A problem with **write** may arise because a line is not printed on the receiving terminal until a carriage return is received from the transmitting terminal. The terminal waits for a carriage return before sending its line. For example, suppose you **write** to another user and a long delay occurs before an initial response. How can you tell if (1) the recipient is perhaps a slow typist and a little verbose as well; or (2) is away from the terminal for a few minutes; or (3) forgot to log out, or (4) is asleep? When a response—especially an initial response—is slow in coming, it's hard to wait staring at a blank screen for a reply that may never come.

Fortunately, the problem is easily remedied. Line-by-line transmission of messages is not dictated by the terminal, but by the UNIX system. A seldom used option to the **stty** command called **cbreak** will cause individual characters to be transmitted as they are typed. If both parties enable **cbreak**, an exact duplicate of screen activity is created, backspace/erasures included. The **cbreak** command does not have to be set *prior* to entering **write**. The following example also shows a **write** to oneself. Once inside the **write** program the escape to the shell can be made using the standard escape character, !, in order to set **cbreak**.

```
$ write chris<CR>
Message from chris ttya4...
when -cbreak is set, each line is
echoed.<CR>
when -cbreak is set, each line is
echoed.
!stty cbreak<CR>
!
WWhheenn ccbbrreeaakK iiss sseett
eeaacchh
cchhaarraacctteerr iiss eecchhooeedd,,
eevveenn ccaarriiaaggee
rreettuurrnnss!!
!!
^d............................................
....
EOF
$ 
```

Normally at login the default value of **-cbreak** is in effect, which means that as each *line* is typed, it is sent back (echoed) to your terminal when a carriage return is typed. You can return **cbreak** to its normal status by typing **stty cbreak**. You have seen many examples of escaping a program to execute one shell command line. This same technique is employed here to set **cbreak** using **stty**, and return to the **write** program. Of course, you could just as easily have set **cbreak** from the command line before entering **write**.

After **!stty cbreak⟨CR⟩**, the **write** program acknowledges your departure from the shell by printing a ! on a line by itself. The output of any command(s) executed during an escape from **write** are *not* included in the transmitted message.

After setting **cbreak**, each *character* is echoed back to your terminal as it is typed. All characters are echoed, spaces and carriage returns included.

Unfortunately, there is another problem that occurs. When you have completed your **write** session and attempt to escape to the shell (perhaps to set **-cbreak**) you find that you cannot. Instead, the escape character, !, is echoed back as an ordinary character. Nor will the normal end-of-file character, control-d, terminate the session. Again, the solution is simple. The **interrupt** character will allow you to exit the **write** program and return permanently to the shell. This is not particularly troublesome, except that once **cbreak** is set, it is no longer possible to use escapes to shell commands.

write and Redirection

The output from **write** cannot be saved in a file, but its input can come from a file. This is handy if another user wants to take a quick look at one of your files without the formality of transferring it via electronic mail. For example, if Sandy wants a copy of your memo to her on August 8, you could send it directly to her screen with the following command.

```
write sandye < Words/Memos/se_jc8aug.mem<CR>.
```

COMMUNICATING WITH OTHER USERS BY MAIL

UNIX **mail** works much like the U.S. mail, but faster. The system post office, whose address is **/usr/spool/mail**, contains a "box" to hold incoming mail for each user. ("spool" is a computer acronym (**s**imultaneous **p**eripheral **o**utput **o**verlay) for an area where output is stored while waiting for the command to execute.) You have encountered spooling before in the discussion of how output is queued for a line printer. If someone sends mail to you, it is held in **usr/spool/mail/chris** until you deal with it (read it and save or delete it). In addition to the system post office, you may have a local mail box **mbox** anywhere in your directory structure. When the mail is "delivered," you are allowed to discard any junk letters and save the important letters in **mbox** to read, file, or answer at your leisure.

Each letter you send or receive will bear the postmark of the sender, together with the time and date of posting. You can even forward mail to other users, keeping a copy for yourself, and you can send "carbon copies" to other users.

Although there are many variations of the **mail** command, there are really only two basic **mail** functions, composing and sending mail, and receiving and disposing of mail.

Composing and Sending mail

The syntax of the **mail** command is

    mail (username)...<CR>

This command puts you in a text entry mode similar to that obtained with **cat**⟩**filename**⟨CR⟩. Text is entered until a control-d is entered or until a period is typed as the first character of the last line. Since using control-d is liable to log you out if you inadvertently hit it more than once, using the period is safer. The example shown is the result of sending some mail to "yourself."

```
$ mail chris<CR>
This is a boomerang letter.<CR>
.<CR>
$ 
```

After a few moments, your letter should have arrived in your post office box. You can look at it there before it is delivered.

```
$ cat /usr/spool/mail/chris<CR>
This is a boomerang letter.
$ 
```

The next time you log in you will be notified by the message,

```
You have mail.
```

If you happen to be reading your mail at the time, this message is displayed:

```
New mail has arrived,
You have mail,
```

If you do not wish to be notified of the arrival of mail, enter **mesg n** in your **.profile** file. This option will also disable your terminal for **write** messages.

If mail arrives at the post office while you are logged in, you will not be notified until the next time you log in, unless you happen to be reading your mail at the time.

You are alerted to the presence of mail when you log in by the following message.

```
    .
    .
    .
[your company announcements here]
You have mail
[your profile messages here]
$
```

The mail announcement is sandwiched between the system announcements and the **echo** statements in your **.profile** file. If your **.profile** begins with a banner, you will know always to look for your mail announcement on top of your banner.

mail and Input Redirection

Mail does not have to be composed each time you wish to send a letter. Any file in your directory system can be mailed by using input redirection. Suppose Sandy would like her own copy of your August 8 memo. You can mail it to her simply by typing

```
mail sandye </Words/Memos/se_jc8aug.mem<CR>
```

To read your mail delivery, just ask for it by typing **mail⟨CR⟩**.

```
$ mail<CR>
From chris Wed Oct 13 11:21:46 1982
This is a boomerang letter.
?<CR>
$
```

Your letter has been given a "postmark"—a heading which gives the name of the sender, and the time and date the letter was sent. The text of a long letter will scroll off the screen, so be prepared to use ^s and ^q when you read your mail. The **mail** messages cannot be piped through the **more** screen paging filter.

When the text of the letter has finished printing, you are prompted by a question mark. This prompt is asking, "What do you want to do with the current letter?" If you have more letters, entering a carriage return will cause another to be printed. If there are no more letters in the post office, typing a carriage return will cause you to exit from **mail** to the shell.

```
$ mail
[letter #1]
?<CR>
[letter #2]
?<CR>
[letter #3]
?<CR>
$
```

The carriage return is only one of several commands that can be given in response to the ? prompt. Reply to the ? by typing a question mark. This will give you the **mail** menu shown in Table 7.1.

Table 7.1   mail Options

q	**q**uit—leave mail, dispose of letters as indicated.
x	e**x**it without changing mail—return all mail to p.o.
p	**p**rint—display current letter.
s[file]	**s**ave (default mbox)—in **mbox** if no file is named.
w[file]	**w**rite without header—same as save, but no postmark.
-	print previous—display last letter.
d	**d**elete—remove current letter from p.o.
+	next—display next letter.
m user	**m**ail to user—forward a copy of current letter to user.
! cmd	execute cmd—escape **mail** to execute a shell command.

In addition to the formal menu, there are three additional commands:

<CR>	display next message, when done, exit to shell.
?	display this menu.
^d	same as quit: **s**aved, **w**ritten, or undeleted messages are returned to the system post office.

The **mail** descriptions of menu items are a bit terse, so we have expanded them.

The **mail** commands can be remembered more easily if they are rearranged as in Table 7.2.

Table 7.2   mail Commands and Options

Display Commands:

- and +   Print the previous and last letters. These two commands are used to thumb forward and backward through your mail. **+** exits to the shell after the last letter.

<CR>   identical to **+**.

P   redisplays the *current* letter. This is useful when the current letter has been removed from the screen—by the menu, for example.

Your terminal's interrupt character is ignored by **mail**. This enables you to interrupt when a message is printing without exiting to the shell.

Departing the mail Program

x   unceremoniously abandons the mail program. Any deletions requested are ignored. The post office is restored to its condition before **mail** was invoked.

q and ^d   discard **d**eleted, **w**ritten, or **s**aved letters. Mail not explicitly disposed of is returned to the post office.

Disposition Commands

s [filename]   *appends* the current letter to **filename**. If a filename is not specified, the current letter is copied into a file called **mbox** in the *current* directory. If **filename** or **mbox** do no exist, they are created in the *current* directory. Letters saved with **s** are not returned to the post office.

w [filename]   strips the postmark from the current letter and appends it to **filename**. If **filename** is not specified, the current letter is copied into **mbox** in the *current* directory. If **filename** or **mbox** don't exist, they are created in the *current* directory. Letters saved with **w** are not returned to the post office.

d   deletes the current letter from the mail. Deleted letters are also not returned to the post office.

m [user]   forwards the current letter to **user**'s box in the system post office. The postmark is changed to indicate that the letter was forwarded and by whom. Forwarded letters are also not returned to the post office.

Escaping mail

The usual escape symbol ! allows you to exit the **mail** program and execute a shell command (including the **mail** command itself).

Setting up a Mail Directory

Before you begin to experiment with mail, it is a good idea to create a **Mail** subdirectory in your home directory. The default filename for the save command is **mbox**. Mail that cannot be delivered is left in **dead.letter**. If these files do not exist at the time, they are created in the current directory. If you use the **mail** program from different directories, you'll leave a trail of **mbox**'s and **dead.letter**'s. To avoid these complications, just return to your **Mail** directory every time you enter the **mail** program.

A sample map of **Mail** is shown below.

Fig. 7.1 Map of the Sample Mail Directory

```
                              chris
                                |
                                |
                              Mail
                                |
                                |
dead.letter    Incoming    archive  |    mbox      Outgoing
_____    _____
            |                                      |
       bob  joel  sandy  others              bob  joel  sandy  others
```

The next examples illustrate the menu commands and the **Mail** directory. Again, if you wish to, you can set up and execute the commands and text shown in the example. Before entering the **mail** program to perform any work, you can preview your incoming mail with the **mail -p** command. This option behaves exactly like **cat /usr/spool/mail/chris⟨CR⟩**, but is easier to type.

```
                             $chris
                              | |
                              | |
                              | |
                             Mail
                              | |
                              | |
                              | |
                              | |
   dead.letter    Incoming    archive    mbox    Outgoing
------------------------------------------------------------------
                    | |                              | |
                    | |                              | |
                    | |                              | |
                    | |                              | |
------------------------------------     ------------------------------
        bob  Joel  sandy  others             bob  Joel  sandy  others
```

```
$ cd Mail<CR>
$ pwd<CR>
/usr/chris/Mail<CR>
$ mail -p<CR>
From bobd Wed Oct 13 08:13:33 1982
Chris: Can you lend me five until payday?
Bobby

From JoelK Wed Oct 13 09:23:35 1982
Chris
One of your people is writing company policy about vehicles.
I want to review it before it's released.
Joel

From sabinp Wed Oct 13 11:06:44 1982
Chris,
This is to let you know that I am retiring from 2nd base.
The old bones Just can't make it any more.
Sabin "Bucky" Phelps
```

```
From davida Wed Oct 13 12:20:15 1982
Chris, I spoke to Allison Co. about our "lost" order p.o.
#22020. They will follow up by Friday, Oct 15.
da

From allenp Wed Oct 13 14:23:35 1982
Chris: Can you tell me the name of the general ledger data file?
Allen Parker (new guy in sales).
$ □
```

The following screen shows the mail and the commands used to handle the messages. The screen was narrowed to allow room for the list on the right which details the responses.

```
$ mail<CR>
From bobd Wed Oct 13 08:13:33 1982
Chris: Can you lend me five until
payday?
Bobby
```
1. Message deleted

```
? d<CR>
From joelk Wed Oct 13 09:23:35 1982
Chris
One of your people is writing company
policy about vehicles.
I want to review it before it's released.
Joel
```
2. Saved, put into a file called **Incoming/sandy**

```
? s Incoming/sandy<CR>
From sabinp Wed Oct 13 11:06:44 1982
Chris,
This is to let you know that I am
retiring from 2nd base.
The old bones just can't make it any
more.
Sabin "Bucky" Phelps
```
3. The message from sabinp was forwarded **to davida**

```
? m davida<CR>
From davida Wed Oct 13 12:20:15 1982
Chris, I spoke to Allison Co. about
our "lost" order p.o. #22020. They
will follow up by Friday, Oct 15.
da

? s<CR>
From allenp Wed Oct 13 14:23:35 1982
Chris: Can you tell me the name of
the general ledger data file?
Allen Parker (new guy in sales).

?!ls usr/chris/Accounts/Genledger<CR>
genledger.dat genledger.prog
!
?!write allenp<CR>
The data file's name is genledger.dat.<CR>
Chris<CR>
.<CR>
!
?<CR>
$ □
```

4. Saved in **mbox**
   for review

5. allenp's message
   required an *escape*
   (!) from **mail** to
   set the file's
   name. Then, it
   was necessary to
   escape again to
   write the reply

All mail messages have been read and specific action taken. Had any mail *not* been explicitly handled, it would have been put back in the post office automatically. Repeatedly sending letters back to the post office is one way to remind yourself to take care of a problem. Every time you log in, you'll see, "You have mail." Your mail will always contain the letters you repeatedly leave there. For example, the message from **davida** should not have been put in **mbox**. (Think of **mbox** as your "back burner"; you should clear it out perhaps once a week.) You need to put **davida**'s letter back in the system post office so that it will prod you every time you log in or read your mail. To get the **davida** message out of **mbox** and back into the post office is an easy matter. You may mail files by using the **-f** option to **mail**.

mail -f [filename]<CR>

Note that **filename** is optional. If **filename** is omitted, the default is **mbox**. When you find the **davida** letter in **mbox**, escape to the shell and forward it to yourself.

```
$ mail -f<CR>
 .
 .
 .
From davida Wed Oct 13 12:20:15 1982
Chris, I spoke to Allison Co. about our
"lost" order p.o. # 22020. They will
follow up by Friday, Oct. 15.
da

?!m chris<CR>
!
?
 .
 .
 .
$ 
```

The next time you check your mail, the **davida** letter will be there again, but with a slight change in the postmark to indicate that it has been forwarded.

```
 .
 .
 .
From davida Wed Oct 13 12:20:15 1982
From joec Wed Oct 13 14:02:18 forwarded
Chris, I spoke to Allison Co. about our
"lost" order p.o. # 22020. They will
follow up by Friday, Oct. 15.
da
 .
 .
 .
$ 
```

Remember the letter for Sandy that we stored in **Incoming/ sandy?** By using the forwarding technique described next, **sandye** will get a copy of the letter and you will keep the original in your **Mail** directory.

```
$ mail -f Incoming/sandy<CR>
From sabinp Mon Oct 1 15:10:12 1982
Chris
I want to thank you for referring me to
Sandy about company policy on vehicles.
She was very helpful.
Sabin
?<CR>

From joelk Wed Oct 13 09:23:35 1982
Chris
One of your people is writing company
policy about vehicles. I want to review
it before it's released.
Joel

?m sandye<CR>
 .
 .
 .
$ 
```

Unlike the basic command **mail, mail -f** does not delete letters that are written, saved, or mailed (forwarded) to other users.

Letters saved or written are *appended* to a target file. The existing contents of the file are not overwritten. If **Mail/Incoming/ sandy** contained a single letter, it could be sent using **mail sandye<Incoming/sandy<CR>**, but it would not contain the forwarded suffix on the postmark. The forwarded suffix is a very valuable piece of information. It leaves tracks. Because the recipient knows that you went to a little extra work, forwarded mail somehow is less likely to languish unattended in someone's **archive** file.

If the forwarded suffix is important, you would naturally want *your* copy to indicate that the mail was forwarded. There is no direct way to backdate the original of a forwarded letter. If, however, all mail that is *to be forwarded elsewhere* is sent to yourself before routing it to your **Mail** directory, then the "From chris . . . forwarded" stamp will identify mail that you have forwarded. This process requires a few extra steps, but it may be worth the extra keystrokes to produce proof that a letter of importance was sent to the correct person.

The command syntax shows that **mail** accepts more than one argument. If you want to retain a copy of all mail you send, create "carbon copies" by adding yourself to the command line.

```
$ mail davida chris<CR>
David:
<CR>
I've checked my mail archives for the last 6 months<CR>
and discovered that the Allison Co. "loses" about<CR>
20% of our orders. I want you to investigate an<CR>
alternative source for bearing stretchers.<CR>
<CR>
Chris<CR>
<CR>
cc:<CR>
.<CR>
$
```

The next time you check your mail, a copy of this letter will be there. Indicate to yourself that it is a carbon copy by attaching the cc: to the end of the letter. If you send the letter to several people, include them on the command line and, for reference only, put them on the cc: line.

```
$ mail davida sandye sabinp chris<CR>
David:<CR>
<CR>
I've checked my mail archives for the last 6 months<CR>
```

```
and discovered that the Allison Co. "loses" about<CR>
20% of our orders. I want you to investigate an<CR>
alternative source for bearing stretchers.<CR>
<CR>
Chris
<CR>
cc: sandye<CR>
    sabinp<CR>
.<CR>
$ 
```

Store the carbon copies in your home directory.

As you can see, it will not take long for your **Mail** directory to become huge. After a while your old letters just represent a waste of disk space. Periodically purge your mail files and discard letters that are not worth saving. Store older but important correspondence on floppy disk or tape.

If you try to send mail to someone who is not a user, or if you mistype a username, the results will be much as with a letter sent through the U.S. Post Office. It ends up in the dead letter office.

```
$ mail sandy<CR>
Sandy:<CR>
<CR>
I think your first draft is excellent. We'll go over<CR>
it in the morning first thing.<CR>
<CR>
Chris
.<CR>
mail: can't send to sandy
Mail saved in dead.letter
$ mail sandye <dead.letter<CR>
$ 
```

The undeliverable letter is stored in **dead.letter**. If **dead.letter** doesn't exist, it is created in your *current* directory. When **mail** sends a letter to **dead.letter**, the existing contents of **dead.letter** are overwritten. This saves you from having to retype it. As shown in the example above, use **mail** with a redirected input from **dead.letter**.

One final option to **mail** is worth mentioning, **-r**. Your letters are normally shown to you in last-in, first-out sequence. Reading the most recent letters first, however, may cause some problems. Suppose someone sends you several letters on the same subject. When you read your mail, you'll read references to letters you haven't yet read. The **-r** option causes your mail to be printed in reverse order—first in, first out.

The name, **mail** tends to restrict one's vision about potential uses of the program. In fact, it is an excellent, general-purpose medium through which almost any *file* may be transferred to any user on the system.

CALENDAR AND REMINDER SERVICE

cal

Before learning to use the UNIX reminder service, **calendar**, we should look at the on-line (almost) perpetual calendar, **cal**. This is not an important program, but it can be convenient to have on hand.

cal has just two possible arguments: month (optional) and year. The command syntax is

```
cal [(month)] (year)<CR>
```

The month must be a positive whole number in the range one to twelve. The year must be a positive whole number in the range one to 9999. The system's response to the command is to display a standard calendar page for the month and year requested by the arguments. For example, **cal 10 1982⟨CR⟩** and **cal 10 82⟨CR⟩** would produce

```
$ cal 10 1982<CR>
   October 1982
 S   M  Tu   W  Th   F   S
                      1   2
 3   4   5   6   7   8   9
10  11  12  13  14  15  16
17  18  19  20  21  22  23
24  25  26  27  28  29  30
31
```

```
$ cal 10 82<CR>
    October 82
 S   M  Tu   W  Th   F   S
           1   2   3   4   5
 6   7   8   9  10  11  12
13  14  15  16  17  18  19
20  21  22  23  24  25  26
27  28  29  30  31
$ 
```

The argument **10 1982** refers to a year in the twentieth century while the argument **10 82** refers to a year in the first century.

If you wish to see the calendar for an entire year, omit the month argument.

The UNIX calendar is historically accurate. It allows for leap years and the historical anomaly represented in the calendar for September, 1752:

```
$ cal 9 1752<CR>
   September 1752
 S   M  Tu   W  Th   F   S
           1   2  14  15  16
17  18  19  20  21  22  23
24  25  26  27  28  29  30
$ 
```

In 1752 Great Britain switched from the Julian to the Gregorian calendar. The English Calendar Act decreed that the day following September 2 would be September 14, in order to make up for inaccuracies in the Julian calendar.

calendar, the UNIX System's Reminder Service

The UNIX system's reminder service is implemented through a program/command called **calendar**. When executed, **calendar** sends dated messages to your terminal from an executable file named **calendar** in your home directory. (You must, of course, create a file in your home directory named **calendar**.) Fill the file with "reminder" messages to yourself. Every time you want to remind yourself to do something on a particular date, write the date, then write what you need to do. Add the item to the **calendar** file with **cat)>calendar⟨CR⟩**. You can also append to the file by using an editor.

Suppose that you had **cat**ted the following messages in the file.

```
$ cat>>calendar<CR>
10/14: check with Joel about Sandy's vehicle draft.<CR>
Oct. 14: bug maintenance about noisy vent.<CR>
15 Oct: big boss's birthday.<CR>
Dec 15: get Santa suit cleaned for Christmas.<CR>
Oct 15 pick up stereo at repair shop on the way home.<CR>
oct. 16 saturday: physical inventory begins<CR>
10/17 sunday: antique shopping<CR>
10/18 monday: correlate computer inventory with physical<CR>
inventory gathered over the weekend<CR>
^d
$
```

Note that a message line contains a date, usually in the first few columns. *Only* lines that contain a date are printed by the **calendar** command.

To execute the **calendar** command, you type **calendar⟨CR⟩**. The system responds by sending you all messages bearing two dates: the day and the next day, "today's and tomorrow's" reminders.

The example below is a partial **cat** of a **calendar** file:

```
.
.
.
Chris:

Subject: T.J. confirming lunch Monday, Oct 18 at usual place.

I would love to have lunch. I'll meet you
at 'Chez Jaques Dans le Boit' at noon.
```

```
TJ

From davida Wed Oct 13 12:20:15 1982
Chris, I spoke to Allison Co. about our "lost" order p.o. #
22020. They will follow up by Friday, Oct. 15.
da
10/14: check with Joel about Sandy's vehicle draft.
Oct. 14: bug maintenance about noisy vent.
15 Oct: big boss's birthday.
Dec 15: get Santa suit cleaned for Christmas.
Oct 15 pick up stereo at repair shop on the way home.
oct. 16 saturday: physical inventory begins.
10/17 sunday: antique shopping.
10/18 monday: correlate physical inventory with physical
inventory gathered over the weekend.
   .
   .
   .
$ ▯
```

On Wednesday, Oct 13 your reminder service would present the following messages:

```
$ calendar<CR>
From davida Wed Oct 13 12:20:15 1982
10/14: check with Joel about Sandy's vehicle draft.
Oct. 14: bug maintenance about noisy vent.
$ ▯
```

The first reminder is not much help. It's the postmark from **davida**'s letter. This letter was installed in the **calendar** file by using the **mail** command, **s calendar⟨CR⟩**. The postmark alone is probably worthless since it does not contain any mention of the subject matter of the letter. (Remember, only lines in the **calendar** file which contain today's or tomorrow's date will be printed.) When sending yourself reminders via mail, be sure to send ony mail which combines a summary of the topic *and* the date on the same line.

The **calendar** command on Thursday, Oct 14 would display the following messages:

```
$ calendar<CR>
22020. They will follow up by Friday, Oct. 15.
calendar<CR>
10/14: check with Joel about Sandy's vehicle draft.
Oct. 14: bug maintenance about noisy vent.
Oct 15 pick up stereo at repair shop on the way home.
$ []
```

The first entry is the last line in **davida**'s letter about the Allison matter. This line contains a reference to the date, but not to the subject matter, so it is not much help either.

Every entry in Thursday's **calendar** is printed except "big boss's birthday." This is omitted because dates must be entered with the month first, although **calendar** is very flexible with respect to the exact form of the date. All of the following are acceptable: 10/14, October 14, Oct. 14, and oct 14, but 15 Oct or 10-14 are not.

Although **calendar** normally displays only messages for two consecutive days, the weekend days, Saturday and Sunday, are treated specially. If you type **calendar⟨CR⟩** on Friday, October 15, you will get messages for Friday, Saturday, Sunday, and Monday.

```
$ calendar<CR>
Subject: TJ confirming lunch Monday, Oct 18 at usual place.
22020. They will follow up by Friday, Oct. 15.
Oct 15 pick up stereo at repair shop on the way home.
oct. 16 saturday: physical inventory begins.
10/17 sunday: antique shopping.
10/18 monday: correlate computer inventory with physical.
$ []
```

TJ's letter came from **mail**, but with **w calendar⟨CR⟩** to remove the postmark. This is the ideal format for a letter because it begins with a single line stating both the subject and the date. Notice also that the entry for Monday consists of two lines. The last line, since it does not contain a relevant date, was not printed.

Reminders in Your Mail

If you are so forgetful that you cannot remember to check your **calendar** every day, you can have the system post office put a copy of your **calendar** output in your mailbox every morning. If you install a command in your **.profile** file to append the output of the **calendar** command to your system mailbox, you can collect your reminder messages as you are reading your other mail. To add the **calendar** program to your **.profile** file, type

```
cat >> .profile<CR>
calendar >>/usr/spool/mail/{your login name}
^ d
```

COMMUNICATION BETWEEN UNIX SYSTEMS AND OTHER NETWORKS

This section and the next will be useful to all UNIX users since networks of computers are becoming pervasive in our society, government, and businesses.

The **mail**, **write**, and **calendar** programs provide for communication between users within a single UNIX system. Increasingly, UNIX systems are supporting programs that permit sending messages and transferring files between UNIX machines, and even executing commands on other machines. The implementation of "networking" capabilities between and among UNIX systems are becoming more common as UNIX systems reach the mass market. Networking allows a community of UNIX users to share resources and exchange news. Networks may be either semipublic and open for general use, or private, such as an interoffice network for a business.

The most important technical consideration for successful networking is the coordination of the sending and receiving machines. Since machines are often connected over telephone lines, the effectiveness of the connection depends on the presence of reliable software that is not particularly sensitive to electrical noise present in the telephone connection. Coordination is aided by having identical computer programs for networking installed on the participating systems, although some national computer networks are relatively tolerant of individual differences in machines connecting to them.

Large multisystem complexes such as the one at U.C. Berkeley generally have facilities for sending mail and transferring files among the individual machines of a local UNIX network. Remotely located machines (even when communication is by satellite!) can "call in" to such a network and use the same facilities. In addition to these specialized networks, there are national networks such as USENET, EDUNET™, and ARPANET, and nonrestrictive computer "bulletin board" networks such as The Source and MicroNet. We will briefly describe the Berkeley network and some national networks at the end of this section.

Connecting to Other UNIX Systems via uucp, uux, and cu

In addition to the **mail** program already discussed, the UNIX system has three programs for communication between UNIX systems, **uucp** (**u**nix-to-**u**nix **c**opy), **uux** (**u**nix-to-**u**nix execute) and **cu** (**c**all **u**nix).

These three UNIX programs have been widely distributed, but whether or not they perform as advertised depends upon the correct setting up of system files for each program. Setting up the system files is the responsibility of a system manager. If you are having a problem using these programs, you should consult your local UNIX expert. We will describe the programs from the user level, and give a few tips on how to tell whether your communication to another UNIX system is progressing successfully.

uucp

The **uucp** (**u**nix-to-**u**nix **c**opy) program copies files from one UNIX system (the source) to another (the destination). The program can create directories for the files on the destination machine if necessary. The simplest use of **uucp**, and one which is suitable for testing, is to copy files from one of your directories to another user's home directory on the same machine. In this case, **uucp** calls up the regular **cp** (**c**opy) program. Since access to files in other directories may be restricted (see the section on access permissions in Chapter 5), **uucp** is most often used to *send* files to a remote user's home directory, or to a **uucp** public directory, usually called **uucppublic** and located in **/usr/spool/uucppublic**.

You may request that you be notified by UNIX mail when the copy is complete, and some UNIX systems have an option by which the intended receiver may also be notified.

The syntax of the **uucp** command is

```
uucp {option} source ... destination ... <CR>
```

When specifying the source and destination pathnames, the first thing you need to find out from your system manager is the **system name** of your own and other UNIX systems. The system name is usually a one-word identifier, which may be the company name (such as **Business**) or department name (such as **sdso1**) associated with that particular machine.

A system name prefix may be used before the pathname for the work on your system and for the remote system, although the local system's name may not always be necessary. The system name is always followed by an exclamation point, as in **Business!**.

The user name may be appended to the system name, preceded by a tilde, as in **Business!~sabinp**, or a full pathname may be used. Partial pathnames for the source files are automatically preceded by the pathname of your current directory. Filenames for the destination that begin simply with a slash (/) are translated into the **uucp** public directory.

Copying of files to other systems is frequently done over the telephone line using a modem. In this case, you must obtain the telephone number of the other system, and when the connection has been made, the **uucp** command may be used.

The **uucp** program files are to be found in the **/usr/lib/uucp** directory. During **uucp** command execution, the program makes a copy of each named file on the source machine in the **/usr/spool/uucp** directory. Like other programs employing spooling, **uucp** puts these temporary file copies in a queue. The temporary files may be removed, administratively, when they are no longer needed.

The following **uucp** command would copy all new memos from chris's **Memos** directory into **sabinp**'s home directory on the **Business** system. Notice the exclamation point after the system name and the tilde before the destination user's name.

```
uucp /usr/chris/Memos/*.new Business!~sabinp/memo.copy<CR>
```

The ~**sabinp** in the destination user's address refers to **sabinp**'s home directory. The **uucp** program works better if a filename, such as **memo.copy**, is explicitly named as a file to receive the copies.

Table 7.3 presents several options to **uucp** which are available.

Table 7.3   uucp Options

`-d`	Make all necessary directories for the file copy.
`-c`	Use the source file when copying out rather than copying the file to the spool directory.
`-m`	Send mail to the requester when the copy is complete.
`-esys`	Send this job to system **sys** to execute (if the system **sys** allows **uux9t** to execute a **uucp** command).
`-9letter`	Put **letter** in as the grade in the name of the work file. (This can be used to change the order of work for a particular machine.)
`-nuser`	Notify **user** on the remote machine that a file has been sent.
`-r`	Queue the job but do not start **uucico** program.
`-xnum`	Print debugging information; **num** is a number between 1 and 9. Higher numbers give more debugging output.

The **-d** and **-m** options may not be used when using **uucp** for internal copying on one machine. Moreover, the **-m** option will only work when sending files or when receiving a single file. A **uucp** request to receive multiple files will not activate the **-m** option.

For testing, the **-x9** option may be used. This will give the fullest possible diagnostic information. If you use the **-r** debugging option, the work will be queued for transmission, but the **uucico** (a **u**nix-to-**u**nix **c**opy **i**n **c**opy **o**ut program activated by **uucp**) will not be summoned to do the actual work.

Another version of the sample command is given below, but this time only one file is requested to be copied. The **-x9** debugging option has been requested.

```
uucp /x9 /usr/chris/Memos/jc_seau95.new Business!~sabinp/memo.copy<CR>
```

The report of the command's progress might look something like this:

```
**START**
UID 456, User chris, PATH /usr/chris
file1 - /usr/chris/Memos/jc_seau95.new
all work here 0
xcp calledchild f1 ok f2 ok stat=0
$ ▯
```

If the command succeeds, the last part of the last line will report "stat = 0", which means status is 0; if it fails, some other status number or an error message may appear. Depending upon how your system files have been set up, a certain amount of time may need to elapse before a **uucp** command may be tried again. Check with your system manager to determine whether such a restriction exists on your system.

uulog

In case of repeated failure, the **uulog** command, which prints a summary log of **uucp** and uux transactions, might be of some help. **uulog** gathers information from **uucp** and **uux** log files, which are created in the **/usr/spool/uucp** directory and may be found there under names beginning with **LOG**. The **uucp** program creates a file named **LOGFILE** in **/usr/spool/ uucp/LOGFILE**, which you may examine directly, or you may use the **uulog** command to examine it. The syntax of the **uulog** command is

```
uulog -u {username} -s {systemname}<CR>
```

The **uulog** program must be used with one of two options, **-u** or **-s**.

Table 7.4   uulog Options

-u {user}   Causes **uulog** to print information about work done for the specified username.

-s {sys}   Causes **uulog** to print information about system requesting the work.

An example of **uulog** output is shown below.

```
$ uulog -u chris<CR>
root      unix (1/13-19:28) DONE (WORK HERE)
root      unix (1/13-19:29) DONE (WORK HERE)
root      unix (1/13-19:30) DONE (WORK HERE)
root      unix (1/13-19:30) DONE (WORK HERE)
sandye    unix (1/13-19:32) PERMISSION DENIED
sabin     unix (1/13-19:38) WRONG TIME TO CALL
root      unix (1/13-19:50) COPY (SUCCEEDED)
$
```

uux

The **uux** (unix-to-unix execute) program lets you work with files on different machines. As with **uucp**, access to the remote files may be restricted. In cases of restricted access, **uux** may be usable only with the **mail** command to send mail to remote users.

The syntax of the **uux** command is

uux {-}command-string<CR>

The option - will cause **uux** to take the command string from the standard input. Frequently, **uux** requires that you precede the command with an exclamation point. In other respects, **uux** follows the syntax of **uucp**, using an exclamation point after the local or remote system names, and a tilde in front of a user name to indicate that user's home directory.

The command

uux - "!mail Business!~sabinp < sdo1!~chris/greetings"<CR>

should mail the contents of a file named **greetings** in **chris**'s home directory to **sabinp** on the **Business** machine. It is a good idea to enclose the entire command string in double quotation marks in order not to confuse the shell.

cu

The **cu** (call **u**nix) program can connect two compatible UNIX systems interactively, and may also be used to transfer files. The telephone number of the remote system is an integral part of the **cu** command. There are also options for specifying the speed (baud rate) at which your modem is operating, and the file names of your automatic calling device and communications line device. Your system administrator can supply you with the necessary information.

The syntax of the **cu** command is

```
cu telno {options} <CR>
```

When you type in the telephone number, insert a hyphen at any point in the number where you might expect a new dial tone. For example, 9-4156626771 would be appropriate for a phone system in which "9" is dialed first to get an outside line. Otherwise, the digits are all run together, without spaces or blanks.

The options for the **cu** program are presented in Table 7.5.

Table 7.5   cu Options

-t	used to dial out to a terminal.
-s speed	indicates the transmission speed (110, 134, 150, 300, 1200); 300 baud is the default value.
-a acu	file name for automatic calling device if different from the default (/dev/cua0).
-l line	file name for communications line device if different from the default (/dev/cu10).

After the connection is made, you are directly connected to the remote system and may use any of its facilities or files for which you have permission. You must have an account and be able to log in on the remote system. During **cu** use, there are two processes running, *send* and *receive*. The *send* process transmits from your standard input to the destination's standard output, and the *receive* process reads data from the remote system and displays it on your standard output.

When you want to modify the interaction, type in a line beginning with a tilde, ~.

During the **send** process, the special instructions shown in Table 7.6 may be given.

Table 7.6 Special send Instructions

`~.`	terminate the conversation.
`~EOT`	terminate the conversation. EOT is `^d`.
`~<file`	send the contents of **file** to the remote system.
`~!`	call up the shell on your system.
`~!cmd`	run a command on your system.
`~$cmd`	run the command locally and send it out to the remote system.
`~%take from to`	copy filename 'from' on the remote system to filename 'to' on the local system.
`~%put from to`	copy filename 'from' on your local system to filename 'to' on the remote system.
`~~...`	send the line `` `~....` ``

The use of ~%**take** requires that the terminal on the remote system have tabs set with **stty tabs**, if tabs are to be copied without expansion. ~%**put**, on the other hand, requires that the settings for the erase and kill characters be identical on the two communicating terminals while cu is running. The **receive** process will respond to the following special instructions:

`~>file` or `~>>file` divert or append output to **file**
`~>` stop the diversion

Electronic Mail to Remote UNIX Systems

The UNIX **mail** programs allow electronic mail to be sent to remote UNIX systems. The **mail** programs will automatically call up the **uucp** programs at both the local and the remote computers in order to transmit the mail and have it delivered to the recipient's mailbox. However, the sender of the mail must provide the routing information. That is, a complete pathname for the user at the remote site must be given. Network members gain access to network facilities when they have an account on one or more of the UNIX systems in the network. All the systems in a network can be connected, usually through the phone lines, so that files may be sent from any user on any system to any other user on another system in the network.

Several major networks of UNIX systems exist. Both regional and national UNIX networks are often based at universities. The Berkeley Network at U.C. Berkeley has users from all over the country. This network supports programs for local network use as well as providing long-distance network capabilities through **mail** and **uucp**.

Electronic Bulletin Boards—usenet and netnews

The **usenet** or **netnews** programs work hand-in-hand with **mail** and **uucp** to provide electronic bulletin board facilities for members of news groups. Members can read items posted by others and post their own items. They can even send mail to the originator of an item (the news program will call up the **mail** program, which in turn calls **uucp**). News groups are formed around topic areas, and are named accordingly. Judging by the names of the groups, some of the 160 topics currently under discussion in the **usenet** include: cars (**net.auto**), poems (**net.poem**), ham radio (**net.ham-radio**), travel (**net.travel**), and trivia (**net.trivia**).

Through programs such as **usenet** and **mail** which are layered on top of **uucp**, UNIX networks can use whatever transmission lines are available, so long as sender and receiver both have access to a UNIX system that supports **uucp**. Long-distance error-free transmission of mail and other files is supported by carriers such as the ARPAnet, a network available to institutions under contract with the Defense Department. Commercial long-distance carriers such as Telenet™ are also available, although commercial, nonuniversity access to UNIX networks is still in its infancy.

THE UNIX SYSTEM COMMUNICATING ABOUT THE UNIX SYSTEM

The UNIX system is distributed with several volumes of printed documentation, including both command references and supplemental discussions of UNIX programs. In addition, UNIX has command reference pages available on-line, so that you can get information about a command without having to look it up in the printed documentation. The UNIX **learn** program also provides interactive instruction about basic UNIX tools for editing, file management, and programming.

**On-Line
Documentation—man**

The **man** (**man**ual) command will print out command reference pages on your terminal screen. The syntax of **man** is

`man {option} {section} {commandname}<CR>`

The command **man** {**date**}⟨**CR**⟩, for example, will print out the command manual reference page for the **date** command. UNIX manual pages are formatted by the **-man** formatting macros. Note that in the command name at the top of the screen page the command name *date* is spelled *date(1)*. The 1 means that this is a section-**1** reference page. Commands labeled **1** in the manual reference pages are commands generally available for use by most users. There are other reference sections, but the commands in these sections are used by UNIX programs and do not usually form part of ordinary command lines. However, when reading through a manual reference page you may come across references to commands in other sections that you may want to examine. For example, the **man(1)** entry on the **man** command itself has a reference to **man(7)** under the heading **SEE ALSO**. In order to read **man(7)**, the section number must be used as shown below.

`man 7 man<CR>`

The Section 7 **man** discussion concerns the **-man** macros that are used to print out or typeset the command reference pages.

In addition to the optional section number, **man** has several other options, **-t**, **-n**, and **-w**. See Table 7.7.

Table 7.7   man Options

-t	Phototypeset the section using **troff**.
-n	Print the section on the standard output using **nroff**.
-w	Print the path names of the manual sections, but do not print the sections themselves.

NOTE: The **troff** *program is used to prepare UNIX-created files for typesetting. The program is not discussed in this book.*

The option to find "pathnames of the manual sections" **(-w)** may seem like a strange feature. However, the on-line reference manual is based on the same files as those used to print or typeset the system documentation, and system managers can access command reference files in order to update them as needed. Manual reference files are found in the directory **/usr/man**, which contains nine subdirectories named **man[0-9]**. The full pathname of **man(7)** is actually **/usr/man/man7/man.7**. The **-w** option will report it as "man7/man.7".

All that the **man** command really does is format the requested files from **/usr/man** using the **-man** macros. You could get exactly the same effect with a command line such as

```
nroff -man /usr/man/man7/man.7<CR>
```

Browsing an unformatted manual reference file by **cat**ting it is not recommended, since the presence of the many and complicated **-man** macros make the file very difficult to read.

Printed Documentation

In addition to the on-line command reference pages, your UNIX system will have the same pages in printed form, plus a great deal of explanatory text. Many of the essays on various UNIX features are reprints or adaptations of UNIX documents originally written by programmers from Bell Labs. For this reason, some of the features documented in such papers may not apply to your particular UNIX system. If you find the documentation hard to use at first, be patient! The effort will pay off and you will find the manual an invaluable tool.

Although they are often written in fairly technical language, these papers contain a great deal of interesting information on the operation of UNIX system tools, especially the lists of options to frequently used commands. If there is a discrepancy between the command syntax specified in any form of print and the command syntax obtained on-line with the **man** command, it is usually best to follow **man**'s on-line syntax. The on-line documentation is likely to be the most up to date.

A list of the documents available from Bell Labs is included in the bibliography.

**Computer-Aided
Instruction: On-Line
Tutorials**

The learn Program

The UNIX **learn** program is designed to aid you in learning, at your own pace, the fundamentals of various UNIX system tools. The topics available include: **files**, which teaches about file handling and manipulation: **morefiles**, a continuation of **files**; **editor**, a course in using the **ed** text editor; **macros**, about the **-ms** macro package, and **C**, a course in the C programming language.

To use the **learn** program, you can either type the command **learn⟨CR⟩**, or **learn {subject}⟨CR⟩**, where {subject} is the name of the course you wish to take. On some UNIX systems, **learn** is a restricted user, and logging in as **learn** will put you directly into the program. (Restricted users are discussed in Chapter 10.)

Users who do not specify a subject to **learn** are assumed to be new users, and a list of available subjects is displayed, along with some additional information regarding the use of the **learn** program. If you press the carriage return, you will see a brief description of each course and the suggested order in which to learn them. Also displayed is one very important bit of information, namely, that you must type **bye⟨CR⟩** in order to exit the **learn** program. You should take care to exit **learn** as soon as you have finished with it to prevent confusion with the basic shell program. The **learn** program's prompt (**$**) is identical to the shell prompt. However, you cannot execute a shell command as long as you are in the **learn** program.

Once you have selected a subject, the **learn** program will ask you to answer questions and perform certain tasks pertaining to the subject area. The **learn** program will respond to an incorrect response by asking if you want to try again. A **yes** allows you to do so; a **no** moves you to the next lesson. If you choose to try again, the program returns you to the prompt. The problem which it presented is not repeated. It may have scrolled off the screen. If this is the case, and you don't remember the problem or the appropriate response, you must exit the program, being careful to note the specific lesson number, and reenter to return to that problem.

Many of your answers must be followed by **ready⟨CR⟩** before **learn** will compare your response to the correct answer. The program will tell you when a ready response is required. If you find yourself lost somewhere in **learn** and can't seem to set back to the **learn** prompt, you can escape by pressing your interrupt key. However, **bye⟨CR⟩** is still necessary to exit from the **learn** program to the UNIX shell.

8

FORMATTING TEXT FILES AND DOCUMENTS

Beautifying text for publication can be crucial to your organization's image. Learning the UNIX* system's document preparation and formatting programs will give you control over the appearance of documents.

Introduction to the nroff Formatting Program

Lesson 8.1: Centering, Line Skipping, Breaking, and Resuming of Fill
The **.ce**, **.sp**, **.br**, and **.nf** commands

Lesson 8.2: Resuming Fill and Adjustment; Indentation
The **.fi**, **.na**, **.ad**, **.ad b**, **.ad r**, **.ad c**, **.ti**, and **.in** commands

Lesson 8.3: Line Spacing, Setting Line Lengths, and Setting Page Lengths
The **.ls n**, **.ll n**, **.pl n**, **.de xx**, **.bp**, and **.wh nxx** commands; introduction to macros

Lesson 8.4: Setting the Left Margin; Underlining
The **.po n**, **.cu n**, and **.ul n** commands

* UNIX™ is a trademark of Bell Laboratories.

INTRODUCTION TO THE nroff FORMATTING PROGRAM

Entering text with an editing program such as **vi** is only half of the process of producing finished documents. Under most circumstances, a text file that is to be printed must be formatted. The line lengths must be made even (right justified), hyphens put in place, underlines, boldface, salutations, closings, and addresses all put in correct and conventional form. These details are handled by a separate *text formatting* program, which follows instructions that you put into the document along with the text. The text formatting program in the UNIX system is called **nroff**, pronounced "n-roff." The **nroff** (**n**ew **r**un**off**) program is a descendent of **roff**, an earlier text formatting or "runoff" program. This chapter and the next are devoted to learning the various steps and procedures for preparing a text for formatting by executing the **nroff** program. Other details and procedures involved in producing printed documents are also covered.

The **nroff** program can be used to produce formatted output on line printers, *printing terminal*s, and phototypesetting machines. When used with a *phototypesetter*, it is called **troff** (**t**ypeset **r**un**off**). In this book the **troff** program will not be discussed. The best printers for **nroff** are letter-quality printers capable of *microspacing*. Microspacing means that the printing head and platen (roller) are able to move up and down and back and forth in extremely small increments to produce subscripts, superscripts, overstrikes, and other special effects.

The principle upon which the **nroff** program works is very simple. During the creation and editing of a text file, the writer includes within the text file symbols that the **nroff** program interprets as commands. Each of these commands directs **nroff** to manipulate the text in some way or to perform a specific operation on its format or appearance. The program then copies the file into another location in memory. In the process of copying, it performs the various formatting operations in response to the included commands. The commands incorporated into the text by the writer are in two forms, dot requests and embedded requests.

The **nroff** program also has a set of commands built into it. They are called *primitive* **nroff** operations. They control the elementary movements of a printer or phototypesetter, and if no dot or embedded commands are given to **nroff** when it is run, it will perform the simplest of these primitive operations, *fill* and *adjust*, which simply form the text into neat blocks.

The filling and adjusting operations pack the text into a framework that can be defined with formatting requests. The **nroff** program *fills* text into lines 6 1/2 inches long and automatically hyphenates words at the ends of lines. Line length and hyphenation can be changed, as you will learn. The program also *adjusts* the text while filling it. Adjustment inserts additional space between words in order to create a perfectly straight, or justified, right margin. A margin that is not adjusted is called *ragged*. The **nroff** program allows either the left or the right margin to be made straight or ragged as required.

There are many primitive operations and it is common practice among most users to form sequences of **nroff** primitive requests that are organized, like a program or subroutine, to perform more complex operations. Such sequences of primitives are called *macros*. A macro can control paragraph spacing and indenting, for example, by means of a single dot request rather than two or three of them. Macros are treated in detail in Chapter 9.

A dot request is so called because it begins with a dot (period) in the first column of a blank line between lines of text. It is especially important to note that the command *must* be in the form and location stated, *or it will not be recognized by the* **nroff** *program as a command*. If you inadvertently place a dot in column one of your text (without an escape character preceding it), **nroff** will interpret it as a command and will ignore the rest of the line. An apostrophe in the first column, unless it too is "escaped," will also be interpreted as a **nroff** command signal and will cause the line to be omitted from the text in the printout.

An example of the form of the dot request is shown in Fig. 8.1. The **nroff** command to center a line of text is **.ce**. This command would be written into the file in the location shown.

Fig. 8.1   The Dot Command Form

```
This is a line of text.
This is another line of text.
.ce
This is the line to be centered.
This is the line after the line to be
centered.
```

It is important to note that in the printout, there will only be *four* lines of text, the third of which will be centered; **nroff** commands themselves are not counted.

Embedded commands may be located at any point in the text. An embedded command begins with a backslash followed by the symbols that define the command. For example, the **nroff** command to put a word in italics consists of placing the symbols \fI at the beginning of the italicized word and the symbols \fR at the end of the italicized word as shown in Fig. 8.2.

Fig. 8.2 The Embedded Command Form

```
This is any line of text. Suppose that a
word in this line of text, say, \fI this
\fR one is to be in italics, etc., etc.
```

Since the **nroff** program operates on text after it has been edited, you can change the text without worrying about formatting details. The formatting commands will handle all the work of producing the finished document. Having formatting commands separate from the text means that text and formatting can be changed independently. The lines of text can be edited without affecting the formatting command, and the format of the document may be changed without having to reedit the text. Changing a single formatting command can change the whole appearance of a document.

An edited text file with formatting commands is referred to as input text since it is the input to the **nroff** formatting program. After being formatted, the text is referred to as formatted output.

Fig. 8.3 shows some examples of filled and adjusted text using first, no dot or embedded commands (just executing **nroff** on the file) and second, using dot commands.

Fig. 8.3 Examples of Filled and Adjusted Text

Input Text: Edited text with
              lines of
              any length.

Filled and Adjusted:

nroff request: **none needed**

```
This text has been filled and adjusted,
so that the lines are filled out to the
default line length of 6 1/2 inches, and
the right margin is straight.
```

Adjusting Turned Off:

```
nroff request: .na (no adjust)
```

```
This text has been filled but not ad-
justed, so that the lines are filled out
to the default line length of approxi-
mately 6 1/2 inches, but the right mar-
gin is ragged.
```

Adjusting Only Right Margin:

```
nroff request: .ad r (adjust right)
```

```
You can also specify that the right mar-
    gin should be adjusted, and leave the
  left margin ragged. This text is an ex-
ample of this format, which is sometimes
called "Swiss style."
```

The right-adjusted paragraph could have been entered in the editing program as follows:

```
.ad r
You can
also
specify that the right margin
should be adjusted, and leave the left
margin ragged. . .
```

```
You can also specify that the right mar-
    gin should be adjusted, and leave the
  left margin ragged. This text is an ex-
ample of this format, which is sometimes
called "Swiss style."
```

The dot request **.ad r** will cause **nroff** to rearrange the haphazard, widely varying line lengths of the input text into one ragged left, "Swiss-style" block. There is seldom much relation between how an edited text file looks in raw form and how it will look when formatted. The dot requests and embedded requests installed in the input text determine a document's finished appearance.

For the lessons in this chapter, use the letter you created in the editing tutorials, **jobreply**. If you skipped that exercise, or have deleted the file, enter the following text *exactly* as shown below without skipping lines. Since you have done a great deal of work with this file in the sample exercises, your most recent copy will be slightly different. In this case, it may be simpler just to retype the file as shown.

```
$ vi jobreply
 1 Letter to Andrea Applicant
 2 from General Manufacturing Co.
 3 June 2, 1984
 4 Ms. Andrea Applicant
 5 1312 N. Main St.
 6 Oakland, CA 94612
 7 Dear Ms. Applicant:
 8 Thank you for expressing an interest
 9 in General Manufacturing Co.
10 After reviewing your resume,
11 we find that we do not
12 have any openings suitable to
13 your qualifications at the
14 present time.
15 However, we will keep your application
16 file in the event that something should
17 become available. Please address any
18 future correspondence to:
19 Hiram Hardhart
20 Director of Personnel
21 General Manufacturing Co.
22 1234 Jackson St.
23 San Francisco, CA 94112
24 Sincerely yours,
25 Mary Jones
```

```
26 Manager, General Manufacturing Co.
:wq<CR>
"jobreply" 26 lines, 656 characters
$ ▯
```

If you used the **nroff** program on the file now, the result would be a neat, rectangular (but unusable) block of text. The full syntax of the **nroff** command is

nroff filename<CR>

Unless you redirect the output to another file or send it to a printer, the formatted output will appear on your screen as usual. If the **jobreply** file were sent to **nroff** in its present form, the result would be as shown in the display below.

```
$ nroff jobreply
Letter to Andrea Applicant from General
Manufacturing Co. June 2, 1984 Andrea
Applicant 1312 N. Main St. Oakland, CA
94612 Dear Ms. Applicant: Thank you for
expressing an interest in General
Manufacturing Co. After reviewing your
resume, we find that we do not have any
openings suitable to your
qualifications at the present time.
However, we will keep your application
on file in the event that something
should become available. Please address
any future correspondence to: Hiram
Hardhart Director of Personnel General
Manufacturing Co. 1234 Jackson St. San
Francisco, CA 94112 Sincerely yours,
Mary Jones Manager, General
Manufacturing Co.
$ ▯
```

The text has been formatted, but all the lines have been run together. When a block of text is not interrupted, **nroff** rearranges it all into one block. Interruptions, called breaks, may be caused by dot requests, or by leaving blank space at the beginning of a line. When breaks occur, **nroff** ceases to process text into blocks. Skipping an entire line in the input text, causes both a break and a space; **nroff** resumes formatting after inserting one blank line for every line skipped in input.

The illustrations for this chapter differ from the screen examples elsewhere in the book because they do not always display command input and program output exactly as you would see them on your system. Instead, selected details of the text input and formatted output will be shown, with the relevant portions highlighted in boldface type.

LESSON 8.1:	Centering, Line Skipping, Breaking, and Resuming of Fill
NEW KNOWLEDGE:	The **.ce**, **.sp**, **.br**, and **.nf** commands
APPROXIMATE TIME:	30 minutes

The first step in preparing any document for formatting is to ensure that all the usual or "normal" divisions or breaks in your text, such as paragraphs, headings, salutations, etc., have been correctly separated or identified. Of course, as you gain experience with **nroff** you will not have to begin with so formal a step as writing out a plan for your document. You will simply enter the **nroff** commands as you go along, or make a mental note of what to do, then go back over the completed file and enter your **nroff** commands. For the present though, the formality helps. A written plan will allow you to see at a glance the most frequently used **nroff** commands for the type of document you are formatting. Although this practice letter has some unusual features (the title line and the author line), you will want the finished output to look like a business letter. A plan of action might be as follows:

- center title
- skip a line
- center author
- skip a line
- date
- skip a line
- inside address (not rearranged)
- skip a line
- salutation
- skip a line
- start body of text, with paragraph indent
- skip line and indent second paragraph

- center home address (not rearranged)
- skip lines
- left justify complimentary close
- skip lines
- signature

The **nroff** program has to be informed of all these steps in the plan of action at the specific points in the text where they are required. Note, however, that there are just four different operations to be performed on this text:

- centering lines of text
- skipping lines, that is, leaving blank lines
- indenting paragraph(s)
- left justifying a line

This summary suggests that since there are only four operations to be performed, only four different commands would be needed. Actually more are needed, but in this lesson, you will use just the following four dot commands:

1. **.ce{n}**
    This is the command to center **n** lines of text. If only a single line is to be centered, the number may be omitted.

2. **s.p{n}**
    This is the command to skip n lines (insert blank lines). Again, if only a single blank line is needed, the number may be omitted.

3. **.br**
    This command is called the "intentional break." It is used to cause **nroff** to stop formatting for a single line.

4. **.nf**
    This command is called "no fill." It is used when you want **nroff** to stop filling and adjusting.

As you can see, line skipping is an operation that occurs frequently in the plan (eight times). A simple way to skip lines is by leaving blank lines when you are entering the text. For example, inserting a blank line before "However, we will keep . . ." causes the unformatted file to appear as shown below.

```
 1 Letter to Andrea Applicant
 2 from General Manufacturing Co.
 3 June 2, 1984
 4 Ms. Andrea Applicant
 5 1312 N. Main St.
 6 Oakland, CA 94612
 7 Dear Ms. Applicant:
 8 Thank you for expressing an interest
 9 in General Manufacturing Co.
10 After reviewing your resume,
11 we find that we do not
12 have any openings suitable to
13 your qualifications at the
14 present time.
15                    <---blank line added
16 However, we will keep your application on
17 file in the event that something should
18 become available. Please address any
19 future correspondence to:
20 Hiram Hardhart
21 Director of Personnel
22 General Manufacturing Co.
23 1234 Jackson St.
24 San Francisco, CA 94112
25 Sincerely yours,
26 Mary Jones
27 Manager, General Manufacturing Co.
```

If you execute **nroff** on the file in its present form, when the program reaches the blank line in the input text, it will stop formatting and go on to the next unbroken block of text. The **nroff** output would apper as follows.

```
$ nroff jobreply
Letter to Andrea Applicant from General
Manufacturing Co. June 2, 1984 Andrea
Applicant 1312 N. Main St. Oakland, CA
94612 Dear Ms. Applicant: Thank you for
expressing an interest in General
Manufacturing Co. After reviewing your
resume, we find that we do not have any
openings suitable to your
qualifications at the present time.

However, we will keep your application
on file in the event that something
should become available. Please address
any future correspondence to: Hiram
Hardhart Directory of Personnel General
Manufacturing Co. 1234 Jackson St. San
Francisco, CA 94112 Sincerely yours,
Mary Jones Manager, General
Manufacturing Co.
$ 
```

Causing breaks by inserting blank lines is acceptable for printed output, but can cause problems in typesetting. It is much better to indicate line skips with the formatting request, **.sp** (**sp**ace). The **.sp** request will skip one line in a single-spaced document, two lines in a double-spaced document.

Dot requests such as **.sp** consist of a period or dot and two letters. A number after a dot request may modify the way a dot request works, indicating how many lines to skip, how many lines to center, etc. For example, **.sp 3** would cause **nroff** to skip three lines *in a single-spaced document*. Again, dot requests are placed between the lines of the text, each on a line by itself. (Dot requests are sometimes used with a single apostrophe in place of the dot, as you will see shortly.)

Remember, the **nroff** program treats every line that begins with either an apostrophe or a period as a formatting command or "control line." Although it is highly unlikely that a line of normal text would begin with a period or an apostrophe, if this should happen and the line cannot be re-written to change the position of the character, you will have to provide an *escape sequence*. Otherwise, as mentioned above, **nroff** will assume that the line is a command. What cannot be executed, will be ignored. The line will not be printed. The escape sequence is \&.

You are now ready to begin entering the formatting commands in the **jobreply** text. The same file is used in this chapter, and since it is not good practice to "nroff" an al-ready "nroffed" file, after making your **nroff** entries in the text you should make a copy of the file under a different name. Then, during each lesson you can **nroff** the copy file, look at it to observe the results, and delete it. At the start of the next lesson, bring up the original **jobreply** file, make the changes called for in the new lesson, and create yet an-other copy file to "nroff." Do the same for each lesson.

If your system is not already up and running, bring it up, log in, and gain access to the **vi** editor.

To center the first line, 'Letter to Andrea Applicant', in-sert the **nroff** dot command **.ce** (**ce**nter) on a line by itself before the line to be centered. Since only one line is to be centered, you do not have to include a number argument. The first line of your file is now **.ce**; the second line is 'Let-ter to Andrea Applicant'. As a general rule, **nroff** requests take effect on the line or lines that immediately follow them. After the formatting request is inserted, the file ap-pears as in the screen below.

```
1 .ce
2 Letter to Andrea Applicant
  ·
  ·
  ·
```

NOTE: *In this and subsequent screens in this chapter,* **nroff** *requests are shown in boldface for emphasis.*

To skip a line following the title, "Letter to Andrea Applicant," insert the dot request **.sp** (**sp**ace). Then center the line "from General Manufacturing Co." with another **.ce** on the next line. The file now looks like the display below.

```
1 .ce
2 Letter to Andrea Applicant
3 sp
4 .ce
5 from General Manufacturing Co.
```

So far, all the input lines and the dot requests are lined up against the left margin of the file. It is best to avoid blank space at the beginning of a line. If a blank space occurs at the beginning of a line, **nroff** might treat this as a break, depending upon where the space occurred in the filling process. If you should press the space bar or tab accidentally at the beginning of a line when you are entering text, the formatting program will break at that point and cause a potentially awkward gap in the output. Suppose, for example, that you have entered the following text:

Input lines are processed and run along, so merrily and smoothly,
    until space is skipped at the beginning of a line.

When **nroff**ed, the formatting breaks at the same point, producing an output such as that shown below.

```
Input lines are processed and run along, so merrily and smoothly,
   until space is skipped at the beginning of a line.
```

You can avoid accidental breaks by explicitly specifying the formatting you want at every point. For best results with **nroff**, use *every* line either for text or for a formatting request.

Intentional breaks are obtained with the **.br** request; **.br** is used when you want **nroff** to stop formatting and pick up again on the next line, without skipping any space. The following is an example of the break request used to keep two lines from being run together:

```
Ms. Mary Jones
.br
Manager, General Manufacturing Co.
```

After the date, which should be included between dot requests for skipping 2 lines (**.sp 2**), comes the inside address, "Ms. Andrea Applicant, 1312 N. Main St.," etc. An inside address usually demands lines which are not rearranged, not filled, and not adjusted. If you want the separate items of the address, name, street address, and city left on three lines, and do not want them adjusted to 79 columns, you will turn off the fill and adjust operations (which **nroff** does automatically) for the inside address. You must turn off default filling and adjusting *before* the beginning of the inside address. Filling and adjusting can be turned off with a single request **.nf** (**no** fill). If text is not filled, it is not adjusted either. Your file now appears as in the screen below.

```
 1 .ce
 2 Letter to Andrea Applicant
 3 .sp
 4 .ce
 5 from General Manufacturing Co.
 6 .sp 2
 7 June 2, 1984
 8 .sp 2
 9 .nf
10 Ms. Andrea Applicant
 .
 .
 .
```

The lines of the inside address will be left as you typed them in.

Write the **jobreply** file to disk with **:wq**. When you return to the shell prompt, perform the copying operation described earlier. Call the copy file **jobreply.1.** Type

```
cp jobreply jobreply.1<CR>.
```

If you wish to verify successful execution of the copy command, you can execute the **ls -l** command. The two files should have the same number of characters. Now **nroff** the file **jobreply.1**, but in order to be able to study the **nroff**ed file, redirect the output to a disk file of the same name but with a different extension. A common practice is to use **.n**. Thus, the nroffed version of **jobreply.1** is **jobreply.1n**.

Type **nroff jobreply.1 ⟩jobreply.1n⟨CR⟩**.

```
$ nroff jobreply.1>jobreply.1n<CR>
$ cat jobreply.1n
        Letter to Andrea Applicant
        from General Manufacturing Co.
June 2, 1984
Ms. Andrea Applicant
  .
  .
  .
```

LESSON 8.2:	Resuming Fill and Adjustment; Indentation
NEW KNOWLEDGE:	The **.fi**, **.na**, **.ad**, **.ad b**, **.ad r**, **.ad c**, **.ti**, **.in** commands
APPROXIMATE TIME:	30 minutes

In this lesson you will finish the formatting plan for the **jobreply** file created in Lesson 8.1. The new **nroff** commands discussed in this chapter are listed below.

1. **.fi**
   This command causes **nroff** to resume filling. However, it only has to be used if filling was turned off by the **.nf** command.

2. **.na**
   This command causes **nroff** to stop adjusting.

3. **.ad**
   This command causes **nroff** to resume adjusting in whatever style it had used previously. Like **.fi**, it only has to be used if adjustment was previously stopped by the **.na** command.

4. **.ad b**
   Adjust both margins.

5. **.ad r**
   Adjust right margin only.

6. **.ad c**
   Center line and don't adjust either margin.

7. **.ti n**
   This command causes the following line to be indented n ems.

8. **.in n**
   This command causes all subsequent lines to be indented n ems, until cancelled.

When you reach the body of the letter, **nroff** should at least fill out the lines, and perhaps adjust them as well. To resume filling and adjusting, use the **nroff** request **.fi** for "turn fill back on." Filling and adjusting will resume.

If at any time you should want to turn off the adjustment of filled text, use the command **.na** (**n**o **a**djust). Adjusting of both margins can be turned on again with **.ad b**(**ad**just**b**oth). There are several styles of adjusting—both margins, right margin only, or centered (ragged right and ragged left). A simple **.ad** command restores the *previous* style of adjusting, whatever that was. If you had changed adjusting styles from **.ad b** (the default) to **.ad r** (**ad**just right margin only) a **.ad** request would restore the previous style of adjusting, namely, **.ad b**. However, if you had progressed from **.ad r** to **.ad c**, a **.ad** request would restore **.ad r**. If in doubt, be specific about which style of adjusting you want turned on. There is no need to turn adjusting on unless you have turned it off.

Now bring up the original **jobreply** file. It should appear exactly as it did before copying it into **jobreply.1**. Since the fill and adjust operations were turned off in order to leave the address in standard form, you have to turn it back on at the beginning of the main body of the letter. Therefore, enter **.fi** at the point shown in the screen below.

```
 1  .ce
 2  Letter to Andrea Applicant
 3  .sp
 4  .ce
 5  from General Manufacturing Co.
 6  .sp 2
 7  June 2, 1984
 8  .sp 2
 9  .nf            <--------[turn fill off]
10  Ms. Andrea Applicant
11  1312 N. Main St.
12  Oakland, CA 94612
13  .sp 2
14  Dear Ms. Applicant:
15  .sp 2
16  .fi            <--------[resume fill]
17  Thank you for expressing...
```

After filling is turned back on with **.fi**, the text of the letter will again be filled and adjusted.

If **nroff** were run now, the formatted letter would appear as in the screen below.

```
            Letter to Andrea Applicant
         from General Manufacturing Co.

June 2, 1984

Ms. Andrea Applicant
1312 N. Main St.
Oakland, CA 94612

Dear Ms. Applicant:

Thank you for expressing an interest in
General Manufacturing Co. After
reviewing your resume, we find that we
do not have any openings suitable to
your qualifications at the present
time.

However, we will keep your application
on file in the event that something
should become available. Please address
any future correspondence to: Hiram
Hardhart Director of Personnel General
Manufacturing Co. 1234 Jackson St. San
Francisco, CA 94112 Sincerely yours,
Mary Jones, Manager, General
Manufacturing Co.
```

Although the format of the main text is now standard, many offices still prefer the indented first line of a paragraph. **nroff** program has dot requests for both permanent and temporary indentions. The **.ti** (temporary indent) command is used to indent only the *first* output line of paragraphs, normal left justification then resumes. The **nroff** program does not provide an automatic or "default" left margin for printed output. If you wish to have a left margin, you have to provide for it by the permanent indent.

Fig. 8.4 Page Offset Diagram

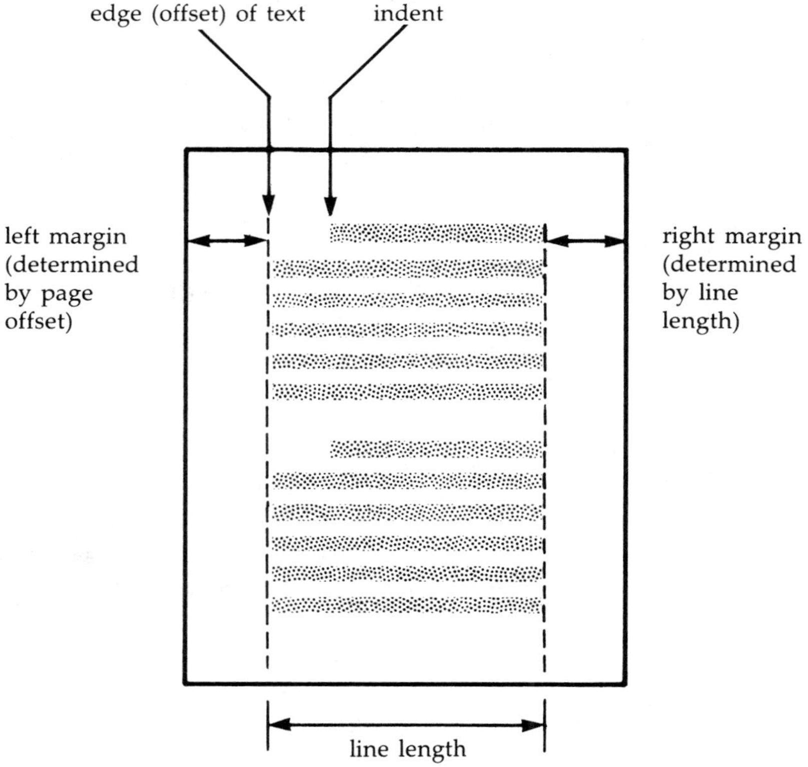

The placement of the text on the page is an indication of the page offset. In the current version of **nroff**, the output text is not offset from the extreme left of the paper. Indenting begins from the page offset.

The amount of indention (and other dimensions) may be specified in inches, centimeters, points, picas, machine units, ens, or ems. We will not cover points, picas, and machine units in detail in this book since they are primarily of concern to the **troff** program, which is covered in *The Advanced Business Guide to UNIX*. Although different on a typesetter, ems and ens are both the same size and width as all other characters on a printer or printing terminal.

NOTE: *The **en** measure is used by some of the macro package programs (see below). If you are not using that particular macro package and have not specified any other unit of horizontal measure, the **nroff** program assumes you are measuring in **ems**.*

Although for this exercise you are not going to use the permanent indentation command, it is necessary to discuss it and show its potential effects.

If you choose to indent *all* the output lines, use **.in**, the permanent **in**dent request. For example **.in 5 (in**dent **5** ems) indents *all subsequent lines* five character widths from the left, as in the following example.

```
         .
         .
         .
13 .sp 2
14 Dear Ms. Applicant:
15 .sp 2
16 .fi
17 .in 5
18 Thank you for expressing...
```

The printed **nroff** output would appear as shown below.

```
        Letter to Andrea Applicant
      from General Manufacturing Co.

June 2, 1984

Ms. Andrea Applicant
1312 N. Main St.
Oakland, CA 94612

Dear Ms. Applicant

          Thank you for expressing an
          interest in General
          Manufacturing Co. After
          reviewing your resume, we find
          that we do not have any openings
```

```
suitable to your qualifications
at the present time.

However, we will keep your
application on file in the event
that something should become
available. Please
                    .
                    .
                    .
```

You can cancel indention with the **.in 0** (**in**dent zero) command. This resets indenting to its original value (none). Another way to reset indenting is to subtract five ems with **.in − 5** (decrease indent by 5 ems).

The **.in 0** command is called an *absolute request* because it gives **nroff** an absolute value. The request **.in −5** is called a *relative request* because it instructs **nroff** to add or subtract a specific number from the existing value. In the example below, we illustrate both techniques. A permanent indention of five ems has been requested for the first paragraph; for the second paragraph, the original indention (none) was restored with **.in −5**.

```
             .
             .
             .
13 .sp 2
14 Dear Ms. Applicant:
15 .sp 2
16 .fi
17 .in 5
18 Thank you for expressing...
19 .in -5
20 However, we will keep...
```

The printed **nroff** output would appear as shown below.

```
        Letter to Andrea Applicant
      from General Manufacturing Co.

June 2, 1984

Ms. Andrea Applicant
1312 N. Main St.
Oakland, CA 94612

Dear Ms. Applicant

        Thank you for expressing an
        interest in General
        Manufacturing Co. After
        reviewing your resume, we find
        that we do not have any openings
        suitable to your qualifications
        at the present time.

However, we will keep your application
on file in the event that something
should become available. Please
    .
    .
    .
```

Because you do not have to remember the previous indention value, absolute requests are preferable to relative requests.

Continue correcting the **jobreply** letter by inserting the standard paragraph indention **.ti 5**, before the first paragraph and between the first and second paragraphs. Replace the line skipped in input with another **.sp** request. When you reach Hiram Hardhart's address, filling and adjusting should again be turned off with **.nf** (**no** fill). Filling and adjusting can remain off for the remainder of the letter.

You can center the five lines of Hiram Hardhart's address by supplying a number argument to the **.ce** command. The number refers to a number of lines in your *input*

text file, not including formatting request lines. Filling will
not occur on input lines that are centered.

After Hiram Hardhart's address, requests may be inserted to skip three lines before 'Sincerely yours' and four
lines before the signature, 'Mary Jones'.

The three **nroff** requests installed before Hiram Hardhart's address could have been inserted in any order. Usually, the order in which **nroff** requests are inserted is not
important so long as they do not conflict. Your file should
now appear as shown below.

```
16 .fi
17 .ti 5               ------>[indent paragraph]
18 Thank you for expressing an interest
19 in General Manufacturing Co.
20 After reviewing your resume,
21 we find that we do not
22 have any openings suitable to
23 your qualifications at the
24 present time.
25 .sp
26 .ti 5
27 However, we will keep your application on
28 file in the event that something should
29 become available. Please address any
30 future correspondence to:
31 .sp                 ------>[skip a line]
32 .ce 5       ------>[center the next 5 lines]
33 .nf         ------>[turn off fill & adjust]
34 Hiram Hardhart
35 Director of Personnel
36 General Manufacturing Co.
37 1234 Jackson St.
38 San Francisco, CA 94112
39 .sp 3
40 Sincerely yours,
41 .sp 4
42 Mary Jones
43 Manager, General Manufacturing Co.
```

You are now ready to **nroff** the **jobreply** file. Again, you should create a copy of the file on which to perform the actual **nroff**, and you should redirect the output file to a file in order to view it. This time, use **jobreply.2** for the copy filename. After creating the copy file, type

```
nroff jobreply.2>jobreply.2n<CR>
```

The formatted output of **jobreply.2** after all the formatting instructions have been inserted and **nroff** run can be viewed by bringing it up in **vi**.

Type **vi jobreply.2n⟨CR⟩**.

```
$vi jobreply.2n<CR>
             Letter to Andrea Applicant
           from General Manufacturing Co.

June 2, 1984

Ms. Andrea Applicant
1312 N. Main St.
Oakland, CA 94612

Dear Ms. Applicant:

         Thank you for expressing an
interest in General Manufacturing Co.
After reviewing your resume, we find
that we do not have any openings
suitable to your qualifications at the
present time.

         However, we will keep your
application on file in the event that
something should become available.
Please address any future
correspondence to:

             Hiram Hardhart
           Director of Personnel
```

```
            General Manufacturing Co.
                1234 Jackson St.
            San Francisco, CA 94112

Sincerely yours,

Mary Jones
Manager, General Manufacturing Co.
:wq<CR>
$ ▯
```

This concludes the formatting plan for **jobreply**. Now that you have had practice in inserting **nroff** primitive dot requests into an input text file and setting formatted output, the remaining lesson in this chapter will discuss some other features of the **nroff** program.

A summary of the **nroff** requests covered so far is shown below.

Fig. 8.5   Summary of nroff Requests Presented in Lessons 8.1 and 8.2

.**ce** **n**   center the following **n** input lines without adjusting.

.**sp** **n**   skip **n** lines.

.**nf**   turn off filling and adjusting.

.**fi**   resume fill and previous style of adjusting.

.**na**   turn off adjusting.

.**ad**   resume previous style of adjusting.

.**ad** **b**   adjust both margins.

.**ad** **r**   adjust right margin only.

.**ad** **c**   center lines and don't adjust either margin.

.**ti** **n**   temporary indent of **n** ems.

.**in** **n**   permanent indent of **n** ems.

LESSON 8.3:	Line Spacing, Setting Line Lengths, and Setting Page Lengths
NEW KNOWLEDGE:	The **.ls n**, **.ll n**, **.pl**, **.de xx**, **.bp**, and **.wh nxx** commands; introduction to macros
APPROXIMATE TIME:	20 minutes

In this lesson you will extend the preliminary formatting plan created in Lesson 8.1 to include setting new line spacing, line length, and page length specifications into a document. You will also write a short macro routine. A full discussion of macros is not part of this chapter; however, it will be helpful to observe the development of a simple macro at an elementary level. The new **nroff** commands discussed in this chapter are summarized below.

1. **.ls n**
   This command is used to set line spacing to **n**. For example, **.ls 2** sets double spacing.

2. **.ll -/ + n**
   This command is used to set the line length to some value **n** inches greater than or less than the default value of 6.5 inches.

3. **.pl -/ + n**
   This command is used to set the page length to some value in inches greater than or less than the default value of 11 inches. The maximum page length is approximately 136 inches.

4. **.de xx**
   This command is used to begin the definition of a macro. The name of the macro is usually two alphabetical characters.

5. **.bp -/ + n**
   This command is used to begin a page. The page begins with the line following the command. The new page number will be **n** greater than or less than the current page number.

6. **.wh nxx**

This command is used to specify *when* another command, **xx**, is to begin execution.

We will make use of the **jobreply** file again. If your system is not already up and running, bring it up, log in, and gain access to the **jobreply** file in **vi**.

Double-spaced printouts are usually made for rough drafts. They allow room to scribble corrections between lines. **.ls 2** means "line spacing 2." This request, placed at the beginning of the input text, doubles the space between lines, including doubling lines skipped. Single spacing can be restored throughout simply by *removing* the **.ls 2** request at the beginning of the file, or you can switch to single spacing at any time by inserting a **.ls 1** request. The **.ls** command will not be included in the **jobreply** file for this exercise; whenever it is included in a file it is placed before any text that it is to affect. If the entire document is to be double spaced, the **.ls 2** would be placed before the first line of text, as in the example below.

```
1 .ls 2
2 .ce
3 Letter to Andrea Applicant
```

Setting Line Length and Page Length

The **nroff** default page length is 11 inches and its default line length (text width) is 6 1/2 inches. Line length may be changed by specifying a new line length with the **.ll** (line length) request. A new line length of 5 1/2 inches would be obtained by inserting **.ll 5.5i** just before the line that is to have the "new" length. The **i** appended to the number argument signifies that the request is made in inches.

An alternative way to change the line length is to add **+** or **−** relative to the previous line length. The request

.ll − 1i

would subtract one inch from the default of 6.5 inches (= 5.5 inches). Usually, it is easier to state the desired line length and other page dimensions in absolute terms. This command will not be included in the **jobreply** file.

Setting Page Breaks and Top and Bottom Margins

The **nroff** program uses a default page length of 11 inches, which means that it will automatically start a new page every 11 inches and number the next page in sequence if page numbering is turned on. However, **nroff** does *not* automatically supply a top and bottom margin. Unless you take steps to stop text processing an inch or so before the end of the page, you will set *continuous output* without visible page breaks.

A trap must be set for the end of the page. When text fills to within one inch of the bottom margin, for example, **nroff** will begin a new page, skip a specified amount of space for the top margin on the next page, and then resume formatting text on the new page.

The process of "setting" a trap for paging is a useful one for our purposes, since it introduces the concept of macros. Without going into great detail, we will illustrate the basics of defining and using a page-break macro.

A macro is fully analogous to a program or routine. Just as a program contains a sequence of instructions and can be given a name that, in turn, can be used as a command, so a macro (in this context) is just a sequence of **nroff** commands that has a name. When the macro name appears in the text file, all of the **nroff** commands in the sequence are executed. Macros save typing and produce predictable results. Macros are covered in some detail in Chapter 9, but the topic of page-break traps gives a preliminary glimpse of this powerful formatting feature.

To set one-inch margins for the top and the bottom of every page, **nroff** must be instructed to stop processing text one inch before the bottom of the page, skip to the top of the next page, then space down one inch.

To define a macro called **xx** (any two alphabetical characters), you begin with the **.de xx** command. This command tells **nroff** that you are now going to write a sequence of **nroff** dot commands that make up the macro. The last command in the sequence is **..**, which informs **nroff** that the sequence is complete. In the present example, you will write a macro for establishing the bottom of page and top of page margins described above. Call the macro **.Np** for "New page."

.de Np	Begin **de**finition and name macro "Np" for "new-page".
/bp	Begin new page.
/sp 1i	Space down one inch.
..	End definition.

In order to avoid confusion with standard macro names, user-defined macros should be named in some special way, say, with any two-letter name using one uppercase and one lowercase letter. See the example above.

Insert this macro definition near the beginning of your input file. Note that we used /**bp** and /**sp** instead of .**bp** and .**sp**. Using the single apostrophe instead of the dot causes the new page to begin only after the last line on the previous page has been completely filled and adjusted. Thus, a page is formatted as completely as possible before a new page begins so that there is no abrupt break in text processing.

The page-break trap uses the apostrophe form of the .**bp** command, /**bp**. To *force* a page break in order to start a new section or chapter at a specific point in the text, use the dot form .**bp** (begin **p**age). The .**bp** request causes a new page to begin unconditionally.

```
Diagram:

     The request
     .bp
     breaks for a new page abruptly;
     between the words "request" and
     "breaks," in this case.

     The
     /bp
     request causes the last line of
```

```
              formatted output to be completed
              before the page break occurs:

              Output: The /bp request causes the last
              . . .
```

Now that the "new-page" macro has been defined, you have a formula for top margins for the second and following pages. To set a bottom margin, **nroff** should be instructed to start the new page when text has reached one inch of the default page end; that is, when text has filled 10 out of 11 inches of a page. **When** text is within one inch of the ordinary page bottom, the new page macro should take effect. This conditional new page is obtained by using the **.wh (wh**en) macro with your new macro name as follows **.wh -1i Np**. No dot is necessary in front of **Np**.

A version of **jobreply** using the new-page macro, **Np** is shown below. In order to demonstrate page breaks with this short letter, the page length has deliberately been changed to 4 inches with the page length command, **.pl 4i**, and the line length to 4 inches with **.ll 4i**. These values are used just for the purpose of illustration. They are not included in the final file. However, make all entries shown in the figure. You should **nroff** it and observe the results.

```
 1 .ll 4i              line length of 4 inches
 2 .de Np              begin New page macro
 3 /bp                 definition
 4 /sp 1i
 5 ..            <---- [end New page macro definition]
 6 .pl 4i        <---- [page length of 4 inches]
 7 .wh -1i Np    <---- [after every 3 inches, New page]
 8 .ce
 9 Letter to Andrea Applicant
10 .sp
11 .ce
12 From General Manufacturing Co.
13 .sp 2
14 June 2, 1984
```

```
15 .sp 2
16 .nf
17 Ms. Andrea Applicant
18 1312 N. Main St.
19 Oakland, CA 94612
20 .sp 2
21 Dear Ms. Applicant:
 .
 .
 .
```

If you have made all the entries shown above, you are ready to execute the **nroff** program on the file. First you should make a copy as in previous lessons. Type **cp jobreply jobreply.3**⟨**CR**⟩. Then **nroff** and redirect copy file by typing

nroff jobreply.3>jobreply.3n<CR>

When the **nroff** program has completed execution, gain access to **jobreply.3n** through **vi**. The **nroff**ed document should appear as below.

```
        Letter to Andrea Applicant
       from General Manufacturing Co.

June 2, 1984

Ms. Andrea Applicant
1312 N. Main St.
Oakland, CA 94612

Dear Ms. Applicant:

     Thank you for expressing an
interest in General Manufacturing Co.
-----[page break]--------------------
After reviewing your resume, we find
that we do not have any openings
```

suitable to your qualifications at the
present time.

However, we will keep your
application on file in the event that
something should become available.
Please address any future
correspondence to:

Hiram Hardhart
Director of Personnel

-----[page break]--------------------
General Manufacturing Co.
1234 Jackson St.
San Francisco, CA 94112

Sincerely yours,

Mary Jones
-----[page break]--------------------
Manager, General Manufacturing Co.

LESSON 8.4:   Setting the Left Margin; Underlining
NEW KNOWLEDGE: The **.po n**, **.cu n**, and **.ul n** commands
APPROXIMATE
TIME: 10 minutes

In this lesson you will put the final **nroff** commands into the **jobreply** file. The new **nroff** commands discussed in this lesson are summarized below.

1. **.po n**
    This command is used to put a margin between the left side of the page and the first column of text. The margin is **n** units (inches or ems) wide.

2. **.ul n**
    This command is used to underline **n** lines of text *one word at a time.*

3. **.cu n**
    This command is the same as the **.ul** command except that it causes *a continuous underline.*

Setting the Left Margin

Another feature of an attractive text is page offset, which is the amount by which the first column of text is set off from the left. By default, **nroff** left-justifies text by placing it at the extreme left of the paper. This gives you no left margin at all. Right margins are determined by the line length.

If your system is not up and running, bring it up, log in, and gain access to the **jobreply** file in **vi**.

Page offset can be modified by inserting the **.po** (**page offset**) request at the beginning of your file. Page offset may be specified in inches or ems. For an offset of 10 ems, insert the request **.po 10** at the beginning of the file. Although it may seem more natural to specify a page offset in inches, typeset output may be more pleasingly proportioned if page offset (and indenting) is specified in ems, the default unit of measure.

If you use ems, indention and offset will change proportionally even if characters change size, as in typesetting.

As a final touch, you can underline Mr. Hardhart's title with the **.ul** (**underline**) command. The **.ul** command can also take a number argument, again related to some number of lines in input text. The command **.ul 4** underlines four input lines. The **.ul** command underlines each word separately. For a continuous underline, use the command **.cu** (**c**ontinuous **u**nderline).

A picture of the entire text of **jobreply** with its complete set of **nroff** requests in place is shown below. In Lesson 8.3 you entered the page break commands in order to observe the action of the **Np** macro. You should now remove these commands. Check your final document against the diagram shown below. If your **jobreply** does not match the example line for line, make the necessary changes so that it will.

```
 1 .po 10
 2 .de Np
 3 /bp
 4 /sp 1i
 5 ..
 6 .wh -1i Np
 7 .ce
 8 Letter to Andrea Applicant
 9 .sp
10 .ce
11 From General Manufacturing Co.
12 .sp 2
13 June 2, 1984
14 .sp 2
15 .nf
16 Ms. Andrea Applicant
17 1312 N. Main St.
18 Oakland, CA 94612
19 .sp 2
20 Dear Ms. Applicant:
21 .sp 2
22 .fi
23 .ti 5
24 Thank you for expressing an interest
25 in General Manufacturing Co.
```

```
26 After reviewing your resume,
27 we find that we do not
28 have any openings suitable to
29 your qualifications at the
30 present time.
31 .sp
32 .ti 5
33 However, we will keep your application on
34 file in the event that something should
35 become available. Please address any
36 future correspondence to:
37 .sp
38 .ce 5
39 .nf
40 Hiram Hardhart
41 .ul
42 Director of Personnel
43 General Manufacturing Co.
44 1234 Jackson St.
45 San Francisco, CA 94112
46 .sp 3
47 Sincerely yours,
48 .sp 4
49 Mary Jones
50 Manager, General Manufacturing Co.
```

Again, make a copy, **jobreply.4.** Then type

```
nroff jobreply.4>jobreply.4n<CR>
```

You may look at the finished copy, **jobreply.4n** with **vi**.
You could also send it to your printer with

```
nroff jobreply.4n | lpr<CR>
```

The final copy should be as follows:

```
              Letter to Andrea Applicant
            from General Manufacturing Co.

June 2, 1984

Ms. Andrea Applicant
1312 N. Main St.
Oakland, CA 94612

Dear Ms. Applicant:

     Thank you for expressing an
interest in General Manufacturing Co.
After reviewing your resume, we find
that we do not have any openings
suitable to your qualifications at the
present time.

     However, we will keep your
application on file in the event that
something should become available.
Please address any future
correspondence to:

              Hiram Hardhart
            Director of Personnel
          General Manufacturing Co.
             1234 Jackson St.
           San Francisco, CA 94112

Sincerely yours,

Mary Jones
Manager, General Manufacturing Co.
```

9

ADVANCED TEXT FORMATTING WITH nroff

Command Reference for the -ms Macro Package
Paragraphs
Section Headings
Changes in Indentation
Emphasis and Size Changes
Boxes Around Text
Title Page and Cover Sheets
Dates
Multicolumn Formats
Footnotes
Keeps
Displays
Tables and Equations

Working with the -ms Macro Package
Title and Author
Displays
Keeps
Paragraphs

Fancy Formatting with the -ms Package
Indented Paragraphs
Quoted Paragraphs
Section Headings
Numbered Headings

Resetting -ms Default Values
Number Registers
String Registers

This chapter discusses **nroff** *macros*, which were touched upon briefly in the last chapter. Macros save you time. A single macro can be used each time a long sequence of **nroff** commands appear in the document. This is especially useful when there is a problem in the formatted document and it is necessary to read through the list of formatting commands checking for an error.

An **nroff** macro is a sequence of **nroff** commands that carries out some specific function. Both the term and the concept of macro came from the mainframe computer world. The term *macro* began life as *macroinstruction*, a term used to define a type of instruction that is at a "higher level" than the machine language instructions of the microprocessor, called *microinstructions*. A macroinstruction is "executed" by executing a specific set of microinstructions.

Why bother learning both macros and basic **nroff** commands? Why not just concentrate on macros? Many operations require a single motion or manipulation of text, and in the **nroff** program all requests affect the text format one motion at a time. Whether it is a command to the printer or to the formatting program, every motion or operation requires a separate request. Even though it is frequently possible to use many macros, almost every document will require some individual **nroff** commands.

Macros are very powerful, even an apparently simple operation such as setting a margin or indenting the first line of a paragraph can easily require four or five or more separate **nroff** dot requests. Since many of these operations can recur frequently in a document, the same set or sequence of instructions has to be repeated for each occurrence. The result is that the document soon has as many or more lines of **nroff** commands as it has lines of text. Replacing each of these sequences with a single *macro* dot request can reduce the number of commands on a page to a fourth or fifth of the number without macros.

It is possible to design your own macros as you did in the last chapter with the **Np** macro, and we will discuss creating "customized" macros at the end of this chapter. However, the UNIX* system has provided several sets of macro packages such as **-ms**, **-me**, **-mm**, and **-man**. Each of these packages is designed for a particular type of document or application.

* UNIX™ is a trademark of Bell Laboratories.

When used as a command line option (for example, **nroff -ms filename⟨CR⟩**) a macro package name causes **nroff** to read a file containing macro definitions and to use these definitions in formatting text files.

In this chapter we will demonstrate the use of the **-ms** macro package by using the **jobreply** file again and wherever possible replacing **nroff** requests with **-ms** macro commands. No lessons are provided in this chapter since the operations performed are virtually the same as those performed in the preceding chapter. It would be helpful and provide useful practice if you carry out the operations described on your system. For this reason, we have organized the actions taken along the same lines as for interactive lessons, but without the usual heading information and screen displays.

We have chosen the **-ms** package because it is the most widely used and because it is especially suitable for the business office environment.

NOTE: *Originally, the **-ms** macro package was developed at Bell Laboratories for the preparation of released papers and other documents. It contains macros for titles, authors, abstracts, and bottom-of-page dates. Some of the **-ms** macros pertain particularly to Bell Labs documents and are of little interest to people outside Bell Labs.*

Both **nroff** requests and **-ms** commands can be used in the same file as long as they are not contradictory. In cases of contradiction, the **-ms** macros usually contain internal commands to reset **-ms** default values. An **-ms** paragraph request would cancel an **nroff** indentation request such as **.in 20**, which would otherwise take effect until changed by another **nroff** request. However, if you're still in the rough draft stage, **.ls 2** may be placed at the beginning of a file, and you can then use the **-ms** macros. The printed output will be double spaced.

In addition to providing handy formatting commands, the **-ms** package sets up pages automatically. It assumes a default page length of 11 inches and a default line length of 6 inches. It provides no page offset, but it sets top and bottom page margins, and numbers and dates each output page. This default page setup may be changed in order to customize your document.

COMMAND REFERENCE FOR THE -ms MACRO PACKAGE

The following pages are from **Document Formatting on UNIX®** **Using the -ms Macros**; Joel Kies, University of California, Berkeley, California 94720, a reference manual for the **-ms** macro package; the intention here is to provide a concise but complete description of the operation of each command. Certain typographic conventions are used in presenting command syntax. Command names appear at the left margin, followed where appropriate by the arguments available with the command, separated from the command and from each other by a space. An argument which contains one or more spaces within it must be surrounded by double-quote marks except where noted. **Boldface** indicates what must be typed literally as shown in the syntax statement; thus each command name appears in boldface. A word in italics represents an argument which you supply.

The contents of the argument are sometimes entirely your choice (for example the *label* after the command **.IP** can be anything). Sometimes the argument is restricted to a predetermined set of choices (for example, the *level-number* after the **.NH** command must be an integer from 0 to 5). Details about what can be supplied as an argument are contained in the description opposite each command.

An argument enclosed in square brackets is optional—the command has meaning either with or without that argument. Conversely, an argument not enclosed in square brackets must be supplied whenever the command is used. An argument enclosed in square brackets and printed in boldface is optional, but, if used, must be typed literally as shown.

Paragraphs

.PP

Begins a standard paragraph, separated vertically from preceding text by the value of number register PD. First line is indented by the value of register Pl, and following lines begin at the current main indent level.

.LP

Begins a left-block paragraph, set off vertically by the value of register PD. No first-line indentation. All lines begin at the main indent level.

.IP [*label*] [*indent*]

Begins an indented paragraph, set off vertically by the value of register PD. The entire block is left-adjusted and then, by default, indented the value of register PI to the right of the main indent level. If one argument is given, it is a label to be placed at the main indent level opposite the first line of the paragraph. If two arguments are given, the second must be numeric and is an amount of indentation (in ens unless indicated otherwise) to supersede the default indentation for the paragraph. Nonstandard indentation must be specified if the label is too wide to fit within the default indentation. This nonstandard indent persists in subsequent .IP's in a series, disappearing when the series is ended by a return to some other format such as a section heading or a .PP or .LP paragraph.

For nonstandard indentation without any label, the first argument should be simply a pair of double-quote marks with nothing between them.

.QP

Begins a block-quote paragraph, preceded by vertical space as for other paragraphs. Every line is indented from the main indent level by the value of register QI. The right margin is moved in toward the left by an equal amount (the line length is shortened). Successive .QP's maintain the same indentation; it does not accumulate.

Section Headings

.SH

Begins a heading that is left-adjusted at the main indentation level and separated by one vertical space from whatever preceded it. In **nroff** the heading is underlined; in **troff** it is set in boldface.

.NH [*level-number*]

Produces a heading similar to .SH except that it is automatically given a consecutive number. The optional level number, from 1 to 5, causes the macro to generate the next consecutive section number of that level (e.g., 1.2.5 is a third-level section number). A level-number 0 (zero) may be used as the argument; this cancels the numbering sequence in effect and generates a heading numbered 1.

Note: When either .SH or .NH is used, all text up to the next paragraph command or section heading command is considered part of the heading.

Changes in Indentation

.RS

Moves the indentation to the right by a value based on register PI. More than one .RS may be used, producing additional indentation.

.RE

Moves the indentation to the left by the same amount as the corresponding .RS moved it to the right. To restore the original indent, each .RS must be balanced by a corresponding .RE.

Notes: It is not possible to move the indent level to the left of the page offset. The value of register PI should not be changed within a series of .RS and .RE commands at any point except after the indentation has been returned to its default starting position.

Emphasis and Size Changes

.I [*word*] [*punctuation*]

Without an argument, this macro causes a switch to font number 2 (italic) in **troff** or underlined typing in **nroff**. If one argument is given, it is one word to be italicized, and the effect of the command is limited to that word. A second argument may consist of trailing punctuation to be printed directly after the word, in the typeface (usually roman) in use for the text prior to the italicized word.

.B [*word*] [*punctuation*]

Produces text in font number 3 (boldface) in **troff**, underlining in **nroff**. Usage is analogous to that of .I.

.R

Switches back to font number 1 (roman) in **troff**, non-underlined typing in **nroff**.

.UL *word*

Causes the word supplied as the argument to be underlined. This is the only -ms command to produce an underlined word on the typesetter. It works for one word at a time, or for "a few words" enclosed in double quotation marks.

.LG

Increases the type size by two points in **troff**. May be repeated for added effect. Ignored by **nroff**.

.SM

Reduces the point size by two points. May be repeated for added effect. Ignored by **nroff**.

.NL

Resets the point size to the normal setting, i.e., the value of the PS register. Ignored by **nroff**.

Note: If changing the type size by two points results in a non-existent type size on the typesetter, the next larger valid size is chosen. Valid point sizes are 6, 7, 8, 9, 10, 11, 12, 14, 16, 18, 20, 22, 24, 28, and 36.

Boxes Around Text

.BX *word*

Draws a box around {word}.

.B1

Begins a longer passage of text to be enclosed in a box.

.B2

Ends passage of text and draws box.

**Title Page and Cover
Sheets**

.RP

Causes a cover sheet to be generated containing any of the following information, if included with the appropriate macro after .RP: title, authors, authors' institutions, and abstract. The current date is printed on the cover sheet unless suppressed with the command .ND.

.TL

When used for cover sheet and/or title page (prior to regular text), .TL causes the title text to be filled, without hyphenation, on a 5-inch line length. The resulting lines are individually centered when printed. To break lines of title text differently, use the command .br. **Troff** sets the title in 12 point boldface.

.AU

Centers the author's name, included on the following line of the input file. More than one name can be included, in which case they will be printed on separate lines if entered on separate input lines. **troff** sets names in 10 point italic.

.AI

Centers lines of information about the author's institution. .AU and .AI commands can be repeated, if desired, for multiple authors from different institutions.

.AB [*no*]

Begins the abstract. When printed, this is preceded by a centered heading of the word ABSTRACT unless suppressed by use of the paragraph or section heading commands before the regular text begins. If .RP is used, all of the title/author/abstract material is put on the cover sheet and all except the abstract is repeated at the top of page one. Otherwise, all of the material is placed on page one prior to the beginning of regular text.

Dates

.ND [*date*]

When used without an argument, this macro suppresses printing of the date on the document. (By default, if .ND is omitted, -ms causes **nroff** to print the current date at the bottom center of every page, and on the cover sheet in .RP format; with **troff**, the date is printed only on the cover sheet). If a date is given as an argument to this macro, it appears on the cover sheet in .RP format but nowhere else.

.DA [*date*]

Without an argument, .DA causes the current date to be printed at the bottom of every page of output in **troff**, as well as on the cover sheet. (This is the default condition in **nroff**.) With a date as an argument, the command causes the specified date (rather than the current date) to be printed at the bottom of every page, and on the cover sheet, for both **nroff** and **troff**.

Note: When typing the date as an argument to either of these macros, you can include spaces without having to enclose the whole thing in double-quote marks as you ordinarily would in an argument to a command.

Multicolumn Formats

.2C

Switches to 2-column format. Column widths are 7/15 of the current value of the LL number register, gutter width is 1/15 LL.

.1C

Switches to single-column format (the default format). A switch from two or more columns to single-column causes a page break before output is resumed.

.MC [*column-width*]

Switches to multi-column format. The number of columns is computed automatically; it will be the largest number of the specified width that can fit without the regular line length (the value of register LL). The column-width argument must be numeric (it may be an integer or contain a decimal fraction), and is understood to be a number of ens unless a different unit is indicated. If no column-width is specified, .MC means the same as .2C. Any change in the number of columns, except from one to a larger number, causes a page break first.

Footnotes

.FS

Begins text of footnote. This macro, and the accompanying footnote text, should be placed in the input file immediately after the reference to the footnote. Footnote text is automatically saved and printed at the bottom of the current page, separated from the main text by a horizontal rule. If not enough space remains on the page for all of the footnote, it continues at the bottom of the following page. The line length of footnotes defaults to 11/12 of the normal line length (in multi-column output, this means 11/12 of the column width). In **troff** output, footnotes are set in 8 point type.

.FE

Marks the end of footnote text.

Keeps

.KS

Begins a standard keep. Text on following input lines will be kept together on one page if possible. If not enough space remains on the current page, a new page is begun at this point.

.KF

Begins a floating keep. If not enough space remains on the current page for the keep, the current page will be completed with the input text that follows the end of the keep; the kept material then begins the next page.

.KE

Marks the end of either standard or floating keep.

Note: In formats of two or more columns, the effect is to try to keep the material together in one column; if there isn't room in the current column, the material starts in the next.

Displays

.DS [*format*] [*indent*]

Begins a display, i.e., unfilled text. Set off by vertical space before and after the display (1v before and after in **nroff**, 0.5v in **troff**). A format indicator may be given as an argument. The possible format indicators are:

L   left-adjusted
I   indented 0.5i (**troff**) or 8n (**nroff**)
C   each line is centered individually
B   left-adjusted lines are centered as a group

.DS with no format indicator means the same as .DS 1. Either of these forms may also take a numeric argument representing a nonstandard indentation in ens. Any of the displays described above automatically invokes a keep.

.LD

Left-adjusted display without invoking keep.

.ID [*indent*]

Indented display without keep. Default indentation is the same as for .DS I. Other indentation may be specified as an argument.

.CD

Lines individually centered, without keep.

.BD

Left-adjusted and then centered, without keep.

.DE

Marks the end of any display.

Tables and Equations

.TS [H]

Signals the beginning of material to be preprocessed by *tbl*. When used with -ms, it also has the effect of supplying half of a vertical space separation between the table and any preceding text. When used with the argument "H," table data up to the command ".TH" is understood as a running head for the table and recurs on following pages of a multi-page table. (This effect is obtainable only when -ms is used.)

.TH

Signals the end of the running table heading.

.TE

Signals the end of material to be preprocessed by tbl, and, with -ms supplies half of a vertical space at the end of the table.

.EQ [*format*] [*number*]

Marks the beginning of material to be preprocessed by *eqn* or *neqn*. When used with -ms, generates vertical separation before the equation is output and, by default, centers the equation in the output line. Placement of the equation can be controlled by use of a format indicator as an argument; use **.EQ L** for left-adjusted, **.EQ I** for indented, and **.EQ C** for centered. An equation number, whatever you choose, may also be given as an argument to **.EQ**. If both arguments are used, the format indicator should be placed first.

.EN

Signals the end of material to be preprocessed by **eqn** or **neqn**.

WORKING WITH THE -ms MACRO PACKAGE

To see how a macro package can make formatting simpler, let's start by editing **jobreply**, replacing most of the **nroff** requests with **-ms** macro commands.

Title and Author

Before the first line 'Letter to Andrea Applicant', replace the .ce with the dot command **.TL** (TitLe). This will center and *underline* the title of the document, and provide a blank line after it. Next, add the command **.AU** (AUthor) before the line 'from General Manufacturing Co.' This will center the line 'from General Manufacturing Co.', underline it, and insert another blank line.

Since the **.TL** and the **.AU** macros automatically skip space between lines, you can now remove the **nroff** **.ce** and **.sp** requests to center text and skip lines. Also remove the "page-break trap" macro and the **wh** command. They are no longer needed.

Now the beginning of the **jobreply** file has been reduced from the eleven lines using just **nroff** requests to the four lines shown in the sample display below.

```
1 .TL
2 Letter to Andrea Applicant
3 .AU
4 from General Manufacturing Co.
```

After 'from General Manufacturing Co.' use a **.LP** (Left Paragraph) macro. The **.LP** macro skips a line and left justifies the next line or lines. The date, 'June 2, 1984' will now be left justified. Again, remove superfluous **.sp** (**sp**ace) requests.

Displays

The inside address, as before, should not be adjusted or filled. You may turn off filling and adjusting in **-ms** with the display commands.

Whenever you begin a display, filling and adjusting are automatically turned off and lines are not rearranged. Use **.DS**, (Display Start) and **.DE**, (Display End).

To left justify a display, which is otherwise automatically indented, you must use **.DS L** (Display Start Left). Until you turn the display off, with a **.DE** (Display End), the subsequent lines will be left-adjusted, not filled, not right-adjusted, and not rearranged. **.DS L** would be used before 'Ms. Andrea Applicant' and **.DE** after 'Oakland, CA.' The salutation, 'Dear Ms. Applicant,' can be set off with another **.LP** (Left Paragraph).

```
 1 .TL  ------------------- [center & underline]
 2 Letter to Andrea Applicant
 3 .AU  ------------------- [center & underline]
 4 from General Manufacturing Co.
 5 .LP  ------------ [skip space & left justify]
 6 June 2, 1984
 7 .DS L  ---[skip space, left justify, & no fill]
 8 Ms. Andrea Applicant
 9 1312 N. Main St.
10 Oakland, CA 94612
11 .DE  ------------------------ [end display]
12 .LP  ------------ [skip space & left justify]
13 Dear Ms. Applicant:
```

Other styles of displays are also possible.

.DS C centers each line of the display.

.DS B left-justifies a centered display.

.DS I same as **.DS;** indents each line about 8 ens.

Keeps

A display is automatically placed inside a *keep*, which means that the lines of the display will be kept together on one page. If the lines of the display won't all fit on the current page, the **-ms** program will break and start a new page for the display. By default, the **-ms** program assumes you are working with 8 1/2 × 11 paper, and will give you a page with a text length of 9 inches and a top and bottom margin of one inch. As soon as the text grows to within one inch of the bottom margin, **-ms** will automatically break for a new page. The **-ms keep** recognizes where pages will break and prevents text that should be kept together from being divided across page boundaries.

To keep sets of lines together that need to be filled and adjusted, you may use **.KS** (Keep Start) and **.KE** (Keep End).

```
.KS
These lines will be kept together on one
page, and the text between the keep
```

```
start and keep end will be filled and
adjusted. If the lines won't fit on the
current page, a new page will be started
before the first line after .KS.
.KE
```

Floating keeps which are started with **.KF** and ended with **.KE**, let you keep lines together without arbitrarily starting a new page. Instead, the text after the end of the keep (**.KE**) fills out the remainder of the current page, and the kept lines begin on the next page.

```
.KF
These lines will "float" through the
text until space on a page exists
to print them out as a unit.
.KE
```

Kept text is diverted until the diversion is stopped. If you don't end a display or keep with **.DE** or **.KE**, the program will attempt to divert *all* the text from the beginning of the display, or keep until the end of the document, and you will get an error message: "Macro diversion overflow."

If, on the other hand, you don't care whether a list is broken across page boundaries, you may use displays (turning off fill and adjust) *without* keeps. In this case, the names of the display commands are reversed. For displays without keeps, use:

.CD for **.DS C**	centers each line of the display.
.ID for **.DS I** or **.DS**	same as **.DS**; indents each line about 8 ens.
.LD for **.DS L**	left-justifies a display.
.BD for **.DS B**	left-justifies a centered display.

```
.CD
This centered display is not placed
inside a keep, and may be broken across
page boundaries.
.DE
```

Paragraphs

The **-ms** package also provides a macro for the standard indented paragraph. **.PP** (**PP**aragraph) causes a line to be skipped before the paragraph. The first line of the paragraph is indented five ens, then the rest of the paragraph is filled and adjusted.

Before each of the paragraphs in the main body of the text, insert the **.PP** macro, removing old **.ti 5** and **.sp** requests. The **-ms** standard paragraph macro indents each paragraph 5 *ens*; recall that 5 ens is equivalent to five character widths on a printer. However, an *en* is about half the width of an *em* on a phototypesetter, so that in typeset copy the **-ms** paragraph indent will be about half of an **nroff** indent of **.ti 5**, where the default value is *ems*.

Here's the formatting we've done so far:

```
 1 .TL  ------------------ [center & underline]
 2 Letter to Andrea Applicant
 3 .AU  ------------------ [center & underline]
 4 from General Manufacturing Co.
 5 .LP  ------------ [skip space & left justify]
 6 June 2, 1984
 7 .DS L  ---[skip space, left justify, & no fill]
 8 Ms. Andrea Applicant
 9 1312 N. Main St.
10 Oakland, CA 94612
11 .DE  -------------------------- [end display]
12 .LP  ------------ [skip space & left justify]
13 Dear Ms. Applicant:
14 .PP
15 Thank you for expressing ...
 .
 .
 .
 .
22 .PP
23 However, we will keep ...
```

You may want to indent or center Hiram Hardhart's address, another type of display. This display may be indented with **.DS**, or centered with **.DS C** (Display **S**tart **C**entered). After Hiram's address, be sure to end the display with **.DE** (**D**isplay **E**nd).

The **nroff .ul** request to underline Hiram Hardhart's title may be left in.

Then insert **.LP** (Left Paragraph), before 'Sincerely yours'. Leave the **nroff** request, **.sp 4** (**sp**ace) before the name 'Mary Jones', because the spacing provided by **.LP** will probably not be sufficient. At this point, an intentional **.br** (**br**eak) request must be inserted before Mary Jones' title, or else the title will be formatted into the same output line as her name. If you wanted to skip one space between the name 'Mary Jones' and her title, a **.sp** request could be inserted here, and **.br** would not be needed.

The **jobreply** file as it appears using **-ms** macros is shown in Fig. 9.1. The improvement in neatness and size is readily apparent.

Fig. 9.1   jobreply File with -ms Macros

```
 1 .TL
 2 Letter to Andrea Applicant
 3 .AU
 4 From General Manufacturing Co.
 5 .LP
 6 June 2, 1984
 7 .DS L
 8 Ms. Andrea Applicant
 9 1312 N. Main St.
10 Oakland, CA 94612
11 .DE
12 .LP
13 Dear Ms. Applicant:
14 .PP
15 Thank you for expressing an interest
16 in General Manufacturing Co.
17 After reviewing your resume,
18 we find that we do not
19 have any openings suitable to
20 your qualifications at the
```

```
21 present time.
22 .PP
23 However, we will keep your application on
24 file in the event that something should
25 become available. Please address any
26 future correspondence to:
27 .DS C
28 Hiram Hardhart
29 .ul
30 Director of Personnel
31 General Manufacturing Co.
32 1234 Jackson St.
33 San Francisco, CA 94112
34 .DE
35 .LP
36 Sincerely yours,
37 .sp 4
38 Mary Jones
39 .br
40 Manager, General Manufacturing Co.
```

In order to include a particular macro package into a file being formatted, use the **nroff** command with the name of the macro package expressed as an option. For example, the complete syntax of **nroff** plus the **-ms** macro package is

```
nroff -ms jobreply<CR>
```

The **nroff** program first reads the macro definitions in the **-ms** definition file. At every point in the file where it finds macro, the program then executes the sequence of **nroff** requests comprised by the macro and processes the text accordingly.

The formatted output will show a couple of **-ms** default options you may *not* want. The **-ms** package automatically prints the current date at the bottom center of every page. To turn off the date, put the command **.ND** (No Date) at the beginning of the file. **-ms** also numbers pages at the center top of each page. Page numbering can be turned off, as will be explained later in the chapter (see **Changing Registers**).

One rule in the use of the **-ms** macro must be observed. The input text for the **-ms** macro package must begin with a "begin-text" macro which alerts **nroff** to the fact that **-ms** macros are in use. The begin-text macros are **.TL**, **.SH**, **.NH**, **.PP**, and **.LP**. Use any one of these before the first line of text. The one you choose depends on how you want your first line(s) formatted.

FANCY FORMATTING WITH THE -ms PACKAGE

Indented Paragraphs

The **-ms** package is so easy to use that even beginners can do specialized formatting. For example, lists can be dressed up by having each item in a list "hang" as a label for a block indented explanatory paragraph.

```
              Indented Paragraph with Hanging Label
   label    paragraph paragraph paragraph paragraph paragraph
            paragraph paragraph paragraph paragraph paragraph
            paragraph paragraph paragraph paragraph paragraph
```

The command **.IP** (Indent Paragraph), when used without a label, indents an entire paragraph five character widths from the left margin. With the **-ms** package, the default indentions are calculated in **ens**, not in **ems** as were the **nroff** requests. Here's an example of how the **.IP** macro is used.

```
.IP
Text text text text text text text text
text text text
text text text text text text text text text text text
```

produces:

```
Text text text text text text text text text text text
text text text text text text text text text text text
```

For a pleasing list format, a label may be added to an indented paragraph with a label, 1, as follows.

```
.IP (1)      ------------------- [label]
Text text text text text text
```

produces:

```
(1) Text text text text text text text text text text text
    text text text text text text text text text text text
  ..
  ¦
  ¦
label
```

Any word or number may be used for the label. Two or more words may be used *if they are enclosed in double quotation marks.* Enclosing a series of words in double quotations causes a phrase to be treated as a single word.

Labels should only be as long as necessary. With long labels, the default value of block indention will be too small, and the label will butt up against the first words of the paragraph as shown below.

```
.IP "This is a long label"
Text text text text text text text text text text text text
text text text text text text text
```

produces:

```
This is a long labelText text text text text text text text
    text text text text text text text text text text text
```

You can increase the indentation with a number argument, *after* the label.

Thus, there are two important points to remember about a longer-than-average label:

1. Enclose the words in the label in double quotation marks (**.IP "For Example:"**);

2. Specify the total length of the indention.

For example, suppose you use the phrase "My Goodness:" as a label. Since 'My Goodness:' has twelve characters (counting the space and the colon) a minimum indentation of fourteen character widths would be necessary, leaving two spaces after the colon. The complete macro command then would be **.IP "My Goodness:" 14**. The label would then hang on a correctly indented paragraph.

```
.IP "My Goodness:" 14
Text text text text text
```

produces:

```
My Goodness: Text text text text text
```

If it is absolutely necessary to use a long label, say one requiring an indentation of more than 20 character widths, it should be on a line by itself, separated from the indented paragraph by a **.sp** request. For instance the sequence

```
.br
.ul
Extremely Long label
.IP
```

produces:

Extremely Long Label
~ ~
~ ~
~ ~
~ ~

Quoted Paragraphs

.QP (Quoted Paragraph) is another way to block indent. The quoted paragraph is indented from both margins to produce a neatly centered block of text.

The automatic indention is five ens. On a printer, the text will be indented five character widths from each margin until your next dot request for a new section or a different type of paragraph. A **.QP** must be used before each paragraph in a set of several quoted paragraphs.

Section Headings

.SH (Section Heading) produces an underlined (boldface in typeset), left-aligned section heading set off by blank lines at the top and bottom. The sequence

```
.SH
Section Heading
.PP
Text text text text text text text text text text text
text text text text text text text
```

produces:

Section Heading
     Text text text text text text text text text text text
text text text text text text text

Numbered Headings

The **.NH** (Numbered Heading) macro automatically numbers headings in traditional "science textbook" style: 1., 1.1., 1.1.1., 1.1.2., etc. The number argument to **.NH** indicates the level of the numbered heading.

A level 1 **.NH** macro produces a section heading numbered **1.**, the first time it is used, incrementing the number by one with each successive use. Level 1 is the outermost level: the first **.NH** request will number a heading as **1.**. A level 2 heading is obtained with **.NH 2**, and it will number a heading as 1.1. the first time it is used.

The sequence below uses two levels of numbered heading macros.

```
.NH
Chapter One
.NH 2
Section one
.NH 2

Section two
.NH
Chapter Two
```

This produces

```
1. Chapter One
1.1. Section one
1.2. Section two

2. Chapter Two
```

Each time a level 1 **.NH** (**Numbered Heading**) is used, the number attached to the next level 1 item in the list is increased by one. Within level 1, level 2 numbered headings behave in a similar fashion. Level 3 headings are of the form: **1.1.1.**, **1.1.2.**, and so forth.

That the item numbers automatically increase is a strong feature of **.NH**. Unfortunately, the levels of section headings don't indent. Indentation would improve readability.

Sections may be indented using the pair of commands **.RS** (**Recess Start**) and **.RE** (**Recess End**), which may be combined with **.NH** if desired.

The **.RS** command indents subsequent lines and aligns them properly, until an **.RE** is reached. Actually, **.RS** changes the current left margin, so that paragraphs within an **.RS** will have the new left margin. **.RS** commands may be nested for several levels of indentation. If two **.RS**'s are nested, two **.RE**'s are needed to cancel them and restore the original level of indentation.

```
.LP
Chapter One
.RS
Section one

Section two
.RS
subsection one
.RE
.RE
Chapter Two
```

produces:

```
Chapter One

        Section one

        Section two

                subsection one

Chapter Two
```

If combined with **.NH**, the input

```
.LP
.NH
Chapter One
.RS
.NH 2
Section one

Section two
.RS
```

```
.NH 3
subsection one
.RE
.RE
.NH
Chapter Two
```

produces:

```
1. Chapter One
      1.1. Section one

      1.2. Section two

            1.1.1. subsection one

2. Chapter Two
```

RESETTING -ms DEFAULT VALUES

Line length, paragraph indent, and other features of the page environment can be modified by changing the default values of **-ms** macros. Default values are stored in the **-ms** definition file in places called *registers*.

There are two types of **-ms** registers: number registers and string registers. As their names suggest, the contents of a number register is a number, and the content of a string register is a string of characters, such as a word or phrase. The default values for line length, page offset, and other format features concerned with *size* are kept in number registers. Values for headings and footings (including the page number) are kept in string registers. The name of each register is an abbreviation for its function. The **FL** register stores the Footnote Length; the **HM** register stores the Header Margin (top margin), and so forth.

To change any **-ms** register, give a command that names the register and gives a new value for it. To change the default value for one of the number registers, use the dot command **.nr**, followed by the name of the register and the new value you have chosen.

The complete syntax for this command is

```
.nr {register name} {new value}
```

To change a string register, you "redefine" it with the define string, (.**ds**) command.

```
.ds {register name} {new value}
```

It is important to remember that a change to a number or string register does not affect the text to be formatted that occurs before the .**nr** or .**ds** command.

For changes that are intended to affect the entire document, it is a good practice to insert register change commands at the beginning of the input file, and follow them immediately with a begin text macro such as .**LP**.

Number Registers

Fig. 9.2 is a summary of the -**ms** registers. This table shows the default values that are kept in the -**ms** number registers. Any of these values can be changed with the command form: .**nr** {register name} {new value}. *You must always specify the unit of measure when changing a number register.*

Fig. 9.2 The -ms Number Registers

Name	Controls	Takes Effect	Default
LL	line length of text	next paragraph	6i
LT	line length of running titles	"	6i
FL	footnote line length	next FS	11/12 LL
PD	vertical offset of paragraphs	next paragraph	1v (nroff)
PI	paragraph indent	"	5 ens
QI	left and right indent for QP (quoted paragraph)	next QP	5ens
PO	page offset	next page	0 (nroff)
HM	top margin	next page	1i
FM	bottom margin	next page	1i

For example, the command **.nr HM .5i** changes top margin to 1/2 inch, and **.nr LL 5.5i** changes line length to 5.5 inches.

As another example, the line length of footnotes, set off by **.FS** (Footnote Start) and **.FE** (Footnote End), is 11/12ths of the line length currently in effect. By changing the value of the Footnote Length register, the footnote length can be changed to a specific value which does not depend on the line length. For example, the command **.nr FL 4i** will make footnotes all exactly four inches long, beginning with the next footnote indicated by **.FS**.

Number registers are referred to constantly by the **-ms** macros in order to format your text. For instance, one version of the **-ms** paragraph macro shows how a standard macro represents several **nroff** requests and makes use of the number registers. A possible sequence for the **.PP** might be the following:

```
.de PP
.RT                \"reset everything to
                   normal
.ne  1.1           \"make sure there's more
                   than one line
.sp \\n(PDu        \"skip one vertical space
.ti +\\n(PIu       \"temporary paragraph
                   indent

..
```

The parenthetical symbols **PD** and **PI** in this macro are references to number registers. These symbols are equivalent to number arguments for the **.sp** and **.ti** commands. Note that explanatory notes (comments) may be included on the same line with dot requests. **nroff** will ignore any characters that are set off with \\".

Although it is not necessary to explain each line in this definition in detail, there are some important things to remember about the **-ms** paragraph macro. First, it automatically resets many characteristics of the formatted output to regular or default values. Second, it defines the amount of space to skip and the amount by which to indent in terms of **-ms** number registers.

As was shown in Fig. 9.2, the default values for the above registers are

PD skip one extra line on a printer,
       and less if typeset
PI indent 5 characters (5 ens)

This example shows that each **-ms** macro contains many elements. It takes into account whether the output is destined for the printer or for the typesetter, and can recognize changed values for number registers and respond accordingly.

String Registers

Other values, such as page numbers, are kept in *string registers.* String registers contain values that control what is printed in six locations on the page: the left, center and right of the page head and left, center and right of the page foot. See Fig. 9.3.

Fig. 9.3 Diagram of the Six String Registers

Left, Center and Right "Heads"	LH	CH	RH
		page	
Left, Center and Right "Foots"	LF	CF	RF

Unless you request otherwise, the **Center Head** string register is automatically filled with the page number, and the **Center Foot** register automatically contains today's date.

To suppress page numbering, define the Center Head string register as empty. This is done by defining the register, but giving no new value. Turning off page numbering would be useful for one-page letters such as **jobreply**

.ds CH define center heading string [no value]

Changing string registers is similar to changing number registers. The **.ds** means "define string," and signals your intention to change the contents of a string register.

If you want page numbers to be in a location different from Center Head, you must both redefine the Center Head register to zero and fill one of the other registers with the page number. Suppose, for example, you wished to have your pages numbered at bottom right, surrounded by hyphens. First turn off center head as above, then redefine the Right Foot register contents as follows: **.ds RF -%-**. (The percent sign (%) represents **nroff**'s page counter. The page counter value will automatically increase by one each time a new page is encountered.) The page number may be surrounded by characters of your choice (we used hyphens here), which are typed around the page counter symbol. If you do not want surrounding characters on page numbers, use **.ds RF %** instead.

You can also change any page number with the **nroff** command **.pn** (**p**age **n**umber), and the page counter will begin again from the new number. **.pn 4** starts page numbering with the number 4.

Headings and Footings

One or more string registers can hold a heading or footing. For a heading which would appear at the Left Head of every page, define the value of the **LH** register using the command **.ds LH Job Letter**. Although **Job Letter** is a two-word label, you need not enclose it in quotation marks: this is an exception to the rule mentioned above for labeling indented paragraphs.

Changing the Date

Unless specifically turned off, today's date will automatically be placed in the center foot register, which causes the date to be printed at the bottom center of every page. Having the date printed at the bottom of the page is helpful for indicating revision dates. The **.ND** (**N**o **D**ate) command will turn the date off. The **.ND** command has the same effect as **.ds CF** (define Center Foot register as empty). You may, if you wish, change the date with the **.DA** (**DA**te) directive to a date other than today's date, **.DA July 4, 1996**.

SPECIAL FEATURES

We have now covered most of the standard features of the **-ms** macro package. The **-ms** package also has some special features. It can produce accents on characters and handle multicolumn output.

Accent Marks

The **-ms** package provides special character sequences for some accent marks (acute accents, grave accents, and umlauts). The accent characters are **embedded** in the text lines. As you will recall, there are two ways to issue **nroff** commands: **dot** requests, which must appear on a line by themselves and **embedded requests**, which are inserted into the text lines.

On most printing terminals, the printer is capable of back-spacing over characters for special effects such as acute accents. The formatting program, however, must supply the instructions for this type of local motion using special symbols embedded in the text.

In **jobreply**, an acute accent might be put over the final 'e' in 'resume.' To do this, the line containing the word 'resume,' should be changed so the 'me' at the end becomes **m*'e**.

Other accents and symbols are available as follows:

acute accent	*'	á
grave accent	*`	à
umlaut	*:	ö
circumflex	*^	ô
cedilla	*,	ça
sueno	*~	mañana

Multicolumn Output

The **-ms** macro package can format your output in two or more columns. The usual request is for two columns, and is specified using the command **.2C**.

Your printer may not be able to process multicolumn output correctly without the use of an additional program called **col**. In order to guarantee that your output will be processed by the **col** program before the printer attempts to display multicolumn format, "pipe" the **nroff** and output it through **col** on the command line. Type

```
nroff -ms {filename} | col | lpr <CR>
```

The **.MC** (**m**ulticolumn) macro can format text in *more than two* columns. Column width may be specified in inches or in any other printing scale measure. The multicolumn option determines the maximum width available from the "line length" value, and formats the text into as many columns of the specified width as will fit on the page.

For example, with a line length of 8 inches, the **.MC** macro would create three 2-inch columns leaving one inch for the left and right margin as shown below.

```
.nr LL 8i
.MC 2i ------- [formats text into three two-inch columns]
<--------2"-----> <-------2"---------> <-----2"------->
```

Switching from a one-column format to a format of two or more columns does not cause a page break. However, switching from two back to one, or from more than two to any other number, will always generate a new page.

Footnotes

Footnotes are a type of display that is automatically placed inside a keep. A footnote with a line above it is printed out in space reserved at the bottom of output page. More than one footnote may be included between **.FS** (Footnote Start) and **.FE** (Footnote End) commands, but the **-ms** package will not automatically put a blank line between footnotes or mark them with numbers or other symbols. Here's an example of how footnotes are specified in the input text.

```
.FS
1. This is the first footnote.
2. This is the second footnote.
.FE
```

Footnotes between **.FS** and **.FE** should be inserted in the input text close to the footnote reference in the text as shown in the example above. They are then output at the bottom of the appropriate page. Remember to enter your own footnote numbers together with your footnote text.

CONSTRUCTING YOUR OWN MACROS

The topic of constructing your own macros has been discussed in the recipe for making a page-break trap. Recall that the **nroff** command .de., for "**de**fine macro," begins a definition. The definition always ends with double dots (..).

Your own macros should also be given a unique two-letter name which does not duplicate either **nroff** requests or the predefined macro names. To avoid duplication, we recommend that you name your custom macros with one capital letter and one lowercase letter. For example, to define a macro for centered and underlined section headings, you will need **nroff** commands to:

```
skip a line before the heading
center the heading
and underline it
```

You could name this macro "Cs," say, for "Center section," and the definition recipe would be

.de CS   define a macro called "Cs".

.sp   skip a line.

.ce   center the heading.

.ul   underline it (italics, in troff).

..   end definition.

Now, for one-line headings, you can use your new **Cs** macro just as you previously used **.SH** (Section Heading) with **-ms** macro section headings.

```
$ cat memo
: a
.ND       ---[no date]
.ds CH    ---[no page numbers]
.de Cs    ---[Center section macro
.sp                  definition]
.ul
.ce
..        ---[end definition]
.LP       ---[make macros take effect]
.Cs
For Your Information
.LP
It has come to my attention that
management personnel have been seen
wearing white sneakers after hours.
```

```
Proper footwear [brown oxfords, Part
No. 73211-0] should be worn at all
times.
.sp 2      ---[skip 2 spaces]
.ce        ---[center the signature]
The Boss
$ □
```

The initial sequence in the example above shows the standard formula for beginning (opening) a new document to be processed by **-ms**. Specifically, you turn off the date and the page number, and define any new macros, then initialize macros (so they will be processed) with a left paragraph directive (**.LP**) or other begin-text macro.

When the above input is formatted with the command **nroff -ms memo** ⟨**CR**⟩ the output will be

```
          For Your Information
It has come to my attention that
management personnel have been seen
wearing white sneakers after hours.
Proper footwear [brown oxfords, Part
No. 73211-0] should be worn at all
times.


                  The Boss
```

When you use headings that take up more than one line in input text, you need to specify the **.ul** request with a larger numerical argument, such as **.ul 5**. Or even **.ul 100**. The number argument does not have to match the number of input lines exactly, since **nroff** would then continue underlining until canceled by the next macro request, such as **.LP** shown above.

Creating your own macro definitions may require some trial and error. Although the **nroff** commands and macros described so far are fairly straightforward, combinations of commands sometimes interact unexpectedly, especially when you are striving for unusual special effects.

Additional **nroff** dot requests for use in your own macros or elsewhere, are described in the Bell Labs documents *A Troff Tutorial* and *The Nroff/Troff User's Manual.*

USING YOUR OWN MACROS

A more efficient way to use your own macro definitions without having to type them into every text file where they are needed is to put them into a separate file. This filename can then be included on the command line, in the same way the standard macro packages are included. Your customized macro package should appear on the command line after the standard macro package but before the name(s) of the text file(s) to be formatted. For example, if you wished to include both **-ms** and a file of custom macros in a file named **mine** in a standard command to execute **nroff**, the complete syntax would be

```
nroff -ms mine {filename}<CR>
```

Note that the file **mine** is not specified with a hyphen. Your custom macro file can be used in more than one directory by linking its name to all the relevant directories. See the discussion of linking in Chapter 5. Header files containing standard opening macros for various types of documents may be "read in" while editing, or even be specified on the command line:

```
nroff -ms {header} mine {filename}<CR>
```

Your custom macro file may contain all the definitions you have created so far, and will work whenever *any* of your custom macro names are inserted as dot requests in your text file.

Another way to cause **nroff** to read other macro files is to use the **.so** (**so**urce) "include file" directive at the beginning of your document, before the initializing macros.

The request/command line

```
.so {filename}
```

will cause the indicated file to be included in the document file. This method obviates having to remember to type the name of other files to be included on the command line. Note, however, that if you happen to use a **.so** request for a file that does not exist or for which you do not have permission, an error message from the program will appear in your formatted output.

WHERE MACRO PACKAGES ARE LOCATED

The macro definitions for the standard macro packages are contained in files located in the **/usr/lib/tmac** directory. These files are named with the **tmac.** prefix. For instance, **-ms** macro definitions are stored in **/usr/lib/tmac/tmac.s**. The **-mm** macro package occurs in **/usr/lib/tmac/tmac.m**. The **/usr/lib/tmac/tmac.an** contains the macro definitions for the **-man** macro package, which is used to format standard command reference pages for the *UNIX Programmer's Manual.*

Standard macro packages contain many complex definitions, and changing them is not recommended. If it is necessary to alter a standard macro package for some special purpose, you must first copy the file into one of your directories. To distinguish it from the unchanged macro package, give it a different name, such as **newms**. The altered macro package can now be read in along with your custom macro files, by specifying its name on the command line. Since **newms** is a file, it is not preceded by a hyphen, as shown in the following command:

```
nroff newms mine {filename} <CR>
```

Combining your own macros and standard **nroff** requests with a regular macro package should be done with caution. Preview your formatted output on the screen, and on paper with the printer. If you are getting unexpected results, **lpr** (line **pr**inter) the entire file, unformatted and examine the sequences of requests to make sure the **nroff** program can understand what you want.

OTHER MACRO PACKAGES

Although we have confined discussion to the **-ms** package, other macro packages are worth examining for comparison. The **-me** macro package is distributed with the Berkeley software, and the **-mm** macro package is available on systems that have the Programmers Workbench software (including System III UNIX systems).

The **-man** macro package formats pages for the *UNIX Programmer's Manual.* The **-mm** macro package is included in System III and V Bell UNIX system and will soon be widely distributed.

The **-me** macro package is popular at U.C. Berkeley, and is made available with the Berkeley UNIX software distribution. We mention them here only in passing; additional information on them can be found in the publications mentioned in the bibliography.

Like the **-ms** macro package, the **-me** and the **-mm** macro packages are collections of definitions for formatting printed output. However, the macro codes and capabilities differ. For example, the **-me** macro package relies heavily on single character designations for various operations, with opening and closing parentheses to indicate start and end.

The **-me** macros for quoted paragraphs, for example, surround the text to be quoted with **. (q** and **.) q**.

In the **-me** macro package, the equivalent to an **-ms** "display" is called a "list." The display is opened with **.(1** and closed with **.)1**, as shown in the sample sequence below.

```
            Example of -me list macros
.(1
This text will not be filled,
adjusted,
or rearranged.
.)1
```

The **-me** package will accumulate and automatically number footnotes, printing them either at the bottom of the current page, or at the end of the document. This package can also generate an index, or even more than one index, automatically.

HOW TO USE MACRO PACKAGES

The following "rules" or suggestions have been either mentioned or hinted at, but are here summarized for convenience:

Input

- *Rule 1* A formatting request line is the only line you should begin with a dot (period) or an apostrophe ('). If you happen to have a dot or an apostrophe as the first character on a line of text, **nroff** will attempt to interpret the line as a formatting request, and, when it fails, will ignore the entire line and not include it in your formatted output.

- *Rule 2* Keep lines short. Since **nroff** and the macro packages rearrange lines, input lines in a text file ought to be short in order to facilitate editing. This is particularly important for long documents.

- *Rule 3* Text lines to be processed by **nroff** alone or in conjunction with one of the macro packages should always begin with some other character than a space. The **nroff** program always inserts a space between the last character in one input line and the first character in the next. Any space left at the beginning of a line will cause a break in formatting. Input lines should always *end* with a complete word.

- *Rule 4* Limit files to a maximum of 1000 lines. Longer documents may be divided into separate files. This makes each file more manageable during the formatting and printing process.

Output

To set formatted output with macro packages type the command **nroff** followed by the name of the file containing the macro definitions. The **-ms** is an option to **nroff**, which causes **nroff** to read the file containing the macro definitions, followed by one or more file names.

Multicolumn output is generated by piping **nroff** output through **col** and then through the line printer. The complete syntax for this command is

```
nroff -ms filename | col | lpr
```

Certain **nroff** command line options stop output at a specified page, or begin processing at a specific page. You can stop output after every page with the **-s1** option. The syntax for this command is

```
nroff -ms -s1 {filename}<CR>
```

You can stop output every two pages with **-s2** although it is not a very common operation. To restart the output after a **-s** (stop) command, use ^d. The **-s1** option can be used to print your text onto single sheets of 8 1/2″ by 11″ paper or letterhead.

The **-o** (origin) option will begin formatting text at a specified page in the *formatted* output. If, for example, you have noticed some mistakes on page 4 of your formatted output, you can correct the mistakes, and then restart formatting at page four with **nroff -ms -o4-** {**filename**}⟨**CR**⟩. The extra hyphen after the 4 means "go on from 4 through the end." You could also specify a range of pages, as in

```
nroff -ms -o4-10 {filename}<CR>
```

Finally, you can begin numbering pages with a specific number with the **-n** option:

```
nroff -ms -n12 {filename}<CR>
```

Since formatting with the **nroff** program can be time-consuming, it is often faster to split a long file into several shorter files, and assign the appropriate page numbers with the **-n** option when the files are formatted.

nroff command line options can be combined as in the following command

```
nroff -ms -s1 -o7- {filename}<CR>
```

Previewing Formatted Output

The **more** program can assist with the previewing of formatted output on your video screen.

The command line to display the formatted output with the **more** command is

```
nroff -ms filename | more<CR>
```

To see each succeeding screen page, press the space bar.

Although a video display monitor does not print in as fine a detail as the average printer and does not show proportional spacing, the video display should give you a general idea of whether you have made any serious mistakes in the formatting commands. Previewing also saves wasted paper and printer time.

10 SYSTEM MANAGEMENT AND MAINTENANCE

Learning the duties of the system manager will aid you in managing your UNIX*-based microcomputer. Larger multiuser systems often require a full-time system manager who is responsible for daily administrative routines and maintenance.

What Does the System Manager Do?

Who Does System Management?

Types of Users on a UNIX System
   Ordinary Users
   Privileged Users
      root
      bin
   Restricted Users

Changing Access Permissions

The Password and Group Membership Files
   The **/etc/passwd** File
   Groups
   The **/etc/group** File

Maintaining the UNIX File System
   Types of Storage
   Defined Units for Data Storage

* UNIX™ is a trademark of Bell Laboratories.

The UNIX system you are working on today is a sophisticated multiuser system. Multiuser, *multitasking* operating systems are used by more than one person and perform many tasks simultaneously, in contrast to simpler single-user systems. The operating system must manage the large amount of internal and external memory required to accommodate several users. A multiuser operating system, unlike a single user system, must provide a more complex file structure, a logical partitioning of space on the disk, and user name recognition to allow users to manage their own separate data areas. Access to the system itself must also be controlled.

This chapter will acquaint you with some of the tasks and responsibilities of the system manager. You will apply the concepts presented here to the management of your directory/file system. If you are working with a small group of users on your UNIX system each of you will probably have to assume the role of system manager from time to time. Detailed tutorials on system administration are given in *The Programmer's Guide to the UNIX System.*

WHAT DOES THE SYSTEM MANAGER DO?

System administration for a large UNIX installation can be a full-time job. The system manager must have a solid knowledge of the UNIX system and understand production requirements. There are many details to handle every day. Most managers are not only responsible for the physical maintenance of the equipment, they also supervise, train, and assist other users.

Precautions must be taken against damage to the system. Possible damage includes physical damage, which may result from the failure of an electronic component, and damage to the file system. Files may be inadvertently deleted or overwritten, and the manager must maintain a scheduled program to create spare copies of valuable files. The process of creating these backup copies is essential to good system management.

A multiuser operating system must be started up carefully. Checks and observations must be made on important hardware and software functions as the system comes online. The system cannot simply be unplugged at the end of the work day; the manager must be sure all users are logged off the system, and the correct data are backed up. Whenever the system is turned off for maintenance, field service, or other purposes, users must be notified to log out, and the system must be halted in an orderly fashion.

The day-to-day handling of these situations, questions, and problems is the job of the *system manager* or system management team. In large UNIX installations, system management is usually assigned to an official system administrator.

WHO DOES SYSTEM MANAGEMENT?

Several kinds of people are needed to support a UNIX system. The system manager's duty is to carry out the maintenance and upkeep of a healthy system and take care of routine software problems. For more difficult software problems, a more knowledgeable person is required. A UNIX expert is generally used only for the truly severe problems. A hardware technician repairs the system after it has failed. Usually, this person handles both hardware and software problems.

TYPES OF USERS ON A UNIX SYSTEM

The term "user account" has a special meaning for system administration. When you are assigned a username and password, a user account is established for you on the system. Accounts are a way of keeping track of system use and are not used for billing.

Ordinary Users

An *ordinary user* has access to the general commands of the UNIX system and to the shell program which runs after login.

Privileged Users

In addition to regular user accounts, UNIX has a number of special accounts set up for system management purposes. These login names are termed *special users*. Special users have greater access to system programs and utilities than regular users. There can be any number of privileged accounts, but there must always be a user named **root**; **root** is the name of the all-powerful *superuser*.

root

The superuser **root** can have access to any file in the file system, regardless of the access permissions on the file or on the directories leading to it; **root**'s unlimited access privileges are required for the maintenance of the UNIX system. For example, **root** must be able to gain access to all files to perform system backups or create new user accounts.

The superuser **root** can remove any file, change any password or deny any ordinary user access to any file (or device). The superuser can also free up disk space by removing unwanted **core** files. Core files are created by the UNIX system when a program crashes or when a forced quit has been executed by the ^\ command.

root's unlimited access permission can be dangerous. Ordinary users and other privileged users can be restrained from causing accidental damage to files by the use of write-protect access permissions. The superuser is unaffected by access permissions, and may write on or erase any file, bypassing all security.

To avoid difficulties, the superuser account should be used only to perform system administration. If a job does not require superuser privileges, the system manager should just log into an ordinary user account.

bin

Another privileged user is the owner of the directory **bin**. **bin** has special powers, but they are not equal to those of **root**. The **bin** user is the owner of the files in the **/bin** and **/usr/ bin** directories. These files contain the UNIX system commands available to ordinary users. Aside from **root**, **bin** is the only user who can change the access permissions on system files.

There is no limit to the number of privileged user accounts. For example, an account named **macro** might be responsible for maintaining and updating the **nroff** macro packages. Even though there may be many privileged accounts, there does not have to be a different *person* for each. The system manager is usually all of them. Privileged user accounts are different hats the system manager puts on for different jobs.

Restricted Users

These users have less access to the system than ordinary users. A restricted user account is created to limit the scope of a user's powers by limiting access. There are two kinds of restricted user accounts. One type has access to a single program or group of programs. The payroll program is often such an account. The person whose job is to produce your payroll would log in as **payroll** and automatically be put into the payroll program; upon exiting the payroll program, this user would automatically be logged out. Such a user would not be able to exit to the shell and would therefore be unable to change directories, create files or execute any system commands that were not part of the payroll program.

The second type of restricted user account is more utilitarian. Frequently, a system manager would like to find out who is on-line without having to sit through the login procedures such as message-of-the-day and announcements from **.profile**. To accomplish this, a restricted account name **who** is sometimes created. It requires no password, so anyone can log in as **who**, execute the command **who**, and then is automatically logged out.

CHANGING ACCESS PERMISSIONS

The owners of files and the superuser can change access permission with the command **chmod** (**ch**ange access **mode**). In some environments, all users have this privilege. In others, the privilege of changing access permissions is limited to the system manager.

The significance of access permissions is slightly different for files and directories. The summary in Table 10.1 shows how each access permission affects both files and directories:

Table 10.1 Access Permission Summary

READ
Files: allows the user to examine the file (by **cat**, for example).
Directory: allows the user to **ls** the directory, but not to do a long listing. Directory read permission does not automatically grant the right to read the files in a directory.

WRITE
Files: allows the user to alter the file or **rm** (**rem**ove) it.
Directory: allows the user to create new files and **rm** (**rem**ove) files within the directory. Permission to alter existing files depends on the permissions on the individual files.

EXECUTE
Files: allows the user to treat the file as a UNIX command. Execute permission does not ensure that the file will actually function properly as a command, only that the shell will *attempt* to execute it.
Directory: allows the directory to become the user's current directory using **cd** (**c**hange **d**irectory). Both read *and* execute permission are required for a long listing. Execute permission is sometimes called *search permission*.

THE PASSWORD AND GROUP MEMBERSHIP FILES

Information on ownership of files and access permissions is stored in two files, the **/etc/passwd** file, which contains information about ordinary, special and restricted users, and the **/etc/group** file, which contains data about groups.

The /etc/passwd File

The **/etc/passwd** file contains the pertinent information about each user, login name, password, group memberships, etc.

Groups

Every user account with the same group ID number in **/etc/passwd** belongs to a group, but members of a given group do not *automatically* have access to files having the same group ID. Any member of a group may exclude other members by altering the group access permissions with **chmod**. Although only one group ID is associated with any particular file, users may be members of more than one group, and can change to other groups with the **newgrp** command. User's membership in groups is denoted by entries in the file named **/etc/group**.

The /etc/group File

The **/etc/group** file defines group accounts. Its entries are similar to those in **/etc/passwd**. Four types of information are in **/etc/group**.

- The group name.
- The group passwords. At present, there is no easy way to install a password in the **/etc/group** file, although it is possible to do so.
- The group ID number.
- The list of members of the group account.

To change groups, user's account names must appear in the list of group members in the last field of **/etc/group**. The last lines of the sample display are shown below.

```
$ cat /etc/group
sys::1:root,drivers,stand:
staff:G2^o&P4_ffaj@:200:marc,mike,paul,steve,jeff,bill,ralph:
guest::100:admin,guest,guest1,cherry,rik,ralph:
$ 
```

Notice that in the **/etc/passwd** entry for the account **ralph**

```
ralph::223:200:Ralph Minkler:/usr/ralph:bin/sh
```

the group ID number is 200. The account **ralph** thus automatically has access to other accounts with the same group ID, 200. **ralph** is also granted membership to the **guest** group by the presence of his name in **guest**'s membership list in **/etc/group**.

MAINTAINING THE UNIX FILE SYSTEM

The UNIX file system has tools to organize information, and fail-safe mechanisms to prevent information from accidental disorganization.

Types of Storage

The UNIX system has two types of storage for files, temporary and permanent. The computer's memory provides temporary *internal storage*. The *external* magnetic storage media, which may be floppy disks, hard disks, or tapes, provide the permanent storage.

When a user issues a command, the UNIX system makes a copy of the corresponding command file from an external storage medium and writes it into internal memory, where it becomes an *active process*. As internal memory is modified, it is periodically copied to permanent storage, to update previous versions. Writing to the disk occurs automatically, every few seconds, as part of system maintenance programs.

Internal memory can store information only when the computer is running. When power is turned off, the contents of internal memory are lost. Because internal memory is not permanent, your UNIX system periodically and automatically updates the disk data by a special update program (**/etc/update**). The update program is performed about every thirty seconds, providing continuous protection against loss of your work in case of a power failure or other system disaster.

Defined Units for Data Storage

The defined units understood by the UNIX system are the *bit*, the *byte*, and the *block*. The *bit* and the *byte* are the means by which letters, numbers, and other characters are coded into electronic signals that the computer can use.

The UNIX system formats disks into groups of bytes called *blocks*. The size of UNIX blocks may be either 512 or 1024 bytes, depending upon your system. These blocks are available for file storage. Every 512 or 1024 bytes of a file are considered to be one full block; blocks that are not full are called *partial blocks*), but this merely means "partially full." Only whole blocks are allocated for file storage, and the remaining bytes of partial blocks are not used by other files.

File Systems

To manage the blocks of internal and external memory, the UNIX system uses the logical structure of the file and directory system. As discussed in Chapters 4 and 5, a file system is a complete directory hierarchy that occupies all or part of a disk. When the system is booted up, the first or **root** file system is opened. Although most system programs and files are usually in the **root** file system (including all the files that belong to **root** and to the privileged users), other file systems that connect to the **root** directory may be created. One or more file systems may exist on a floppy or hard disk.

The process of opening a file system so that its contents are known to the system's kernel is called *mounting the file system*. When the system is shut down, all of the file systems are first brought up to date, and then *unmount*ed.

Part of the booting up process causes the system to follow a script that instructs it to mount file systems. Frequently, one file system will contain all the system programs and related information, while another will be dedicated to storage of users' files and directories.

File systems are mounted by naming the device on which the file system resides and the directory on which the file system is to be mounted for use. The names of file system devices are found in the **/dev** directory. Names such as **/dev/hd02** or **/dev/usr** may be found. These names denote file system devices (usually, a hard disk) that have been formatted for file system storage.

Although more than one file system can be mounted at one time, they store information independently of each other. If you run out of user space on one file system device, such as a flexible disk, the information cannot cross a file system boundary and be stored on some other disk. It is also impossible to link files across file systems as with the **ln** command. An attempt to do so will result in an error message such as "**ln:** cross-device link".

Structure of a File System

Every UNIX file system is divided into four different areas.

1. *The boot block.* The very first block in a file system is set aside for a boot program that brings the UNIX system into core memory from the disk. Once the system is present, it causes this file system, which becomes the root, to be mounted.

2. *The super block.* The second block in a file system, it contains information describing the size of a particular file system and how the rest of the file system is divided up. A file system's size in blocks is determined when the file system is created. It does not necessarily occupy all the space available on a flexible or hard disk. Several file systems can reside on the same hard disk. Ensuring that the super block remains healthy and up-to-date is crucial to system maintenance since it is the key to its system.

3. *The i-list.* The i-list blocks contain a list of file definitions. Each definition in the i-list is called an *inode*. Inodes uniquely identify the size, date last modified, and location on the disk of any file in a particular file system.

4. *The data blocks.* After the inodes come the data blocks, which contain data and information about directories.

Monitoring and Administering Disk Use

Part of system maintenance is to format new floppy disks, to create and mount additional file systems, and to make backup copies of one or more file systems.

Monitoring and administering disk use is aided by UNIX commands that report any file systems currently mounted, and the space available on storage devices.

The following commands, while used primarily by the system manager, are useful to know, and may be used by anyone. They will sometimes explain why your system is responding slowly.

The **mount** command, used by itself, reports which file systems are currently mounted. For example, the display shown below indicates that a **f**loppy **d**isk file system is mounted on the **sandy** directory, one level down from **root**. **root** file system is not reported since its presence is assumed.

```
$ /etc/mount
/dev/fd02 on /sandy
$ □
```

The df (disk free) Command

The **df** (**d**isk **f**ree) command displays the number of free disk blocks. If used without an argument, the **df** command shows the number of free blocks from a default list of file systems.

An example of a **df** report is shown below. The report from your system may differ. The **df** command displays the name and the number of blocks available for use in each file system.

```
$ df
/dev/root        2667
/dev/usr      155647
$ □
```

When a file system fills up, additional data cannot be written to the disk. This condition should cause an error message to appear on the system console, usually something such as "device 0,64 full," which refers to the file system device by its major and minor device numbers. An overloaded file system means that old and unused files should be removed and either discarded or archived.

The du (disk use) Command

The **du** (**d**isk **u**se) command reports the number of blocks in use, beginning with the current directory and proceeding through all subdirectories. The **./Epson** directory, for example, in the display below is using 14 blocks.

```
$ du
14    ./Epson
1     ./Words/Memos
```

```
11    ./Words
9     ./Profiles
5     ./File.index
1     ./Newdir
58    ./Nroff.test.sh
64    ./Shellscreens
10    ./New
3     ./Mail
204   .
$ ▯
```

The **du** command with the **-a** option shows the number of blocks in use by each file in every directory and gives totals for each directory. Special subsets or even individual files may be "**du**ed" by giving arguments to the command.

```
$ du New
10 New
$ ▯
```

The quot Command

The **quot** command reports the number of blocks owned by each user, in descending order for each file system device as shown.

```
$ quot
/dev/rusr:
3828 bin
 974 root
 485 learn
 298 becca
 210 sandy
 186 sylvia
 147 uucp
 126 sys
 113 joanne
```

SYSTEM MANAGEMENT AND MAINTENANCE — CHAPTER 10 ———————————— 413

```
70 demo
70 rathomas
64 rikf
13 ellen
12 joe
 8 daemon
 4 alex
 3 chris
 1 joel
$ ▯
```

To warn users that the disk is becoming full, the system manager should monitor the amount of free disk space remaining on each regularly used file system device.

HOW TO TRANSFER FILES AND FILE SYSTEMS TO TAPE OR DISK

Commands for Transfer

The UNIX operating system provides several different methods for making copies of files or file systems. The methods are designed for the size of the copy, **cp** for individual files; **tar** for groups of files; and **dump** for the entire file system. The **tar** program's function overlaps both **cp** and **dump** in that it can also copy individual files or provide partial backups of the entire file system

This section explains the preservation of data on permanent, "archived" storage devices, primarily tape. The **cp** command is explained in Chapter 5. The **dump** and **tar** programs are usually run by the system manager. Since many system managers allow ordinary users to run **tar**, a discussion of the program is included in this chapter. Before running the program for the first time, you should go through it with a knowledgeable user or read your manual carefully.

The tar (tape archiver) Command

The **tar** (tape archiver) command has two important features:

1. It can be used both to make and to restore copies.
2. It preserves the directory structure.

When restoring files, **tar** can create the directories it needs to replace files with their original pathnames.

Using tar

The command syntax for **tar** is

```
tar {key} [{options}] [{devicename}] {name1} [{name2}...]
```

The {name} can be a filename or a directory name. When a directory name is used, all files and subdirectories within that directory will be archived.

The use of **tar** requires a *key*. The key tells **tar** to perform a function such as create, extract, update, or table of contents on a listing of files from the media. The **tar** command must be used with one of the following keys in Table 10.2.

Table 10.2   Keys for the tar Command

- c   Create a new tape with the files named in the argument list. Writing always begins at the beginning of the tape, and old files are overwritten.

- u   Update a tape. The named files are added to the tape if they are not already present or have been modified since they were last written to tape.

- r   Read the tape until the EOF is found and append the named files.

- x   Extract the named files from an archive tape. If the named file is a directory, the contents of the directory are (recursively) extracted. If no names are given, all of the files are extracted. Missing directories are created as needed on the destination file system to preserve the relationship of the files to the system hierarchy. Existing files with the same names are overwritten. The last entry of a file on the tape overwrites previous entries on the destination file system.

- t   Table of contents of the argument names from a tape. If no names are given, each file is listed as it occurs.

After one of the required keys, the additional modifying options listed in Table 10.3 are recognized by **tar**.

Table 10.3 Modifying Options for tar

f Use the argument filename as the device name. This allows the selection of the name of the device if it is not the default tape drive. If the name of the device is -, **tar** reads from the standard input or writes to the standard output.

0-7 Selects the drive number of the default tape device, **/dev/mt1**. For example, **tar c0** creates a tar-formatted tape on **/dev/mt0.**

v Makes **tar** verbose. The command normally proceeds quietly except for error messages. With **v**, the name of each file is displayed as it is treated, with a function letter preceding it (**a** for append, **x** for extract). When **v** is used with the **t** option, more information is displayed for each file.

w Waits for user confirmation before proceeding. **tar** prints a message and performs the action described if the response begins with "**y.**"

1 **tar** complains (notifies you by a message on your screen) if it cannot resolve all of the links to the files named.

m Sets the **m**odify time in the file to the time of extraction. Normally, the modify time of the file is unchanged from the modify time present when archived.

b Sets the **b**locking factor to the next argument. This is used to specify blocking sizes for tape devices. The default is 1 (512 byte block) and the maximum is 20.

k Sets the size of the media to the next argument in **k**ilobytes. This is useful with devices with fixed volume sizes, such as floppy disks. Very large files are split into "extents" across volumes, and **tar** will prompt for additional volumes if they are needed to fully restore a split file.

To illustrate, typing

```
# tar cf /dev/rdf0 /usr/chris
#
```

creates a **tar** copy on a floppy disk of all of the files and directories beginning with the directory **/usr/chris**.

[@Warning: the device names for file systems differ widely from system to system.@]

If you have a floppy disk, it will have to be formatted. Consult your reference manual or system manager for exact instructions.

tar is sensitive to the presence or absence of a complete pathname. For example, **/usr/chris** is a complete pathname. When this directory is extracted from the **tar** media, it will be restored to its former position in the file system hierarchy. On the other hand, if a file specified by a partial pathname is archived from the working directory, it may be restored in any working directory.

In the example below, **tar** creates a **tar**-formatted disk, beginning with the current directory, (.) and requesting the **c** key (**create**), the **v** (verbose) option, and the **f** (archive file) option. Because the verbose option has been requested, a listing of **tar**'s activities is printed on the terminal. Note that the names of the files and directories extracted are not complete pathnames. When the files are extracted from this disk, they may be written into any working directory.

```
# cd /usr/chris
# tar cvf /dev/rdf0 .
sort.h
sort1.c
Tables
...
Tables/hash2
#
```

Restoring Files with tar

The x (extract) key of the **tar** command is used to read **tar**-formatted tapes or disks. Remember that if a file is extracted with a complete pathname (that is, if it begins with /) it will be restored to its previous location in the file system hierarchy. If the name of the file is not a full pathname, it is copied into the working directory from which the **tar** command is issued. For example, the command

```
tar xf /dev/rdf0 /etc/passwd<CR>
```

copies **/etc/passwd** without regard to the current working directory. Had this file been archived from the **/etc** directory, the working directory would have to be changed to **/etc** before typing

```
tar xf /dev/rdf0 passwd<CR>
```

By combining the **t** key and **v** option, the listing of filenames on a **tar** tape can be expanded to a format similar to the **-l** options of **ls**. The following display illustrates the use of **tar** with and without the **v** option.

```
# tar tf /dev/rdf0
/etc/motd
/etc/passwd
# tar tvf /dev/rdf0
rw-r--r-- 0/1          768 Jul 9 1984 10:42
                                   /etc/motd
rw-r--r-- 0/1          225 Oct 2 1984 14:01
#                                  /etc/passwd
```

Incremental Backups with tar

The **tar** command may be used to archive a set of files. When the files are needed again, they may be restored to the file system. While **tar** preserves directory structure, it cannot determine which files must be backed up. However, **tar** may be used with the **find** command to generate a list of selected filenames. First, the **find** command selects those files that have been modified (or created) since a given date. The resulting list of names, which is directed to a file which might be named, **tar.09.23,** may be given to **tar** as the names of files to archive. In the display below the **find** command locates the files that have been created or modified since a previous **find**.

```
# find / -newer tar.09.23 -print > tar.09.24
# tar ckf 1200 /dev/rdf0 `cat tar.09.24`
# ▯
```

The previous **find** command produced the list that was sent to file **tar.09.23**. The list of names selected by the **find** command is all files with modification dates newer than those in the last list of names (**tar.09.23**). This list is redirected into the file **tar.09.24**. Then, the command **cat tar.09.24** ⟨**CR**⟩ provides the list of files to be archived on the disk. When archiving several files, you must specify the size of the tape or disk so that you do not overrun the end. With **tar** you use the **k** option. Consult your reference manual or system manager for the exact size.

Lists such as **tar.09.24** may be saved for future reference. Note that use of the **k** (size in blocks) and **f** (device name) options require additional arguments (**1200** blocks) and **/dev/ rdf0**, a **tar** device name. These should be stated on the command line in the same order as the modifying options (here, **k**, and **f**) which require them.

The dump and restor Commands

The **dump** command and its counterpart, **restor**, are also used to copy files and directories. The **dump** command, like **tar**, creates disks or tapes that can be read only by special commands. The volumes created by **dump** are in a different format from **tar** archives. The first volume in a set of **dump** disks or tapes begins with a listing of all filenames and inode numbers that follow. This listing may be read with the command **dumpdir**.

The **dump** command can perform incremental backups based upon the date a file was last modified and the date of the last **dump** backup. **dump** reads a file, **/etc/ddate** (for **dump** date), to determine when the last incremental **dump** was performed, and compares this date with the date last modified information in every inode of the file system being backed up. **dump** will optionally update the **/etc/ddate** file with the date of the backup.

A separate command, **restor**, is used to restore files from **dump** tapes. The process of **restor**ing files is more complicated than the process of extracting files from **tar** tapes. But because of **dump**'s incremental backup ability, **dump** is the command most often used for making regular backups of large file systems.

Backing up

Remember that one of the system manager's most important jobs is *backing up the file system.*

Despite all of your care and training, computer failures do occur. If you have vested your computer with a great deal of responsibility, you need to protect yourself from a catastrophic loss of precious data.

The simplest form of insurance is a spare copy of all your files. This spare copy is called a backup. UNIX provides a wide variety of backup functions to enable you to make spare copies of selected files or of your entire system.

System data and system files can usually be divided into two broad categories, files whose contents seldom change (such as tax tables) and files whose contents are changed every day (accounts payable, for example). Backing up your system becomes much simpler if daily spare copies are made only of the files whose contents have changed.

New computer users tend to be careless about backing up. The few extra minutes required at the beginning of a work day seem wasted on a smoothly running system. However, data files can be irretrievably lost through no error of the computer. A simple typographical error when entering a command with a * wildcard character can erase every file on your system. A power failure miles from your office can occur during a disk write. A careless employee might format the wrong disk. The possibilities are limitless, and so are the financial consequences. We cannot stress strongly enough that the system manager should design a consistent backup routine. If you back up every day, the most you will lose is one day's work. If you back up once a month, you can lose a small fortune's worth of work.

The system manager must have everyone off the system during a backup. Backups should be performed at a time convenient for most users, not necessarily for the system manager.

Directions for the various methods of backing up will be given at the end of the next section.

ROUTINE DUTIES

Start-up and Shutdown

The system manager is responsible for bringing up the system and for shutting it down in an orderly fashion. The process of turning on the system and bringing key system programs into memory is called *booting* or *booting up*. After booting, the system is in a special state called *single-user mode*. Only a single terminal, referred to as the *console*, is active. A shell program is active on the console in single-user mode.

Once the system has booted up, the file system(s) can be checked and the date set. The system may then be made multiuser, by mounting the file systems and activating the terminals. Because the process of bringing up the system has many stages, it is usually automated by a shell script. Similar shell scripts may be developed for shutdown and other common maintenance activities.

Shutting the System Down

User Logout

When the user types the end-of-file code **^d** [@or **logout**, @] the shell program exits, and a login prompt reappears. All regular users should log out before the system manager shuts the system down.

[@The Shutdown Command

Executing a script like **/etc/shutdown** is the recommended way to bring the system down. **/etc/shutdown** is a file of shell commands that must be executed by root from the system console, **/dev/console**. The syntax of the command line for one such script is

```
# /etc/shutdown [ time ] [ su ]
```

Here **time** is the number of minutes until the shutdown cycle is initiated and must be an integer between 0 and 15. If **time** is not specified, **/etc/shutdown** will prompt for the delay to allow users to log out. If the **su** argument is specified, the shutdown cycle will halt when the single-user mode is reached. Otherwise, the program **/etc/haltsys** will be invoked to complete the system shutdown.

An **/etc/shutdown** script should perform the following tasks:

1. Warn users that the system is about to go down. If there was a delay specified, then users will be sent a message every minute warning them to log off.

2. Terminate most processes (except those generated from the console).

3. Dismount all mounted file systems.

4. Leave the system in single-user mode if the **su** argument is specified; or half the system automatically with the command **/etc/haltsys**.

The haltsys Command

The **/etc/haltsys** utility is the recommended program for halting the system from the single-user mode. This program is normally invoked automatically by **/etc/shutdown**. However, if the system is already in single-user mode, **/etc/haltsys** must be specified explicitly. The **/etc/haltsys** program will perform the following tasks:

1. Stop all potential writes to the disk by flushing out write buffers, such as editor buffers.

2. Mark the file system clean.

3. Halt the CPU. @]

Manual Shutdown

[@If a system problem prevents the running of the UNIX **shutdown** or **haltsys** commands, the system can be brought down manually.@]

The following steps bring the system down manually:

1. The **wall** (**w**rite to **all**) utility is run to warn logged-in users of the imminent shutdown. (**wall** behaves like

422 — A BUSINESS GUIDE TO THE UNIX SYSTEM

write except that the message is broadcast to all users and it overrides the user's **msg n.**)

2. Issue the command **kill -1 1⟨CR⟩** to terminate all multiuser related processes and put the system in single user mode.

3. Issue the commands **sync;sync⟨CR⟩** from the console. This forces all outstanding I/O on the system to complete.

At this point the system may be powered down or rebooted.

OCCASIONAL DUTIES

Adding a New User

The superuser is responsible for adding new user accounts. After deciding where to install the new user's home directory, the system manager or superuser looks over the **/etc/passwd** file and selects user and group identification numbers. The superuser then takes the following steps:

1. Edits the **/etc/passwd** file and adds an entry.
2. Edits the **/etc/group** file and adds the user's name to the groups to which he or she belongs.
3. Creates the home directory, changes its ownership to the new user, and perhaps adds a login profile.
4. Creates a mailbox file for the new account.

Installing passwords as root

The superuser can install a password using the **passwd** command with the username, **chris**, as in the command

```
passwd chris <CR>
```

The system will then prompt for the password and ask that the new password be retyped.

In systems that require any degree of security, passwords are mandatory except for restricted users. When ordinary users use the **passwd** command, they must first type in the existing password. When **root** uses the **passwd** command, however, any user's password may be changed without knowing the existing password.

The system manager should *always* install a password as part of the procedure for establishing an account. The new user can change the password later if necessary or desired.

Establishing a User Directory

At this point, a new account, **chris**, has been added to the system. The superuser still needs to create a login directory for this user. The superuser makes a directory for the new account with the pathname in the home directory field of the **/etc/passwd** entry. The home directory should be part of the same file system as the remaining accounts in the user's group.

Four steps are involved in setting up a new home directory.

1. Making the directory.
2. Copying a [@.login or@] .profile to the directory.
3. Changing the ownership from **root** to the account name.
4. Changing the group from **root**'s group to the user's group.

The following screen illustrates the creation of **chris**'s **HOME** directory:

```
# cd /usr
# mkdir chris
# cp /.profile chris
# chown chris chris/.profile chris
# chgrp doc chris/.profile chris
# 
```

As with most system administration commands, only **root** can execute the **chown** (**ch**ange **own**er) command and the **chgrp** (**ch**ange **gr**oup) command. If **root** forgets to change the ownership of a user's home directory, the user will not own the directory and, therefore, will not have owner's access permissions.

A standard login profile may be installed by the system manager for each user. The presence of this file is not essential, but is so useful that it is almost always installed for a new user. Usually a few commands generally used on the system are included in the original file. The owner of the account can customize it as required.

Deleting a User Account

As you might suspect, an account can be removed by reversing many of the procedures described above.

1. The entry in the password field for that user is changed to **:deleted:**.
2. The user's name is removed from all membership lists in **/etc/group**.
3. If necessary, the contents of the home directory and the user's post office box, **(/usr/spool/mail/{username})** are archived onto floppy disk or tape.

SYSTEM SECURITY AND PRIVACY

System security means that all information is safe from hardware failure—fortuitous events such as power surges; safe from damage or loss resulting from inadvertent carelessness in the operation of the system; and safe from intentional damage.

Hardware Failures

Occasionally, a hardware failure will result in damage to system data, but the checks and cross-checks made every day by the system manager should reveal these kinds of problems before they have a chance to spread. There can be no assurance that a hardware failure will not occur. Sooner or later it is almost certain that one will. Your best insurance against such failure is a conscientiously applied program of preventive maintenance and a responsive vendor or contractor.

Hardware failures are usually readily apparent: a printer that prints gibberish, a dead terminal, a disk drive that reports many read or write errors, etc.

Bugs

When a computer system is first installed, there are likely to be *bugs* to iron out. An inexperienced computer user is apt to blame such problems on the hardware. How can you determine whether your problem lies in software or hardware? If the problem has existed from day one, a software bug is likely. However, if your problem began after some time of trouble-free operation, you should consider reinstalling the UNIX system from the original diskettes. If the problem disappears, it was probably due to a form of failure called a *glitch*. On the other hand, if your problem remains after regenerating the system programs, you might have a hardware problem. Consult your computer vendor or contractor.

Glitches

A glitch is a random, nonsystemic error in a data or program word. Often the magnetic pattern on a disk or tape has been affected by external magnetic noise and causes a bit to change or be removed. Glitches sometimes result from a worn disk, but usually are caused by careless handling of the media. Remember that the *read/write head* in your floppy disk drives is engaged by the closing of the disk door. If this head is touching the diskette during powerup or power down, transient pulses may cause spurious data to be written onto the disk's magnetic surface—a glitch.

The following precautions can be helpful in reducing glitches.

1. Always store your media away from electronic equipment. Magnetic fields turn up in the most unexpected places: television screens (electrostatic fields), loudspeakers (permanent magnets), magnetized paper clips, and ballpoint pens.

2. The static charge built up on your body from contact with carpets can glitch a diskette or tape. Areas where media are likely to be handled or exposed should be equipped with antistatic mats. Store all media in antistatic sleeves and boxes.

3. Do not allow media to lie about when not in use. Return them to safe-keeping as soon as you are finished with them.

4. *Write-protect* all media until it is necessary to write on it. Although the procedure is different for each type, generally you must
   - cover a notch on a 5 1/4-inch diskette;
   - uncover a notch on an 8-inch diskette;
   - turn the save screw on a cassette;
   - remove the write-ring on a tape.

Security from Operator Error and Carelessness

Prevention of this type of security problem has already been covered in this chapter. Remember to perform frequent system backups and to exercise caution when using commands that affect large amounts of data. If you are in doubt as to the effect of a wild card option, don't use it! Having to retype 200 pages of text because you misused a wildcard is an unnecessary painful reminder of this point.

Security Against Intentional Damage

No computer is likely to be 100 percent safe from unauthorized tampering. The old adage is as true of computer security systems as it is of locks. "They only keep an honest person honest; they won't stop a thief." Ultimately, the best security system is a conscientious application of the basic UNIX security systems: the password, access permissions, the group, and the restricted user. You also should be aware, when possible, of who is authorized to use the system. If unauthorized persons make obvious attempts to find out a user's password or appear to be tampering with the machine, do something about it!

Even though password protection is the only basic defense against unauthorized access, it is sufficient protection for virtually all circumstances if passwords are guarded and used intelligently. Once a password has become public knowledge, it is, of course, useless. (At one university installation, some passwords for frequently used administrative accounts were typeset and posted!) Such practice is, at best, foolhardy in a business environment. Employees should be discouraged from exchanging passwords. The system manager should be especially careful not to divulge the **root** and **bin** passwords. If the system manager finds it necessary to delegate the responsibilities of system administration to someone for a day or so, the privileged passwords should be changed as soon as possible.

CONCLUSION

So you finished the book! You have completed a major effort and should be able to handle a UNIX-based business computer with some authority. Try the reference manuals now to enhance knowledge of your particular system. Use this book as a continuing terminal-side reference. If you want to go on to more advanced materials, look for other Yates books on UNIX at your bookstore, or try some of the papers and books listed in the bibliography.

APPENDIX A
THE BASICS OF COMPUTER TERMINOLOGY

Every discipline has its peculiar vocabulary or jargon. Usually this special vocabulary arises out of the need to accurately describe new devices and to define new concepts and ideas. Certainly the most extensive special vocabulary ever produced is that associated with the computer industry, and it continues to grow. Most of these terms are important only to the specialist and need not concern us in the study of the UNIX* system. Nevertheless, there is a certain minimum set of essential, general terms which must be acquired. Many of these terms define or refer to the computer's hardware, architecture, or *peripheral devices* and are so pervasive in the whole computer milieu that any discussion involving computers assumes they are understood.

Fig. A.1 is a functional diagram of the basic elements of a computer system, including the operating system. It identifies the major divisions of a computer and a fundamental computer operating system. The callouts on Fig. A.1 have been included to draw a comparison between a typical office structure and a computer system.

As shown in Fig. A.1 a minimum computer system consists of certain devices, collectively called resources:

1. A *CPU* or *Central Processing Unit*

The CPU is the brain of the machine. It is this element that executes all of the instructions and commands issued by the software.

* UNIX™ is a trademark of Bell Laboratories.

427

Fig. A.1 The UNIX Operating System

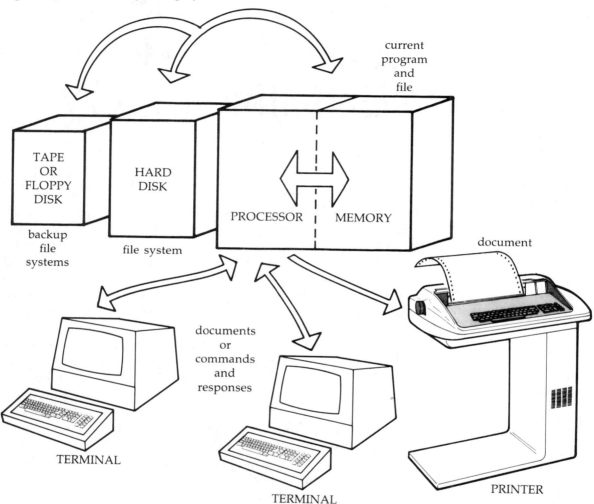

2. Memory, Sometimes Called "On-Board" Storage

Memory contains all the information and instructions used by the machine as it executes or runs programs. For the purposes of this text, it is important to know how memory is organized. Memory can best be thought of as a sequential array of equally sized containers, each of which is capable of holding one computer "word." For the present it can be thought of in the same sense as an ordinary English word with a fixed number of letters. However, the computer word is made up of *bits* rather than letters. Whenever memory "size" is spoken of, for example, 64 *kilobyte*s or 1 *megabyte*, the figure refers to the number of these containers. Moreover, each container is identified by a number, called an "address."

3. Permanent Storage, Magnetic Disk and Magnetic Tape

This type of storage device is permanent only in the sense that if power is removed, the information contained in it is normally not destroyed, as is the case with on-board memory. However, whenever a system is up and operating, data is constantly being changed and moved around in the system and to and from the disk or tape.

a. **Disk**

Although the organization of data on a disk is systematic, it is not quite the same as it is in the on-board memory. There are three basic organizational units in a disk system: the sector, the track, and the record. Each of these units has a fixed size within a given formatting system. Each sector has an "ID number" which the disk handler (part of the operating system) keeps track of. Whenever information is "written" onto the disk, it is uniquely located by the sector(s), track(s), and record(s) in which it is written. In the on-board memory, information is moved in and out a "word" at a time. On the disk, however, information is written around each track a bit at a time, and it is moved to and from the disk a bit at a time. One of the main functions of the disk controller is to convert from the bit-at-a-time format to the word-at-a-time format and vice versa, as required.

b. **Magnetic Tape**

Magnetic tape (usually shortened to "magtape") is comparable in most respects to magnetic disk, except that it has only two basic organizational units, the record and the track. However, there are usually just 7 or 9 tracks, depending upon the particular machine, and information is moved a word at a time like with the on-board memory. (Actually, it is moved a *byte* at a time, which in all cases may not be a full word.)

4. Printer

As the name implies, this device is used to provide "hard copies" of the information handled by the computer. Printers, depending upon the particular machine, can handle information a bit at a time or a word at a time, and some can handle information in either way.

5. Terminal/Monitor

These terms are usually thought of as a single entity called the terminal since they constitute the users' word station. Actually, the terminal is just the keyboard and its associated electronics, and the monitor is the CRT display or screen.

6. The Operating System

The operating system is actually a program or, more accurately, a group of interrelated program elements, each of which is responsible for performing some administrative task within the computer system. Insofar as the user is concerned, the operating system is the link with the computer. The operative feature of this link is the command. Commands have names that usually (but not always!) describe their functions, for example, "copy," "move," "list," and "print." Whenever the operating system is prepared to accept and execute a command, it informs the user by issuing a *prompt*, which is a symbol printed on the CRT monitor. The user then types in his or her command at the keyboard. When the command has been fully entered, the order to execute it is given, normally by pressing the carriage return. The definitions, descriptions, and execution of UNIX commands are the principal subject matter of this book.

APPENDIX B
GLOSSARY

These terms have been italicized in the text. Note: numbers in parentheses after the term refer to the chapter(s) in which the term is mentioned.

absolute request (8)

An absolute formatting request (in **nroff**) has an absolute value as an argument for the instruction. For example, "**5**" could be an absolute value argument to the indentation request, instructing **nroff** to indent exactly 5 ems. See also: **relative request**.

access codes (5)

A nine-character field associated with a file that can be set to permit or deny access to a file. Access codes may be seen on a long-form directory listing. The codes indicate read, write, and execute permission for three separate types of users: the file's owner, members of specific groups, and the general public. See also: **access permission**.

access permission (4)

Access permission allows the user to read, write to, or execute a file. Access permissions are granted or denied by the file's owner. See also: **access codes**.

account name (2) See **username**.

active process (10)

When a command is issued, the UNIX* System gathers copies of the necessary data and files, and generates an active process for the command's execution.

adjust (8)

In formatting with **nroff**, the insertion of additional spaces between words as necessary in order to obtain a straight, or justified, right margin. A variant form of adjusting centers the text. See also: **filling**.

application packages (1)

Programs written to perform specific tasks, such as accounting, payroll, inventory control, or database management.

archiving (4)

The process of making an archive copy of files, or of an entire directory, when such files are no longer in current use.

argument (2, 4)

The object of a UNIX system command, often a filename. Many

---

* UNIX™ is a trademark of Bell Laboratories.

UNIX commands can take more than one argument.

ASCII collating sequence (4, 5)
Each character, including numbers, symbols, and control characters, is represented within the computer by a number between 32 and 127, according to the **ASCII** ("American Standard Code for Information Interchange") code. The order of the character codes denotes ASCII collating sequence, used by UNIX commands such as the **comm** program to compare sorted lists.

background (3)
To avoid having to wait for a time consuming command to finish executing before going on to other work, commands may be run in background. This is accomplished by placing an ampersand (&) at the end of the command line.

backup (3, 4, 10)
Backup copies of files should be made periodically in order to insure against loss due to hardware failure or human error. The frequency and extent of file system backups is determined by the user or users responsible for system management and maintenance.

bit (10, Appendix A)
The smallest unit of information used by the computer. The term "bit" stands for **b**inary dig**it**. A bit can be either a "1" or a "0".

blanks (2)
A blank, or space, is considered a character in the UNIX system, even though no character appears on the screen. UNIX commands will not work properly with blanks mis-

placed, although extra blanks in command lines are typically ignored.

block (10)
A logical construct for referring to stored data. A UNIX block may have a size of either 512 or 1024 bytes, depending on the particular UNIX system.

booting (10)
The process of turning on the system and bringing key system programs into memory. Usually automated by means of a shell script. Also known as booting up.

booting up (10) See **booting**.

buffer (3)
A place in memory where information can be temporarily saved. Buffers are not as secure as disk files, but they are easier to access. See also: **edit buffer**.

bugs (10)
Errors in computer programs which cause commands to produce unexpected and sometimes damaging results. Also used to refer to malfunctions of computer hardware.

byte (10, Appendix A)
A group of eight binary bits, whose values are usually assigned to characters according to the ASCII code. Each eight-bit byte represents a single character.

central processing unit (Appendix A)
The central processing unit ("cpu") is the hardware that controls the interpretation and execution of commands by the system. The

computer chip(s), such as the 68000, reside in the central processing unit.

command file (5)

A file containing a set of commands to be executed as a group. Command files may be used for editing or other tasks.

command line (2)

Comprises all characters, including blank spaces, that are used to build a command. A command line is typed in response to the shell prompt.

command lists (6)

A command sequence consisting of multiple commands separated by semicolons.

command mode (3)

When the screen editor **vi** is in command mode, cursor motion commands may be issued to move the cursor to any position in the text.

command syntax (2)

The structure of a UNIX command language sentence. Generally: **command** { **options**}... {**arguments** }...

console (10)

The terminal that is used to boot up the system, and for system management and maintenance.

control character (2)

Generated by pressing the CONTROL key simultaneously with another key, **control characters** have special meanings in the UNIX system. Control characters are usually not displayed on the video screen.

cpu (1, 2, Appendix A) See **central processing unit**.

current directory (4)

The directory from which a user is currently issuing commands. The name of the current directory may be obtained with the **pwd** (**p**rint **w**orking **d**irectory) command. When a user logs in, the home directory is usually the current directory.

current line (3)

In editing, the line of text most recently written or edited is called the current line, and can be addressed in command mode using the period, or dot.

cursor (2)

A small lighted rectangle or bar which appears on the screen, indicating location of next entry or command.

default value (2, 3)

The value used by a command if no alternative value is supplied in the command line.

directory (4)

Directories are data files that contain the names and locations of other files. A long-format directory listing provides additional information. Directory names may, by convention, begin with a capital letter so that they can be easily distinguished from other filenames.

edit buffer (3)

A temporary working area for text being edited. Changes made to an edit buffer are not saved unless a write command is issued.

erase (2)

By default, the **#** character erases, or more correctly, cancels individual characters. One **#** is echoed on the screen for each canceled character. The erase character may be changed with the **stty** command. (*stty not covered in book*)

error message (2)

The UNIX system responds with an error message when a command is given incorrectly. Errors can be either typographical or syntactical in nature.

escape (2, 3, 6)

(1) The special meaning of a character to the shell or to an editor may be escaped, or temporarily turned off, with a backslash (\), including \ itself. (2) Also refers to a temporary exit, or escape, from an editing program in order to issue commands.

escape sequence (8)

In formatting, a sequence of characters beginning with \ used to embed formatting requests in lines of text.

extension (4)

The latter part of a filename, separated from the rest of the filename by a dot. Helps identify the file.

filename (3, 4)

A sequence of up to 14 non-blank characters used to identify a file. Characters having special meanings to the shell should not be used in filenames. Filenames should be made unique and meaningful, yet still kept as simple as possible. Separating parts of a filename with underscore and dot, as in **mary_new.acct**, can improve readability. Filenames should begin with a lowercase letter to easily dis-

tinguish them from directory names, which should be capitalized.

file system (4)

The logical structure which contains all text files, program files, and files that control the logical interfacing among system components such as terminals, printers, and disk drives.

fill (8)

The **nroff** process of rearranging lines of unequal length into lines about 6 1/2 inches long. The line length may be changed. See also: **adjust**.

filter programs (6)

A UNIX program (command) that takes only one input from standard input and produces exactly one output on standard output. A filter program may participate in a command pipeline in which the output of the previous command forms the input for the filter command, which may in turn transmit its output to other commands.

glitch (10)

A hardware failure, often as a result of damage to a magnetic medium such as a disk. Silicon Valley Guy language.

headers (3)

A line or line of information printed at the top (or head) of a page—usually on every page of a document.

home directory (4)

A user's home directory is the directory present at login. This directory is usually named with the user's login name.

implementation dependent (2)

Signified by [@, material that is implementation dependent only applies to certain UNIX systems. For instance, the U.C. Berkeley version of UNIX has some commands which may not be available on systems running other versions of UNIX.

inode (4, 5, 10)

A file system element that points to the exact location of the file's bytes on the disk.

i-number (5)

The i-node number, uniquely associated with a particular file. The i-number associated with a given filename may be seen using the -i option to a directory listing command.

i-list (10)

The list of i-nodes in a file system that are being used to point to existing files.

interactive (shell function) (6)

A shell command, like **cp**, **rm**, or **cat** which receives an immediate response from the system. See also: **programmed** (shell function).

interrupt (2)

Issuing an interrupt signal stops a shell command or other command in progress and returns user to the previous level at which work was being done. By default, the interrupt signal is sent using the key labeled RUB, or DEL; on some UNIX systems the interrupt signal may be reassigned to another character.

keep (9)

An element of the formatting macro package which temporarily stores lines that should be kept together until they can be inserted at the appropriate place in the formatted output.

kernel (2)

Set of UNIX internal system programs.

key (10)

In a **tar** (tape archive) **command**, the key tells which function is to be performed.

kilobyte (Appendix A)

One kilobyte equals one thousand bytes. However, because of the use of binary numbers to represent computer data, one kilobyte is accepted as meaning 1,024 bytes (2^{10} bytes).

line kill (2)

A character that cancels an entire command line or text entry line and allows it to be retyped. The line kill character, set by default to @, may be reassigned with the **stty** command.

line-oriented (1)

A line-oriented editor uses the line numbers of input text to determine the operation of text editing commands. Editing is performed on a line-by-line basis, often using an address range of line numbers.

line printer (3)

A printer used only for obtaining printed output; does not permit two-way comunication between the computer and the printer.

line printer queue (3)

When more than one **lpr** command is issued to a line printer, the files named in the commands are accumulated in a buffer, or queue, until the printer is available.

login name (2) See **username**.

login shell (6)

The login shell is the shell assigned for initial use after logging in. The login shell is specified in one field of a user's entry in the **/etc/passwd** file.

logout (2)

The process of exiting the UNIX system by sending a control character (usually the end-of-file character, **^d**). Logging out causes another login process to be started at that terminal.

macro (8, 9)

A set of **nroff** requests collected under a single name, so that several formatting requests may be issued using a single dot command.

macro packages (9)

A complete set of macros for formatting files. The **-ms** macro package is frequently used for formatting text files.

megabyte (Appendix A)

Approximately one million bytes. The actual figure, because of the binary nature of computer number, is 1,048,576 (1,024 × 1,024). See also **kilobyte**.

menu driven (6)

A menu-driven shell simplifies the process of giving commands by offering a list of commands from which the user makes a selection. Each command may actually be a combination of commands designed

to accomplish a specific task, such as file sorting, list printing, etc.

metacharacters (5)

Characters which have special meanings to the shell or other program. Metacharacters such as *** $? . / [ ]** may be interpreted differently by a shell than by another program.

microspacing (8)

The ability of a printer to move its printing head and platen (roller) up, down, back, and forth in very small increments to produce subscripts, superscripts, overstrikes, and other special effects. A letter-quality printer with microspacing is the most desirable type to use with the UNIX formatting program, **nroff**.

mnemonic (2)

Most UNIX system commands are mnemonic abbreviations which remind the user of their full-word meanings. Some examples include **cd** for change directory, **cat** for catenate, and **mkdir** for make directory.

modem (2)

An electronic device which allows communication between terminals and computers via telephone lines. Modems convert analog signals to digital signals and vice versa.

multitasking (10)

A multitasking operating system allows several tasks to run concurrently. The system performs a portion of each task until tasks are completed.

multiuser (1)

A multiuser operating system allows users to work at the same time at different workstations.

multiuser mode (2)

The status of a computer system when more than a single user is logged on to the system.

named buffers (2, 3)

Temporary, named storage spaces used to hold text **yanked** or **deleted** when using a UNIX text editor.

null lines (3)

In **vi**, lines in the screen display that are marked with a tilde to indicate that the end-of-file has been reached. See also: **tilde**.

operating system (1)

The software programs that manage the logical operations and physical devices of a computer system. The UNIX system is an interactive operating system.

options (2, 4)

Options modify the meaning of the command in a UNIX command sentence. The options refine the command verb's actions.

ordinary user (10)

An ordinary user has permission to create, remove, read, and write files and directories and has access to other files and directories on the system if the appropriate permissions are set.

overwrite (3)

The text editing write command or any of its variants (**wq**, **x**) will overwrite the disk copy of the file with the contents of the edit buffer, replacing the file's previous contents.

owner (4)

The user account name from which a file or directory is created becomes the owner. The owner may change access permissions on owned files and directories.

partial blocks (10)

On disk, a block of size 512 or 1,024 bytes that is not completely filled by the bytes of a file.

partial pathname (5) See **pathname**.

password (2)

Used in conjunction with a username to allow a user to log in. Each username has a unique password. The password is not displayed on the screen during login.

pathname (5)

Pathnames indicate a file's position in the directory tree. A full pathname, which always begins with a slash (/) traces a file's ancestry all the way back to the root directory. The current directory in which the filename is entered may be named with one dots (.); two dots (..) denote the directory immediately above the current directory. Partial or relative pathnames indicate a file's position in the directory tree without going all the way back to root.

peripheral devices (Appendix A)

Devices which attach to (are peripheral to) the cpu, such as printers, keyboard, disk drives.

phototypesetter (8)

Typesetting machine which uses a photographic process.

PID (6) See **process identification**.

pipe (3)

A pipe connects the output of one command to the input of the next. The symbol is ¦ .

pipeline (6)

A string of commands connected by pipes.

printing terminal (8)

A self-sufficient terminal with a keyboard and switches, that prints commands and responses on paper.

process identification (6)

A unique number that the kernel uses to identify a process.

programmed (shell function) (6)

Storing a set of commands for use at a later time. Regular UNIX commands can be placed in a file, and the shell will sequentially execute them. See also: **interactive**.

prompt (Appendix A)

A symbol used to indicate that a program is ready to receive commands. The shell and the text editing programs are among those that use prompts.

read/write head (10)

A magnetic head on a disk or tape drive.

redirection (6)

Changing either the standard input or standard output from their default values is called redirection.

registers (9)

In text formatting with **nroff** and the **-ms** macro package, values for certain formatting operations are kept in two types of registers: number registers and string registers.

Values for measures such as line length, page offset, etc. are kept in number registers. Values for headings and footings are kept in string registers. Default values for these registers may be changed.

relative pathname (5) See **pathname**.

relative request (8)

A request that uses a relative, rather than an absolute, value. An example is **.in -5**, which instructs **nroff** to subtract five ems from the previous indentation value. See also: **absolute request**.

right justifies (1) See **justified**.

root (4)

The first directory in the root file system. All other files and directories trace their ancestry back to the root.

screen-oriented (1)

A screen-oriented text editor allows the cursor to be moved freely over the screen to the place in the text where editing is to begin. The screen image of the text is updated immediately as changes are made. See also: **line-oriented.**

search permission (10)

This is a directory's equivalent of execute permission on a file. It is necessary in order to list the directory.

secondary prompt (6)

When a command line becomes too long to fit on one line of the video screen, it may be continued on the next line by preceding the carriage return with a backslash. This causes the carriage return to be "escaped," and a secondary prompt ($>$) may appear on the next line, indicating that the shell expects more command input.

shell (2, 3)

The shell program, also called a "command interpreter," controls the interaction between users and the computer system, and interprets commands for the system kernel.

shell command language (6)

Has a vocabulary of built-in commands and shell procedure directives for use in controlling the environment and building command files and shell scripts.

shell escape (3)

A temporary exit to the shell from a text editing program for the purpose of issuing one or more commands to the shell. The first command issued may call up the shell itself, so that a number of subsequent commands may be issued.

shell procedure (6)

Also known as shell script, a file of commands driven by shell procedure directives which may operate on one or more files given as arguments.

shell script (5, 6) See shell procedure.

single-user mode (2, 10)

Immediately after booting up, the system is in a special state called single-user mode. Only a single terminal, referred to as the console, is active, along with a shell program. A user logged in as **root** may use the system in this mode.

spaces (2) See blanks.

special users (10)

Special users have access to system programs and utilities which is usually denied to ordinary users. Special user accounts are generally set up for system management purposes.

spooling (3, 7)

The process of lining up jobs for a peripheral device. Jobs in the queue will be sent to the device one at a time. Acronym for simultaneous peripheral operation online.

standard input (6)

The keyboard is the standard input by default, but input may be redirected.

standard output (6)

The terminal is the standard output by default, but output may be redirected.

subdirectory (4)

A directory whose name is an entry in another directory. All directories except the root directory are subdirectories.

subshells (3, 6)

A shell program invoked as a command becomes a subshell that nests within the previous shell. Only a limited number of successive subshells may be invoked. Each subshell must be exited separately with **^d.** Logout may be done only from the login shell. See also: **login shell.**

superuser (2, 10)

The all-powerful user, whose name must always be **root.** Has unlimited access privileges to files and directories in order to perform system management and maintenance.

system manager (2, 10)

The individual whose responsibility it is to perform system management and maintenance.

target directory (5)

The directory that is the object of a command such as **cp** (copy). May also be referred to as "destination directory."

text editing (1)

Process of entering and/or modifying text or programs. Text editing is a UNIX system utility. The UNIX text editors include **vi, ex,** and **ed.**

text entry mode (3)

The mode entered by giving a text entry command to an editing program. In **vi) ESC** returns the user to command mode.

text formatting (1, 8)

Organizing and arranging text into a desired output. Text formatting programs are usually used as post-processors for text editors. The UNIX text formatting program, **nroff,** has a typesetting version called **troff.**

tildes—˜ (3)

In the screen editor, **vi,** tildes on the screen indicate that the end of a file has been reached. Also, a special character used to stand for a user's home directory (on some UNIX systems).

UNIX command language (2)

The command language sentence has an implicit subject, "UNIX", a command verb indicating the action that the system is to perform, and one or more objects, usually files, on which the command is to act.

unmount (10)

The process of removing a file system from active use.

username (2)

Login name or account name.

wildcards (5)

A character which may have special meaning to the shell or to an editing program. Shell wildcard characters used in filenames are expanded to refer to a specified set of files. The **echo** command should generally be used to preview the effects of a wildcard character in shell commands. See also **metacharacter.**

word processor (3)

A combined text editing and text formatting program. Editing and formatting are separate functions in the UNIX system.

write-protect (10)

A means of preventing a floppy disk or other storage media from being overwritten.

APPENDIX C
BIBLIOGRAPHY

*Aho, A.V., Kernighan, B.W., and Weinberger, P.J. "AWK—A Pattern Scanning and Processing Language."

Allison, D.R. "A Comparison of CP/M and UNIX." In Digest of Papers Spring Compcon 82, High Technology in the Information Industry, IEEE Publications, 1982.

Anonymous. "Vendor's Software Musts: Function, Portability." *Computerworld Special Report*, May 1981, p. 32.

Balocca, R. "Networking and the Process Structure of UNIX: A Case Study." In *Proceedings of Compcon Fall 78*, Computer Communications Networks, 1978.

Bourne, S.R. "An Introduction to the UNIX Shell." *Bell System Technical Journal* 57 (1978):2797–2822.

Boughton, D.A. "A Multi-User Software Development System for Microprocessor-Based Products." In Colloquium on Development Environments for Microprocessor Systems, London, England, 1982.

Computer Business News Comment. "Overcoming the Hurdles in the Path to UNIX." *Computer Business News*, 27 October 1980, p. 8.

Cermak, I.A. "An Integrated Approach to Microcomputer Support Tools." In *1977 Electro Conference Record*, 1977.

Cherlin, Edward. "The UNIX Operating System: Portability a Plus." *Mini-Micro Systems*, April 1981, pp. 153–159.

*Cherry, L.L. and Morris, R.H. "BC—An ARbitrary Precision Desk-Calculator Language."

*The documents so marked are distributed with the Version 7 Edition of Bell Labs UNIX. They are public domain documents and may be obtained from a university UNIX installation, or from Bell Labs.

Certain references were found through a search performed on the Dialog Information Retrieval System of Dialog Information Services, Inc. of Palo Alto, California and were obtained from the Magazine Index file 47, produced by Information Access Corporation of Menlo Park, California; from the ABI/INFORM file 15 produced by Data Courier of Louisville, Kentucky; and from the INSPEC file 13 produced by the Institution of Electrical Engineers of London, England and are published here with permission.

Chesson, G.L. "The Network UNIX System." *Operating Systems Review* 9 (1975). Also in *Proceedings of the 5th Symposium on Operating Systems Principles,* 1978.

Colony, George F. "AT&T Deregulates—There's a New Kid on the Block." *Computerworld (Office Automation Issue),* March 1982, pp. 39, 42–43.

Corbett, C. and Witten, I.H. "On the Inclusion and Placement of Documentation Graphics in Computer Typesetting." *Computer Journal,* (GB), May 1982, pp. 272–273.

Dolotta, T.A. and Mashey, John R. "An Introduction to the Programmer's Workbench." In *Proceedings of the 2nd International Conference on Software Engineering,* 1976.

Dolotta, T.A., Haight, R.C., and Mashey, John R. "UNIX Time-Sharing System: The Programmer's Workbench." *Bell System Technical Journal* 57 (1978):2177–2200.

*Feldman, S.I. and Weinberger, P.J. "A Portable Fortran 77 Compiler."

*Feldman S.I. "Make—A Program for Maintaining Computer Programs."

Flournoy, Marina L. "Software 'Workbench' Automates Program Modification." *Data Communications,* February 1982, pp. 107–115.

Geisler, Pamela, "Design Approach for 16-bit." *Systems International* (UK), November 1981, pp. 24–28.

Gillogly, J.J. "Word processing with UNIX. In *1978 Midcon Technical Papers,* 1978.

Glasser, A.L. "The Evolution of a Source Code Control System." *SICSOFT* 3 (1978):121–125.

Gooding,, Claire, "France Builds UNIX Environment with Pascal." *Mini-Micro Systems,* July 1982, pp. 73–74.

Greenberg, Robert B. "The UNIX Operating System and the XENIX Standard Operating Environment." *Byte,* June 1981, p. 248.

Grietzer, John. "UNIX Starts Its Ride to the Top." *Computer Business News,* 26 January 1981, p. 1.

*Haley, C.B. and Ritchie, D.M. *Setting Up UNIX, Seventh Edition.*

*Haley, C.B. and Ritchie, D.M. *Regenerating System Software.*

Heffler, M.J. "Description of a Menu Creation and Interpretation System." *Software-Practice and Experience,* March 1982, pp. 269–281.

Holmgren, S.F. "Resource Sharing UNIX." In *Proceedings of Compcon Fall 78,* 1978.

Horsley, J. "Backing UNIX in the 16-Bit Standard Race." *Computing* (GB), April 1982, pp. 24–25.

Horton, R.E. "Using Personal Computers as Terminals in Computer Networks." In *AEDS Proceedings of the 18th Annual Convention* "A Gateway to the Use of Computers in Education," 1980.

Hughes, P. "The Operating System of the Future." *Microcomputing,* June 1982, pp. 28–31.

Information and Publication Division. "The UNIX System. An Easier Way to Communicate with Computers." Bell Laboratories, 1979.

Isaak, Jim. "Looking at the 'Universe'." *Mini-Micro Systems*, October 1981, pp. 145–148.

Johnson, R. Colin. "Major Firms Join UNIX Parade." *Electronics*, April 1981, p. 108.

Johnson, R. Colin. "Operating Systems Hold a Full House of Features for 16-bit Microprocessors." *Electronics*, March 1982, p. 113.

Johnson, R. Colin. "What is UNIX Anyway?" *Electronics*, March 1981, p. 121.

*Johnson, S.C. "YACC: Yet Another Compiler-Compiler."

*Johnson, S.C. "A Tour Through the Portable C Compiler"

*Johnson, S.C. "Lint, A C Program Checker."

Johnson, Steven C., "UNIX Time-Sharing System: Language Development Tools." *Bell System Technical Journal* 57 (1978):1971–90.

Johnson, Stephen C., and Lesk, Michael E. "Language Development Tools." *Bell System Technical Journal* 57 (1978).

*Kernighan, B.W. "Ratfor—A Preprocessor for a Rational Fortran."

*Kernighan, B.W. and Weinberger, P.J. "The M4 Macro Processor."

*Kernighan, B.W. "A TROFF Tutorial."

*Kernighan, B.W. "UNIX for Beginners (2nd Edition)."

*Kernighan, B.W. "A Tutorial Introduction to the UNIX Text Editor."

*Kernighan, B.W. "Advanced Editing on UNIX."

*Kernighan, B.W. and Ritchie, D.M. "UNIX Programming."

Kernighan, Brian W. "PIC—A Language for Typesetting Graphics." *Software-Practice and Experience* (GB), January 1982, pp. 1–21.

Kernighan, Brian W. and Morgan, Samuel P. "The UNIX Operating System: a Model for Software Design." *Science*, February 1982, p. 779.

Kernighan, Brian W. and Mashey, John R. "The UNIX Programming Environment." *Software-Practice and Experience* 9 (1979).

Kernighan, Brian W. and Cherry, L.L. "A System for Typesetting Mathematics." In *Communications of the ACM* 18 (1975):151–157. Also published as "Computer Science Technical Report No. 17." Murray Hill, NJ: Bell Laboratories, 1977.

Kernighan, Brian W., Lesk, M.E., and Ossanna, J.R., Jr. "Document Preparation." *Bell System Technical Journal* 57 (1978).

*Lesk, M.E. and Schmidt, E. "LEX—A Lexical Analyzer Generator."

*Lesk, M.E. and Kernighan, B.W. "Learn-Computer Aided Instruction on UNIX."

*Lesk,, M.E. "Typing Documents on the UNIX Systems."

*Lesk, M.E. "TBL—A Program to Format Tables."

*Lesk, M.E. "Some Applications of Inverted Indexes on the UNIX System."

Lesk, Michael, "Another View. (UNIX)." *Datamation*, November 1981, p. 146.

Lesk, Michael and Kernighan, Brian W. "Computer Typesetting of Technical Journals on UNIX." In *Proceedings of AFIPS National Comuter Conference*, 1977.

Lettieri, Larry. "Can UNIX Cut It in the Commerical World?" *Mini-Micro Systems*, June 1982, pp. 155–158.

Libes, Don. "UNIX and CP/M." *MICROSYSTEMS*, January 1983, pp. 26–34.

Libes, Don. "UNIX on Microcomputers." *MICROSYSTEMS*, January 1983, pp. 42–44.

Lions, J. "The UNIX Operating System." In *Commentary*, Murray Hill, New Jersey: Bell Telephone Laboratories, 1977.

Lions, J. "Experiences with the UNIX Time-Sharing System." *Software-Practice and Experience* 9 (1979).

Lowe, Linda. "UNIX Gets Real-Time and Menu Extras." *Electronics*, September 1982, p. 49.

Luderer, G.W.R.; Maranzano, J.F.; and Tague, B.A. "The UNIX Operating System as a Base for Applications." *Bell System Technical Journal* 57 (1978).

Lunn, K. "What's So Nice About the UNIX System . . . Is That It Is Just So Nice and Easy for Users to Operate." *Computer Talk*, (GB), March 1982, pp. 10–11.

Lycklama, H. "UNIX on a Microprocessor." *Bell System Technical Journal* 57 (1978).

Lycklama, H. and Christensen, C. "A Minicomputer Satellite Processor System." *Bell System Technical Journal* 57 (1978):2103–13.

MacDonald, N.H., Frase, L.T., Gingrich, P.S., and Keenan, S.A. "The Writer's Workbench: Computer Aids for Text Analysis." *IEEE Transactions on Communication*, January 1982.

Manning, E.G., Howard R., O'Donnel, C.G., Pammett, K., and Change, E. "A UNIX-Based Local Processor and Network Access Machine." *Computer Networks* 1 (1976).

Marshall, Martin. "UNIX Implemented for 68000 Systems." *Electronics*, January 1982, p. 41.

Marshall, Martin. "Price Cut Makes UNIX Strong Contender." *Electronics*, December 1981, p. 42.

Martin, M.R. "UNIX and Local Computer Networking." In Digest of Papers Spring Compcon 82, High Technology in the Information Industry, IEEE Publications, 1982.

*Maranzano, I.F. and Bourne, S.R. "A Tutorial Introduction to ADB."

Mashey, John R. "Using a Command Language as High-Level Programming Language." In Proceedings of the 2nd International Conference on Software Engineering, 1976.

Mashey, John R. and Smith, D.W. "Documentation Tools and Techniques." In *2nd International Conference on Software Engineering*, 1976.

McCauley, E.J., Doka, Eric N., and Baladi, Nabil A. "Microcomputers: Challenging the Minis." *Mini-Micro Systems*, September 1981, pp. 135–141.

McIlroy, M.D. "Development of a Spelling List." IEEE Transactions on Communications, January 1982, pp. 91–99.

*McMahon, L.E. "SED—A Non-interactive Text Editor."

Miller, P. "A Beginner's Guide to UNIX." In Digest of Papers Spring Compcon 82, High Technology in the Information Industry, IEEE Publications, 1982.

Minnich, Mike. "Where We're Going In the World of Mini/microcomputers." *Canadian Datasystems* (Canada), July 1981, pp. 26–29.

Morgan, Samuel P. "Easy Does It." *Telephony*, March 1979, p. 50,52–53,56.

Morgan, Samuel P. "The UNIX System: Making Computers Easier to Use." *Bell Laboratories Record*, December 1978, pp. 308–313.

*Morris, R.H. and Cherry, L.L. "DC—An Interactive Desk Calculator."

*Morris, R.H. and Thompson, K. "Password Security: A Case History."

Mulrooney, T.J. "An Inexpensive Z-80 Based Microcomputer Development System." In *Proceedings of Micro-Delcon '82, the Delaware Bay Computer Conference 1982*, IEEE Publications, 1982.

Myers, Edith. "UNIX: A Standard Now?" *Datamation*, January 1982, p. 77.

Needle, D. "Look-Alikes Crowd Bell's 'True' UNIX in 16-Bit Micro Market." *Infoworld*, March 1982, pp. 12–13.

Norman, Donald A. "The Trouble with UNIX." *Datamation*, November 1981, p. 139.

Norman, D. "The UNIX Road to Power (Operating System)." *Practical Computing*, (GB), March 1982, pp. 159–164.

*Nowitz, D.A. "UUCP Implementation Description."

*Nowitz, D.A. and Lesk M.E. "A Dial-Up Network of UNIX Systems."

Nowitz, D.A. and Lesk, M.E. "Implementation of a UNIX Network." *Computing Communications* (GB), February 1982, pp. 30–34.

*Ossanna, J.F. "NROFF/TROFF User's Manual."

O'Connor, Rory J. "Users Meet to Voice Support for UNIX Standard." *Computer Business News*, 27 October 1980, p. 1.

Ousterhout, J.K. "Caesar: An Interactive Editor for VLSI Layout." In *Digest of Papers Spring Compcon 82*, High Technology in the Information Industry, IEEE Publications, 1982.

Paul, Lois. "Yourdon Details Software Development Trends." *Computerworld*, February 1982, p. 12.

Perez, Matt M. and Roth, Raymond M. "Terminal Variety Poses Software Problem." *Computerworld Special Report*, March 1982, pp. 25, 28.

Plauser, P.J. and Krieger, M.S. "UNIX-like Software Runs on Mini- and Microcomputers." *Electronics*, March 1981, p. 125.

Plum, Thomas. "Integrating Text and Data Processing on a Small System." *Datamation*, June 1978, pp. 165–175.

Rauch-Hindin, Wendy. "UNIX: An Operating System That Means Business." *Data Communications*, October 1981, pp. 101–110.

*Ritchie, D.M. *The UNIX I/O System.*

*Ritchie, D.M. *A Tour Through the UNIX C Compiler.*
*Ritchie, D.M. *On the Security of UNIX.*
*Ritchie, D.M. The C Programming Language—Reference Manual.
*Ritchie, D.M. *UNIX Assembler Reference Manual.*
Ritchie, Dennis M. "The Evolution of the UNIX Time-Sharing System." In *Proceedings Symposium Language Design and Programming Methodology,* Sydney, Australia, 1979.
Ritchie, Dennis M. and Thompson, Kenneth. "The UNIX Time-Sharing System." *Bell System Technical Journal* 57 (1978).
Ritchie, Dennis M. "UNIX Time-Sharing System: A Retrospective." *Bell System Technical Journal* 57, (1978):1947–69.
Roome, William D. "Programmer's Workbench: New Tools for Software Development." *Bell Laboratories Record,* January 1979, pp. 19–26.
Rose, G. "An Operating System Case Study." *Operating Systems Review* 12 (1978).
Rosenthal, D.S.H. "UNIX as a Basis for CAD Software." *Computer Aided Design* (GB), May 1982, pp. 131–135.
Rochkind, M.J. "The Source Code Control System." *IEEE Transactions in Software Engineering* SE-1 (1975):364–370.
Rowe, Lawrence A. and Birman, Kenneth P. "A Local Network Based on the UNIX Operating System." *IEEE Transactions on Software Engineering,* March 1982, pp. 137–146.

Schindler, M. "Software Awaits a Revolution." *Elektronik* (Germany), July 1982, pp. 89–93.
Simpson, David. Small-Business Systems Solve Big Problems." *Mini-Micro Systems,* June 1982, pp. 201–216.
Stiefel, Malcolm L. "UNIX." *Mini-Micro Systems,* April 1978, pp. 64–66.
Stonebraker, M., Wong, E., Kreps, P., and Held, G. "The Design and Implementation of Ingres." In *ACM Transactions on Database Systems* 1 (1976).
Swain, M. "The Birth and Development of UNIX—Ma Bell's Software Baby." *Infoworld,* March 1982, p. 11.

Teitelman, W. *A Display Oriented Programmer's Assistant,* CSL 77-3, Palo Alto, California: Xerox Corp., Palo Alto Research Center, 1977.
Thomas, Rebecca A. and Yates, Jean. "UNIX." *Computerworld,* Janury 1982, pp. 19–32.
Thomas, R.A.C.; DeLobel, C.; and Litwin, W. "Process Structure Alternatives Towards a Distributed Ingres." In *Proceedings of the International Symposium on Distributed Data Bases, "Distributed Data Bases,"* 1980.
Thompson, Kenneth. "UNIX Implementation." *Bell System Technical Journal* 57 (1978).
Thompson, Kenneth. "The UNIX Command Language." In *Structured Programming—Infotech State of the Art Report.* Berkshire, England: Infotech International Ltd., March 1975, pp. 375–84.

Ursino, Mark. "Introduction to the XENIX Operating System." *MICROSYS-TEMS*, January 1983, pp. 36–40.

Weiner, Bruce and Swartz, Douglas. "Adapting UNIX to a 16-bit Microcomputer." *Electronics*, March 1981, p. 120.

Weiss, H.M. "Ingres: A Data-Management System for Minis." *Mini-Micro Systems*, January 1982, pp. 231–232.

Woodward, J.P.L. "Applications for Multilevel Security Operating Systems." In *AFIPS Conference Proceedings, 1979 NCC.*

Yates, J. and Thomas, R. *A User Guide to the UNIX System.* Berkeley, CA: Osborne/McGraw-Hill, 1982.

APPENDIX D
RESOURCES DIRECTORY

Hardware Vendors:
UNIX* Related Products

Altos Computer Systems
2641 Orchard Parkway, San Jose CA 95134
408/946-6700

16-bit microcomputers
586: 1–5 users (8086-based)
ACS 8600: 1–8 users (8086-based)
ACS 68000: 8–16 users (68000-based)
XENIX, System III UNIX

Amdahl Corporation
1250 E. Arques Avenue, P.O. Box 470, Sunnyvale, CA 94086
408/746-6000

IBM System/370 compatible mainframe computers
UTS Universal Time-sharing System
Amdahl 470 and 580 processors
Modified V7 UNIX
Target: Programming environment

Callan Data Systems
2645 Townsgate Road, Westlake Village, CA 91361
805/497-6837

16/32-bit integrated workstations, 68000-based
Unistar 100: single-user
Unistar 200: 1–10 users
V7 UNIX with Berkeley enhancements
Target: OEMs, large end-users

* UNIX™ is a trademark of Bell Laboratories.

Codata Systems Corporation
285 N. Wolfe Rd., Sunnyvale, CA 94086
408/735-1744

16-bit Microcomputers, 68000-based
Codata 3300: 1–10 users (10, 33, 84 MByte Winchesters)
V7 UNIX with Berkeley 4.1 enhancements
UniPlus+ enhanced System III
Target: OEMs

Fortune Systems
1501 Industrial Road, San Carlos, CA 94070
415/593-9000

16-bit microcomputer, 68000-based
Fortune 32:16: 8 users
FOS: Fortune's version of UNIX
Target: Office environment

Intel Corporation
3065 Bowers Avenue, SC6-290, Santa Clara, CA 95051
408/987-8080

Microprocessors, systems, software
8086, 186, 286: 16-bit microprocessors
86/330 and 86/380: 8086-based microcomputers: 5 users (expandable to 9)
XENIX
Target: OEMs, Systems Integrator

National Semiconductor
2900 Semiconductor Drive, Santa Clara, CA 95051
408/721-5000

16-bit Microprocessors, Development systems
16000 Microprocessor family: 16032 CPU, 16081 FPU, 16082 MMU
Development system: 16032-based microcomputer: support for 8 users; .5
to 3.25 MByte RAM; 20 MByte Winchester; streaming
tape; available: September 1983.
Berkeley 4.1 UNIX User interface
Target: Engineering development for 16000 users

NCR
OEM Marketing Division, Dayton, OH 45479
800/222-1235

16-bit microcomputers, larger systems
Tower 1632: 68000-based: 16 users
System III UNIX
Target: Systems Builders, OEMs

Onyx Systems, Inc.
25 East Trimble Road, San Jose, CA 95131
408/946-6330

16-bit microcomputers
Z8000-based
Sundance 16: 5 users
C5002A: 5 users, 11 users
C8002: 8 users
C8002A: 5 users, 11 users
System III UNIX
Target: Business applications

Perkin-Elmer
2 Crescent Place, Oceanport, NJ 07757
201/870-4712

32-bit minicomputers
Proprietary processor design
3210: 8–32 users
3230: 16–64 users
3250: 32–128 users
Edition VII Workbench UNIX with Berkeley enhancements

Plexus Computers, Inc.
2230 Martin Avenue, Santa Clara, CA 95050
408/988-1755

16-bit microcomputers
P/25: Z8000-based: 16 users
P/35: 68000-based: 16 users

P/40: Z8000-based: 40 users
P/60: 68000-based: 40 users
System III UNIX
Target: Distributed processing and decision support

Sun Microsystems
2550 Garcia Avenue, Mountain View, CA 94043
415/960-1300

16-bit graphics workstation: 68010-based
Sun workstation: Single-user: clustered network
Berkeley 4.2, V7 UNIX
Target: Scientific and engineering markets

Tandy Corporation
400 Atrium, Tandy Center, Fort Worth, TX 76102
817/390-3935

16-bit microcomputer systems
68000-based
TRS 80 Model 16: 3 users
TRS 80 Model 2 with upgrade: 3 users
XENIX
Target: Small businesses

Tektronix, Inc.
D/S-92-635
P.O. Box 4600, Beaverton, OR 97075
503/629-1718

Multi-user development systems
LSI 11/23 processor; 1 MByte of memory optional
8560: 4–8 users
TNIX derived from V7 UNIX
Target: Software development

Three Rivers Computer Corporation
720 Gross Street, Pittsburg, PA 15224
412/621-6250

32-bit minicomputer system
Proprietary processor
PERQ: Single-user
V7 UNIX
Target: Publishing industry, computer-aided design; engineering workstations

---

Zilog
Systems Division
1315 Dell Avenue, Campbell, CA 95008
408/370-8000

16-bit Microcomputer systems
System 8000: 8–24 users; Z8000-based
System III UNIX
Target: OEMs, large end-users

Zilog
Components Division
1315 Dell Avenue, C2-0, Campbell, CA 95008
408/370-8000

16-bit microprocessors
Z8000 microprocessor family
UNIX
Target: Microcomputer development

Software Vendors:
UNIX Related Products

American Business Systems
3 Littleton Road, Westford, MA 01886
617/692-2600

Business application software under UNIX
Hardware Supported: Altos, Onyx, Pixel, Plexus, Zilog, Ithaca
Intersystems
BACS: Multi-user accounting system
FAS: Single-user accounting system
Client Accounting System
Financial Modeling
Real Estate System

Human Computing Resources
10 St. Mary Street, Toronto, Ontario, Canada M4Y 1P9
416/922-1937

UNIX porting, support, software and training
Systems supported: 16032, 68000
Computers: PDP-11, VAX under VMS, VAX standalone UNIX
UNITY: Enhanced System III UNIX (System V available summer 1983)
HCR/BASIC, HCR/PASCAL
HCR/EDIT: Screen editor under UNIX
RT/EMT: RT-11 emulator for UNIX
CIS COBOL
Mistress

Interactive Systems
1212 Seventh Street, Santa Monica, CA 90401
213/450-8363

Systems and Application Software
Hardware Supported: DEC VAX, PDP
Operating Systems: UNIX, VMS
IS/Workbench
IS/WB-XTS: includes screen editor
IS/WB-UCS: includes electronic mail, networking, screen editor
IS/WB-APS: includes word processing, electronic mail, networking, screen
            editor
INword: word processing software
INed: screen editor
INmail: electronic mail
INnet: networking software
INtelex: telex interface
INremote/HASP: remote job entry system
INpost/6670: 6670 post processor
INpost/APS: post processor for Autologic APS phototypesetter
INpost/LQP: post processor for Diablo and Qume printers
Connect: hardware connection program
FTP: File transfer program
C Cross Compilers: Z80, 68000, 8086

Microsoft
10700 Northup Way, Bellevue, WA 98004
206/828-8080

Operating Systems and Application Software
Systems supported: Z8000, 68000, 8086
XENIX: Enhanced UNIX
MS-DOS
Multi-Plan

Relational Technology, Inc.
2855 Telegraph Avenue, Berkeley, CA 94705
415/845-1700

Relational Data Base Management System for UNIX
Systems supported: 68000, VAX
Ingres
Micro Ingres

Rhodnius, Inc.
10 St. Mary Street, Toronto, Ontario, Canada M4Y 1P9
416/922-1743

Relational Database Management systems for UNIX, XENIX,
    UniPlus+, UNITY.
Systems supported: 68000, Z8000, 8086
Computers: All Perkin-Elmer, all DEC, Onyx, Amdahl (UTS), IBM 4300 and
            3030X, Zilog, Altos, Gould SEL, Intel 86330 and 86380, Pixel
Mistress, Mistress-Plus (m-writer, m-vision)

Ryan-McFarland Corporation
Language Products Group
9057 Soquel Drive, Aptos, CA
408/662-2522

Cobol Systems Software under UNIX
Systems supported: Z8000, 8086, 68000-based microcomputers, P-E 32XX,
            VAX
RM/COBOL

SMC Software Systems
Division of Science Management Corporation
1011 Route 22, P.O. Box 6800, Bridgewater, NJ 08807
201/685-9000

System and Application Software
Systems supported: 8086, Z8000, 68000
UNI-DOL: Derived from System III UNIX
SMC BASIC: Enhanced business BASIC
IDOL: DATA base management
M-BOS: Multi-user BASIC Operating System
SMC Business Applications: Purchase Order, Fixed Assets, Order Processing,
        Accounts Payable, General Ledger, Payroll, Ac-
        counts Receivable.

Unisoft Corporation
2405 Fourth Street, Berkeley, CA 94710
415/644-1230

UNIX Porting Support and Software
Systems supported: 68000
UniPlus+: System III UNIX with Berkeley 4xBSD enhancements
4.1 BSD UNIX for VAX Binary Licenses
C Compiler
68000 Macro Assembler

VenturCom, Inc.
139 Main Street, Cambridge, MA 02142
617/661-1230

UNIX Porting Support and Software Tools
Systems supported: DEC (Rainbow, Professional, LSI 11/2, 11/21, 11/23, PDP-
        11 Family, VAX-11); 8088, 8086, 186, 286, 68010
VENIX: Enhanced System III UNIX for real-time applications
SUNIX: Satellite UNIX for single-board computers
TEQ: Mathematical function evaluation package
SigPak: Signal processing package
Matrix: Spreadsheet decision support system
Final Word: Interactive word processor
C Cross-Compilers: Z80, 8086/8088

Wollongong Group
1135A San Antonio Road, Palo Alto, CA 94303
415/962-9224

UNIX Porting Support
Systems supported: Perkin-Elmer, DEC
Edition VII: Enhanced V7 UNIX (4.1 BSD Utilities)
Edition VII Workbench: SCCS Utilities plus 4.1 BSD
Eunice: 4.1 BSD Co-resident with VAX VMS

User Groups

Usenix Association
P.O. Box 7
El Cerrito, CA 94530
415/428-UNIX

Uni-Ops
P.O. Box 5182
Walnut Creek, CA 94596-1182
415/945-0448

/usr/group
P.O. Box 8570
Stanford, CA 94305-0221

Publications

Addison-Wesley Publishing
Jacob Way
Reading, MA 01867
617/944-3700

Business Guide to the UNIX System
Business Guide to the XENIX System
Programmer's Guide to the UNIX System
Programmer's Guide to the XENIX System

International Data Services
11020 Stewart Drive
Sunnyvale, CA 94086
408/730-8649

UNIX Softalk Newsletters

458

A BUSINESS GUIDE TO THE UNIX SYSTEM

Osborne/McGraw-Hill
2600 Tenth Street
Berkeley, CA 94710
415/548-2805

A User Guide to the UNIX System

Yates Ventures
4962 El Camino Real
Suite 111
Los Altos, CA 94022
415/964-0130

The Yates Perspective Newsletter
Documentation and Books on Software
Market Research Reports on UNIX and Standard Software

Training

Bunker Ramo Information Systems
Trumball Industrial Park, Trumball, CT 06609
203/386-2000

UNIX and C Training Seminars
Introduction to UNIX
Programming in C
Advanced C Methods
Advanced UNIX Methods
Shell programming in UNIX
Basic data communications

Institute for Advanced Professional Studies
55 Wheeler Street, Cambridge, MA 02138
617/497-2075

Customer on-site and publically offered UNIX and C training
C Programming
Introduction to UNIX
UNIX System Administration
A Survey of UNIX Software
UNIX Systems Programming
Network Development with UNIX and Microcomputers

Shell Programming
DBMS on UNIX-based Microcomputers
UNIX Management Briefing
Interfacing to UNIX
UNIX Briefing for Sales and Marketing Managers
Introduction to UNIX for Office Automation

Structured Methods, Inc.
7 West 18th Street, New York, NY 10011
212/741-7720

UNIS and C Training Seminars
UNIX Operating System—in-depth
Introduction to C Language Programming
UNIX System Administration
Advanced Topics in the C Language

Request catalog for additional seminars

SYMBOLS INDEX

SUBJECT INDEX